M000169615

A LIFE WITHOUT BORDERS

By sailboat, planes, train, and RV, a funny and inspiring tale of a
family's quest to escape the boundaries of their ordinary life

CARLA GRAY BEDELL

A Life Without Borders

Copyright © 2013 by Carla Gray BeDell. All rights reserved.

First Print Edition: 2013

Cover and Formatting: Streetlight Graphics

Alegria Press books are available at special discounts for bulk purchases for sales promotions or corporate use. Special editions, including personalized covers, excerpts of existing books, or books with corporate logos, can be created in large quantities for special needs. The author is also available to speak at your live event. For more information on sales or speaking events, please call (704) 288-5869.

No part of this book may be reproduced, scanned, or distributed in any printed or electronic form without permission. Please do not participate in or encourage piracy of copyrighted materials in violation of the author's rights. Thank you for respecting the hard work of this author.

To Mom, who waited for me to finish my journey before she left on her own. I love you and miss you so much.

To my husband, Dan, who always sees more in me than I do in myself.

Table of Contents

PROLOGUE

IT IS EARLY AFTERNOON. WE are about 5 miles from our destination, Puerto La Cruz, Venezuela—the feared Venezuelan mainland. The kids are inside doing schoolwork, Dan is at the helm, and I sit in the cockpit, deeply engrossed in my book. The sky is a brilliant blue and the sea calm; it's a great day. Suddenly, I feel a shift in energy. I look up from my book and watch Dan calmly step down from the helm seat and head into the salon. He doesn't say a word, but we have been on this boat together for nearly four years and are so attuned to each other I immediately know something is wrong. The helm seat is Dan's throne. He never leaves it if for anything, which is why the kids and I dubbed him Velcro Butt. It's a term of endearment.

I scan the horizon in front of me, but all I see are the towering mountains from the Venezuelan coast. Dan comes back into the cockpit, holding the handheld GPS. He stares behind me, over my shoulder, and without a word, gently slips the GPS deep into the garbage can. My eyes widen and meet his. I instantly know what he is staring at over my shoulder. Pirates! I take a deep breath, set aside my book, and steel my nerves for what might come next.

A small white boat is fast approaching from the rear. We've heard the stories of sailboats robbed in these waters, and our current position is not far from where an American sailor was recently killed after pirates boarded his boat.

The pirates steal everything, including electronics, GPS systems, and VHF radios, leaving the owners adrift with no idea where they are and no way to communicate. Dan and I have planned for such an incident. If we think an attack is imminent, we will remain calm and not resist. We need a GPS, so we will hide in the trash. We haven't emptied our trash in several days, so it's pretty nasty. The odds are in our favor the pirates will not look there.

My eyes meet Dan's and I give him a brave smile. So this is it. Four years of incident-free sailing are about to end, all because we have been foolish enough to believe our gut and not buy into the fear mongering espoused by some of our fellow cruisers. I glance at Tristan and Tessa busily working on their math, oblivious to what is going on, then turn to face the danger that is speeding our way.

The approaching boat isn't the normal *pirogue* that the pirates use. Maybe they know cruisers are onto them and have switched to a different type of boat. As it grows closer, we can see several people on board. We are definitely going to be outnumbered. It doesn't look good for us.

Wait—that looks like a pleasure craft, not a pirate boat. And isn't that a woman in a swimsuit, holding a baby? Are those beach umbrellas? I turn to Dan, my mouth open, ready to say something, but I see by the look on his face that he realizes it too.

Our "pirates" wave as they speed past. We slowly wave back. Dan sheepishly reaches into the trash and pulls out the GPS, picking off a few strands of last night's spaghetti.

"There's a little bit of sauce on there too," I point out helpfully. He nods and gets a towel. It is understood we won't speak of this again. I return to reading my book.

Part I

Who Said This Was Supposed to Be Fun?

FLORIDA

I LOOKED AROUND THE BOAT AT the stacks of boxes and realized I was in the seventh circle of hell. What was going on here? There were boxes absolutely everywhere. You couldn't move without relocating a box. Boxes were on the salon table, in the cockpit, on the beds, blocking the bathrooms (heads), and on the kitchen (galley) counter; it was overwhelming. Worse yet, we still had two large cars filled with more boxes.

I imagine this is where many people give up their dream. It's a gray area where you've left behind what you know and can see what you want on the horizon, but the space between is dark and scary, and in my case, piled high with boxes. I envisioned us quitting our jobs, jumping on the boat with a backpack and two young kids, and sailing off into the sunset. Truthfully, I hadn't thought it through that far. I stopped thinking at quitting my job and selling our house because the rest was just too pie-in-the-sky to comprehend. But here we were, January 2007, in a marina in very cold Palm Coast, Florida, trapped in a sea of boxes.

Overwhelmed, my first instinct was to totally withdraw. I felt so alone. I couldn't call my friends and complain, even though they were incredibly supportive. I couldn't call my mom. Her last words to me were, "I give you thirty days and you'll be back." When I repeated their grandmother's words to Tristan and Tessa, I told them that I didn't care if the boat sank, they would have to float on a cooler for at least thirty-*one* days.

I couldn't talk to Dan about my fears. I knew he was as scared as I was. We were holding on by a very slim thread, and if one of us said "I can't do this" or "I don't know what I am doing," everything would collapse.

So we didn't talk about it. He went to work on the mechanics of the boat, and I fell, uncomfortably, into my new role. One day I am a successful senior vice president at a Fortune 500 firm, the next day I am a homeschool teacher, homemaker, and first mate. (I was never much for slow transitions.)

I walked off of the boat and sat on the dock. I looked back at the 38-foot catamaran that would be my home for the next few years. Like me, she was reinventing herself. One day she was a charter boat in the Caribbean, a base for overstressed vacationers trying to reclaim lost years in one rum-soaked week. Today she was part of a family, our family, our home as we traveled the seas, looking for ourselves and reconnecting to each other. Even her name was in transition. When we first fell in love with her, her name was *Calypso Quean,* meaning loose woman. We had since christened her *Alegria,* which is Spanish for joy and happiness. Her new name had been applied to the stern and one of her hulls, yet her old name was still visible, symbolically putting me forth into the world as a loose woman—or as I preferred, a happy, joyful woman, now loose in the world.

Soon all our remaining possessions would be on board. The cars would be sold, our cell phones disconnected, and all that was left of our old, constricting life shed. Most of it was already gone: the expensive work suits consigned, winter clothes given away, furniture sold or now in the homes of friends, and clients reassigned. Even our beloved dog was living a new life with my sister. Everything that defined who we were was gone. Now it was time to find out who we are.

"Look Mommy. It's a party," Tessa said, drawing my attention to a group of our dock neighbors setting up for a barbecue. I vaguely remembered a sign being posted about a cookout, but I had no desire to try to be friendly. Besides, it was cold and we had laundry to do.

"No. It's just some people talking." I grabbed her hand and hurried off to the washing machines. A woman approached as I was loading the washer. It was Dottie. Tessa knew her, but the most I had ever said to her was a quick hello.

"Hi! I'm Dottie. We're having a cookout. We'd love for your family to join us."

Immediately Tessa piped up, "See Mom! I told you it was a party!"

I threw Tessa a quick look. "Thanks, but I don't think we can."

"Why not?" Tessa demanded.

"Because," I said. I needed a good excuse here. "We don't have any food for a cookout."

"Oh, we have plenty of food," Dottie assured me.

"Well," I stalled. "We have all this laundry to do."

"We can do it later, Mom. Please!"

"I don't think so. But thanks."

Dottie stared at me for a moment. She was trying her best to include us, but I was shutting her down. "Alright. But if you change your mind, stop by."

She walked away, but Tessa wouldn't give up.

"Why can't we go?"

"Because we have a lot of work to do."

"We can do it later."

"We don't have any food to cook on the grill."

"She said she had plenty of food."

"No."

"But it's a party!" In her six-year-old mind, turning down a party was incomprehensible.

I was tired and in no mood to deal with this. "I said no!"

She scowled at me. "This is no fun! We never have any fun!"

I angrily said to her the words that will stay with me forever, "Who said this was supposed to be fun?"

As soon as the words were out of my mouth, I realized how crazy they sounded. Who said this was supposed to be fun? Really? I just said that? If it wasn't fun, then why were we doing it? I let out a deep sigh, relaxed, and gave thanks for being blessed with such an insightful daughter. Giving Tessa a hug, I said, "You're right. This is supposed to be fun. We're going to a party!"

From that moment on, everything changed. We still worked hard, but we also took time to socialize and explore. We drove to the Miami International Boat Show, we visited Cape Canaveral—where we were among the VIP guests for the rocket launch of Themis—we spent time with our neighbors, and in general, had more fun.

Eventually we found a place for everything we'd brought. (Then we would spend the next four years giving away most of that same stuff.) Dan finished the frame for the four solar panels. He did a great job, and we were finally able to get the panels out of the car and mounted on top of *Alegria*. We had sold Dan's car already, so the last piece of business was to sell my car. I think that was when it finally began to sink into our kids' heads that we were really going to do this.

The initial chaos on the boat made it difficult to have four aboard, so Tristan and Tessa spent a lot of time exploring. Palm Coast is a thriving marina, with most slips

4

filled, a small liveaboard community, and a large transient business as boats heading up and down the intracoastal waterway stop for fuel or an overnight dock. It was this amazing marina community that took us under their wing and really saved us those first two months.

Don, whose beautiful trawler, *Over Indulgence,* was docked nearby, was a constant source of encouragement to us. He took ten-year-old Tristan under his wing, showing him dock-line management and knot-tying skills. I loved watching Tristan, who was normally shy, blossom and become more outgoing. He became so confident in his line-handling abilities that within a very short time, he was earning tips helping boats coming in to the fuel dock. Let me go on record to say that he was officially the only one of us with a paying job.

Most of the boat work was done, and we were finally close to leaving Palm Coast. Dottie and her husband, Rich, were a big help to us the last few days. Rich left his truck at the marina in case we needed to borrow it. They took Tessa and Tristan out for dinner, giving us much needed time to ourselves to finish things up. Don also offered to help run last-minute errands. The marina staff was always supportive. As anxious as we were to get going, we were really going to miss the community we had at Palm Coast Marina.

Sunday, March 4, 2007 we left the marina. Don memorialized the occasion by taking a picture of the four us standing anxiously on the bow of the boat. As we pulled away from the dock, Tessa closed her eyes, smiled, and said with a big sigh, "This feels like freedom." It really did.

To say we were nervous was an understatement. It was the first time we were all alone on the boat away from the dock. When we bought the 38-foot Voyage catamaran in the British Virgin Islands (BVI) in July of 2006, neither

Dan nor I had any open-ocean sailing experience. We had chartered boats in the BVI many times, but that was not the same as a ten-day passage from the BVI to Charleston, South Carolina. At that time, we hired a captain, and Dan and his buddies Alan and John were the crew. Once our boat was in Charleston, Dan and I were still unsure of our sailing skills. We had only taken *Alegria* away from the dock one time and that was with friends. The maneuver ended disastrously, a story I won't retell here, and we never took her out again. Later that same year, Dan, Alan, and another captain moved the boat to Palm Coast, Florida, where it hadn't moved again until the day we left Palm Coast Marina for good.

Maybe we should have had more experience before we started the trip, but I believe you will never be prepared for everything. I remember reading an article warning the "The Ten Things You Must Know Before You Head Offshore!" A "man overboard" drill was on the list as something everyone had to know how to perform. It seemed very complicated. I read it and thought, I don't have time to learn all this—the trip is off, the dream is over.

Then I read a book about a Canadian family with limited sailing experience who sailed around the world. And I read a blog about *Bumfuzzle*, two twenty-somethings with no sailing experience who bought a boat and also sailed around the world. If they could do it, so could we. Until we learned the man overboard drill, I told the kids it was probably in their best interests to make sure they didn't fall out of the boat. Problem solved.

How did it go our first day out? We left at 10:15 a.m. and motored down the Intracoastal Waterway (ICW). There's a saying that everyone runs aground on the ICW, and anyone who says they haven't is lying. So I got that out of the way early. I was steering us to a fork in the

ICW, and Dan told me to keep to the right. I kept to the right all the way until the depth finder showed less than the clearance under our keels, and *Alegria* slowed to a gentle stop, stuck. Since I had successfully completed the requisite running-aground drill, I surrendered the helm to Dan who worked his magic, coaxing *Alegria* back and forth with the engines until she pulled free. We managed to make it the rest of the day without another incident and anchored for the night at Sheepshead Cut, New Smyrna, Florida at 4:45 p.m.

Did I mention we had never anchored this boat before? Anchoring had always been my job on our bareboat trips in the BVI, so it was only natural it became my permanent job on *Alegria*. Tristan was my apprentice. The depth finder showed 12 feet. The guide book said the bottom was mud and sand, not bad for holding. We were in pretty tight quarters, located just off the channel and backed up to some condos. I let out a 7 to 1 scope—7 feet of chain to each foot of depth. We'd normally then dive on the anchor to make sure it was dug in, but the water was so murky it was impossible to see anything. Dan put the engines in reverse, and Tristan and I picked a spot on the bank to use as a marker to see if the boat was on the move, an indication of whether or not the anchor was holding. It held. Our first day ended in success.

It was very strange being anchored overnight for the first time, especially since it seemed we were right in the backyard of the waterfront condos. As the night wore on, the current shifted. *Alegria* had been facing one direction but was now facing another. This was natural and the anchor was designed to adjust.

Dan was sure the anchor wasn't holding. "I think we're dragging," he said. This was the phrase I would hear nearly every single time we anchored over the next several years. I'm not making this up. Just typing those words today still makes me crazy.

My response was always the same. "We have a great anchor. I know how to drop anchor. We're not dragging."

"Yes we are," he said.

"No, we're not."

Back and forth we went with this witty banter until the next day proved I was right, and we were still in the same spot. But that first night, I was not so sure of myself, and the stakes were pretty high. It would look very bad if we dragged and lost our boat the first night out. Because Dan would be steering all the next day (while I would be homeschooling), and because we weren't sure if we would hear the anchor alarm, I agreed to be on anchor watch all night. I spent the dark hours watching movies and checking our position. Our Spade anchor never moved. The next morning I served a breakfast of biscuits and gravy with a big side of "I told you so."

We made our way steadily down the ICW, stopping in the marina at North Palm Beach to have a watermaker installed. The watermaker allowed us to convert saltwater to drinking water and ensured we could take freshwater showers. I know there are many old-school cruisers out there who look on a watermaker as a luxury, but not us. With two kids on board, conserving water was not something I wanted to worry about. Our Village Marine Tec watermaker averaged a little over 8 gallons an hour, never gave us any trouble, and didn't need a generator since it worked off our boat batteries. It was vital to the enjoyment of our trip.

But that didn't stop us from staying aware of our water usage. The first year on the boat, Dan made sure everyone understood that they didn't take long showers. If water was low, and we didn't want to make any because we were in a dirty harbor, he would give the kids their showers, which we later unpleasantly referred to as "prison showers." I will never forget Dan's voice as he stood outside the door holding the shower sprayer on either Tessa or Tristan in the bathroom. It went like this:

"Brad (as in Pitt, as in armpit), Angelina (other armpit), privates, now spin. Grand Canyon. Spin again." I am sure my kids will need counseling for that in the years to come.

We used our marina time well. Tristan put his new line-handling skills to work and helped out as a dockhand. His tips increased dramatically. Tessa celebrated her seventh birthday. Normally her birthdays consisted of a lot of kids at an expensive and extremely loud party place that was fun for the kids but miserable for us, the parents. This time, while we couldn't give her a lot of friends, we could give her our time. For the whole day, she called the shots, and we gave her all our attention. She loved it. With our family slowly getting adjusted to the boat, we could concentrate on enjoying the trip and each other.

When the watermaker installation was finished, we left the marina and headed farther south to Lake Worth, our staging area for our passage to the Bahamas. From Lake Worth to West End, Bahamas was 55 miles as the crow flies and could be very challenging. The Gulf Stream is a current, usually extremely strong, that flows south to north. To compensate for being pushed north, you should first head south. It is important to wait for low seas and extremely important to never leave in high winds from the north. A strong current flowing north into winds also coming from the north causes huge waves and is a recipe for disaster.

Crossing the Gulf Stream, sailing at night, bringing *Alegria* into a foreign country—all of these were firsts for us as a family. I knew Dan was being extra cautious, waiting for the best weather window. Though some cruisers wait weeks in Lake Worth for the right conditions, we were lucky and only had to wait a few days. A quick departure was good so we wouldn't have time to overthink what we were about to do. We just might have thought about how crazy it was that a family who had never taken their boat into the open ocean together was about to cross the Gulf Stream to the Bahamas and changed our minds.

Tristan and Tessa were still sleeping when we hauled the anchor at 3 a.m. and motored out into the inlet. We expected to find calm seas and winds under 10 knots. What we found instead were high winds and waves that pounded the boat. The wind was so strong, we had to yell at each other to be heard. *Alegria* was slamming up and down in the short-period waves. It was pitch-black and I was scared to death. After a few minutes of being battered, we realized this wasn't for us. Neither of us wanted to continue, but neither of us wanted to admit we were scared.

Suddenly we saw the bright light from the large, metal, dredging barge, which ran back and forth across the inlet all night. It was heading right for us. We debated what we should do. The barge was coming up on us fast. With a strong incoming current against us, we had no hope of getting ahead of it. Dan yelled for me to flash the spotlight on the barge so the captain could see us. I did, but it didn't seem to make any difference. I feared it was on autopilot and there was no one on watch to see what was going on. Even if we'd been able to raise the crew on the VHF, the barge was too close for them to take evasive measures. We had to act quickly. If we didn't turn back at that moment, we would be crushed.

Turning around wasn't easy. The inlet was narrow, and we were totally disoriented. Dan pulled the wheel hard to port. The sharp rocks on the side of the inlet seemed so close. *Alegria*'s rudders and engines strained against the current. The rocks were getting closer. It seemed there was no way we were going to turn in time to miss them. Dan was doing all he could. Finally the bow came around, and we headed back into Lake Worth.

We anchored *Alegria* almost in the same spot we had left, and I went back to bed, trying hard not to show my frustration. Dan tried to assure me that this was a minor setback, no big deal. He reminded me that sometimes you couldn't tell the conditions until you got out there, but to me it felt like a complete failure. It was a really low point for me, but I didn't feel like talking about it. Instead, I put on a happy face for the kids, and we agreed to try again the following night.

The next night, the alarm rang again at 3 a.m., but it wasn't necessary. I was already awake. I had tossed and turned the whole night, worrying about the crossing. What if we got out there again and failed because we were afraid? What if we just couldn't do it? Other people had made the crossing. What was wrong with us? My stomach was full of knots as I pulled on my clothes and mentally prepared to try it again.

I stepped into the cockpit, shivering from both cold and nervousness. Dan pointed to a boat anchored close in front of us. He said it looked as if the boat was over our anchor. He started our engines, hoping the noise would wake the captain. It didn't. We had to wake him up. After all, his boat was over our anchor. It was his problem too, right? I shined our megawatt spotlight into his boat windows and yelled, "Excuse me. Hello?"

A few minutes later, a man groggily appeared on deck.

"Hi! Um, we are trying to leave and think your boat is over our anchor. Can you move?"

He stared at me for a moment, clearly puzzled at the situation. Finally he replied, "If you get too close, I'll start my engines and move."

Fine. I went forward onto our bow. As I hit the remote control to raise the anchor, I saw for the first time where our chain was positioned. I was shocked to realize *he* wasn't over our anchor, *we* were. *Alegria* had drifted forward on her anchor chain so that our anchor was under *our* boat. This was something I really should have checked before waking up our tired neighbor with a megawatt spotlight. I sheepishly yelled, "Sorry!" but I was pretty sure he knew what was going on all along. Now we had to leave because we were totally embarrassed—more worried about being called stupid than being called afraid.

We motored out into the inlet. Though the winds were still strong, the sea was much calmer. The dredging barge careened toward us once again, cutting close to the front of our boat. Once it passed, we threaded our way through the channel markers and made our way out of the inlet and into the ocean. The waves were about 3 to 4 feet and close together. In the beginning there was a lot of up and down motion, but in a few hours, the seas settled down nicely as we motorsailed across the Gulf Stream.

There was nothing in front of us but open ocean and the Bahamas, and if we missed that, Africa, as Dan would always say on later passages east. Behind us, the lights of Florida were still visible. It was surreal to think we wouldn't see the US again for a long time. We weren't just leaving the country, we were leaving all the things we had been told about how to live our life. From this moment on, our life would be truly ours. I lay down in the cockpit and stared at the full moon lighting a silver path across the ocean. It was the perfect night to start an adventure.

The kids slept late, enjoying the ride. About two in the afternoon, we pulled into Old Bahama Bay Marina. Tristan tied the yellow quarantine flag onto the stay, letting customs know we had arrived. After checking in with immigration and obtaining the first of many passport stamps we would receive over the next several years, Tristan replaced the yellow flag with the blue, black, and yellow courtesy flag of the Bahamas. The long-awaited Bahamas was now ours.

2

Adjusting to Our New Life
ABACOS, BAHAMAS

April 9, 2007 Old Bahama Bay Marina, West End, Grand Bahamas
(from the blog of Alegria)

What started out as an overnight stay in Old Bahama Bay Marina (to simply clear customs) has turned into an ordeal. We were scheduled to leave Thursday morning. Dan checked the port engine and discovered an oil leak. The puddle was under the engine, so he hadn't noticed it when we first stopped. Apparently it now looked as if the *Exxon Valdez* had capsized in our engine room. After discovering the growing oil slick, Dan said, "I think we may need a new engine."

Well, that's not want I wanted to hear. We had just gotten started. This was unacceptable. But, also knowing my husband may be over dramatizing the situation, I sent him back to the engine room with orders not to come out until he found a better answer. He came back later and said there was definitely an oil leak, but it wasn't as bad as he thought. It was probably just a seal. We needed to get someone to look at it though since the leak was under the engine, and he couldn't access it. We needed to find a mechanic. [*End blog*]

Finding a mechanic in the Caribbean was never an easy task. It wasn't that they didn't know what they were doing; we were fortunate to have had some excellent work done during our trip. It was the reliability factor of getting a repair done on time. A mechanic would show up soon enough and start the work but leave us with what became Dan's and my much-quoted phrase, "I go to come back." It meant I am leaving to get a part, to find a tool, to take a nap, we were never sure, but it would usually involve several days. It was our first lesson in island patience.

April 12, 2007 Old Bahama Bay Marina, West End, Grand Bahamas
(from the blog of Alegria)

Another week in an expensive marina. Audley, our mechanic, stopped by to let us know the customs paperwork for the part he ordered was not correct, and he needed to get new paperwork faxed to customs before they would release the part. We went through stages of being upset and then realized we were in the Bahamas where we wanted to be, and the kids were having a great time, so we needed to enjoy ourselves.

It gave us some time to meet two cruising couples on *Makai* and *Magnificat*. Though they left before us, it was nice meeting other cruisers. Tristan and Tessa made friends with three boys from a fishing boat that arrived late in the afternoon. A couple hours later, Tessa ran to us yelling, "Shark!" The kids had seen a shark in the lagoon where they were fishing. Dan and I went out to get a look. I never saw it, but Dan and the kids spotted a nurse shark. We met the parents of the boys and talked for a few minutes. As we left to go back to our boat, we agreed to meet the next night for a shark hunt.

The following night, Tristan and Tessa were very excited

about the upcoming hunt. Their new friends' dads, John and Chris, had fish to clean, so they gave Dan some bait and a fishing pole. Now I'm sure none of us, including Dan, thought anything would come of it. Not long after the line hit the water, I slipped on some rocks at the edge of the lagoon, cutting my leg, so I limped back to our boat to get a bandage. I wasn't gone long before Tessa ran to me, screaming "Mom! Mom! Dad caught a shark! He caught a shark!"

My response? "Oh my God! What are we going to do with a shark?"

I ran to the lagoon, about 50 yards away, as a crowd was starting to gather. Sure enough, Dan had a shark on the line. Dan, who hadn't fished since he was probably eleven and who had never fished in anything besides a river, had now caught a shark. Where was the camera? It was in Dan's pocket. I struggled to get the camera from his pants while he was trying to reel in the shark. I pulled out the camera along with several ten-dollar bills, which were now scattered on the ground and threatening to blow away. What to do? Take the shark picture or go for the cash? I chose the cash, losing valuable photographic opportunities.

Finally I got the money stuffed back into Dan's pocket and snapped a picture of the shark. Hearing the commotion, John arrived to help. A marina guy held a gaff, which the very sight of gave me the willies. I said to Dan, "We are going to let it go right?"

"Yes."

Okay. I couldn't get a good picture of the shark in the water, but I didn't want it gaffed. John cut the line, setting the shark free. "A lemon shark," he said appreciatively. Dan and I looked at each other and said "lemon shark" and nodded as if we knew what that meant.

A lady standing next to Dan exclaimed, "You caught a shark! Wow! What were you fishing for?"

Dan hesitated, a bit confused. "Um...a shark," he replied.

There'll be no living with him now. [*End blog*]

April 17, 2007 Old Bahama Bay Marina, West End, Grand Bahamas
(*from the blog of* Alegria)

Audley promised us he would be back tomorrow "first thing," so we were feeling confident we would soon be on our way. We decided to celebrate. I was tired of cooking and was craving some wings, so we took a taxi into town. Our driver seemed very happy that we were venturing outside the gates to mingle with the locals.

The settlement at West End still hadn't recovered from the last hurricane that went through. Houses were boarded up, there were very few people there, or so it seemed. Oddly, there were at least three sports bars. Our driver told us that most of the places were closed because there was a big political rally that night, and the whole town was turning out. The Bahamian election was coming up, and the PLP party had just opened a campaign office in West End.

Our driver's favorite restaurant was still open, and a short ride later he stopped at a nondescript building called the Triple Play Sports Bar. Outside, several people were milling about, drinking beer, and wearing matching yellow shirts with the letters PLP. As he dropped us off, the driver promised us good food and friendly people. If we wanted to, we should stay and enjoy the political rally.

Skirting the crowd, we entered the building and were surprised to find four large, flat-screen TVs. Three were tuned to basketball, and the other was tuned to a Bahamian news channel covering the election. We ordered wings and conch and settled in at our corner table. The bar started to fill up with more yellow shirts. Tessa, on her way back from the restroom, had discovered a back room with video games. She asked if she and Tristan could check them out while we waited for our food. I said sure. A few minutes later Dan said, "I think those are video-poker machines back there."

"Nonsense," I replied. The kids came back just as our food arrived. The wings and conch were delicious. After we ate, the kids returned to the game room. By this time the bar was busier and louder. The waitress came to take our plates away and mentioned the political rally. As I watched most of the political participants taking bottles of Guinness beer and jugs of wine outside to the rally, I couldn't help but think we would have more enthusiasm in our elections if malt liquor and wine were included.

Dan checked on the kids. He returned with them scurrying ahead of him. "Those aren't video games back there. Those *are* video-poker machines."

I looked at the kids, and they looked at me innocently.

"Were people playing them?" I asked.

"Yes."

"What were our kids doing?"

"They were watching."

I breathed a sigh. "Well if they weren't bothering anyone." Dan shot me a look. My "Mother of the Year" status was in jeopardy.

In our corner white world, we watched as more patrons came and went, each with their yellow shirts uniquely styled to suit the wearer: there was one tied at the side, that one was knotted at the waist, another was off the shoulder. It was a mini political fashion show. As we waited to pay our bill, the kids were getting bored. They wanted to go outside and play. At first we said absolutely not as it was now dark, the restaurant was close to the road, and there was no place to play. They pleaded. In another "Mother of the Year" moment, with Dan looking at me as if I'd lost my mind, I said, "Sure, but don't bother anyone."

Ah, my little militants, off to join the rally. I was proud of myself. Not only was I allowing my children to embrace cultural diversity, but I was pretty sure I could count this as home schooling. (If I could have gotten them on those video-poker machines, math would have been covered!)

The bartender brought our bill, touched Dan on the shoulder, and in a reassuring tone again mentioned the political rally. I wondered, did we have an "Oh my God, what are all these locals doing in a local bar" look on our faces? We paid our bill, and the owner called for the taxi to pick us up. Tessa ran into the bar. The kids were in high spirits after finding a cat to chase and were having a great time. All too soon, however, our driver came and took us back to the marina. [*End blog*]

The repair was finally finished, and we were now free to explore the Abacos, an absolutely beautiful series of small islands in the northern Bahamas. We fell in love with the town of New Plymouth on Green Turtle Cay. The town was originally settled by Loyalists, many from North Carolina, who fled there after the Revolutionary War. The people were friendly, colorful clapboard houses lined the streets wide enough for one lane of golf carts, and the pace was slow. We made the required stop at Miss Emily's Blue Bee Bar to sample her famous drink, the Goombay Smash, and then stopped by Pineapples where we chilled in the hammock by the pool, watching the sun set on *Alegria* in the harbor. We were finally beginning to relax and get the laid-back Bahamian experience we had been looking for.

Manjack Cay, just off Green Turtle Cay, was one of our favorite islands in the Abacos. Except for a very few houses, the island is uninhabited, and those who live there don't mind sharing their beautiful beach, gardens, and well-maintained hiking trails. The windward side of Manjack is wild, with waves bashing the shore, but a short distance across the tree-covered island is the calm leeward side, perfect for swimming, picnicking, and playing with the stingrays that swim close to shore.

We had just secured our dinghy onshore when the

Brendal's Dive Center boat arrived loaded down with a group of tourists. During his dive excursions, Brendal stops here, cooks lunch for his dive group, and feeds the rays. We had met him the night before at Pineapples, and he seemed like a really nice guy. The kids ran down the beach to say hello, and we lazily followed. As we got closer, we saw three large southern stingrays circling in the water near Brendal. We watched fascinated as the divemaster put a small piece of fish between his toes, encouraging the rays to swim over his foot and eat the fish.

There were six people on his tour, and they nicely included us in their group. Soon Dan, I, the kids and a few of the braver tourists were sticking fish between our toes. The rays very gently swam over our feet. They were huge, much bigger than I imagined. It took a leap of faith to have your entire foot disappear under a huge stingray, but what an experience. I felt this slight roughness, almost like a cat's tongue on my toes, when the ray took the fish. It tickled and made me laugh. Brendal was very patient and let us feed the stingrays as much as we wanted.

Surprisingly, the rays liked to be petted. Even if you didn't have food, they would swim close enough that you could run your hand along their velvety wings. Brendal had named the biggest ray Sandy. She was 4 feet across. He had been feeding her for eighteen years, and they had a special bond. We watched mesmerized as Sandy lifted as much of her body out of the water as possible to let Brendal rub his hands across her velvety wings. At one point she even wrapped herself around his leg (as much as a ray can do that). To us, it looked as if she was giving him a hug.

Brendal grilled a fish he'd caught, and while his tour group ate, we stayed in the water to play with the rays. A little later he invited us to have some of the fresh conch salad he'd made. I felt bad at first. These tourists paid for the tour, and we had attached ourselves to them like remoras, but Brendal assured us it was fine. They had plenty, so we enjoyed the food while the kids played. They were having the time of their lives, especially Tessa, who ran up and down the beach with the rays following her.

As we finished our conch salad, Tristan raced to our table.

"There are sharks in the water," he yelled excitedly.

We all ran back to the beach. Sure enough, two hungry sharks were now aggressively circling in the crystal-clear water. The sharks swam very close to shore, coming within 3 feet of the kids. The rays swam protectively between the sharks and the kids, forcing the sharks back if they got too close. I found that very interesting because I was pretty sure that ray was on the menu for sharks.

Brendal threw some food scraps to the sharks, which caused them to become even more aggressive. One obviously clueless German tourist, dressed in a tank top, black Speedos, and water shoes that gave the illusion of wearing socks with sandals, took a leftover fish head and swirled it in the water, enticing the sharks. One shark leapt up at the fish head, coming close to getting both the fish and the man's hand. I yanked the kids back out of harm's way and waited to see if the German was dumb enough to stick the fish head between his toes. Thankfully, Brendal took the sacrificial food offerings from the guy before we could find out, and we were able to spend a little more time watching the marine life without the scene turning into a blood bath.

While we loved the isolation and small town life of the islands around Green Turtle Cay, eventually we needed to buy groceries. The prices for food at the Green Turtle market were very high and there was a limited selection. We held out as long as we could, then weighed anchor and sailed to Great Abaco Island, farther down the chain. We anchored in Marsh Harbour, located about midway down the island. Marsh Harbour is a major town in the Abacos. It wasn't necessarily pretty, but the harbor is fairly protected, and if you need food, supplies, or a variety of restaurants, this is the place.

May 2, 2007 Marsh Harbour, Abacos
(from the blog of Alegria)

Many cruisers love Marsh Harbour, so we were intrigued. After making sure our anchor was set, we took the dinghy to shore. After about four hours in the blistering sun, we had covered all the hardware and grocery stores in the area. On the way back to the boat, we passed a video store advertising DVDs for US$10. We stopped in for a look.

The store didn't have a lot of movies, but it did have a lot of *new* movies; so new they were still out in the theaters in the US. That seemed a little suspicious, but I thought that maybe international releases were distributed early, so we bought two movies. As we were walking back to the boat, we passed a barber shop. Tristan needed a haircut, so we decided to stop.

From the outside, we couldn't see through the blacked-out windows. Dan opened the door. Six locals sat in the chairs along the wall, and one guy occupied the barber chair. Thinking it would be a long wait, Dan let the door close. It quickly opened back up, and a man asked if he could help us. I said our son needed a haircut, but it looked as if the barber was busy. He said no, come on in. He kicked the guy out of the barber chair, and a few of the men graciously gave up their seats for us to sit down.

This was my first visit to a black barber shop. In fact, I think it was safe to say it was our whole family's first visit to a black barber shop. The barber quickly cleaned up the chair and motioned for Tristan to sit down. Tristan bravely climbed into the chair. This was clearly not Supercuts. I know I've never had his hair cut in a salon with blacked-out windows or posters with marijuana references on the walls. Well, cultural diversity, I always say.

The barber quickly went to work with the clippers. After the first couple of swipes, I was starting to think this wasn't a good idea. I made eye contact with Dan. He'd also planned to get his hair cut, but I could tell by the look on his face, he was changing his mind.

To take my mind off Tristan's hair, I decided to concentrate on the pictures of the half-naked women hung on the wall. Interesting. When my eyes had made it all the way around the room, I looked back at Tristan's hair. It was looking good! I glanced to my left. The five guys sitting there had stopped watching the soccer game on TV and were staring at Tristan getting his hair cut. I mean just staring, fascinated. I caught Dan's eye and tilted my head toward the guys. We both smiled.

The door opened and a young man entered. Apparently there was a pecking order in the barber shop because when he walked in, the guy next to me had to once again give up his seat. None of them seemed to be there to get their hair cut. The barber finished with Tristan and his hair looked great. Now it was Dan's turn.

While we waited, Tessa busied herself by looking at the DVDs we'd bought at the store. The guy sitting next to me leaned in and said, "Gino has DVDs" and pointed to the new guy.

I thought that was what he said, but I'm not sure because his accent was pretty thick, and he was talking in a low voice. I looked at Gino. He looked at me. I replied, "Uh huh." That usually covered everything. I went back to looking at the wall art.

"Gino has DVDs," the guy repeated.

Now I was thinking that Gino must own the store I'd bought the DVDs from. I smiled and said to Gino something clever like, "You own the store I bought the DVDs from?"

Gino looked at me as if I was from another planet. I tried again.

"The store down the street?"

No. *He* sold DVDs. Suddenly it dawned on me that Gino ran a black-market DVD operation. I asked him, "Are the DVDs good quality?"

"Of course," he replied.

"Where did you get them?"

He just laughed. He wouldn't reveal his source. I tried again, "This isn't someone taking a video camera into a movie theater, right? I'm not going to see someone eating popcorn in front of the camera?"

Again, he laughed. "No, no. I have them in my car. I'll show you. I have kids' movies."

I told Dan, who was now paying for the haircuts (his hair also looked great), that I was going to look at movies with Gino. Once outside, Gino opened his trunk, revealing several boxes of DVDs. They were all current movies. "Three for twenty," he said.

The kids and I looked through his selection and found two kids' movies. Then I uttered the classic line, one I always regretted, "Do you have any adult movies?"

Dan, who had just joined us, stopped Gino as he was reaching for another box. "She doesn't mean adult movies. She means, not-kid movies." Dan turned to me. "I can't believe you said adult movies!"

I say this wrong all the time. My brain thinks the opposite of kids is adults. So the opposite of kids' movies is adult movies. But what I have just told Gino is that I am looking to buy porn from the trunk of his car while my kids watch. I am off the map here.

Dan saved the day and we bought: *The Robinson's* (kid movie), *Are We Done Yet?* (kid movie), and *Premonition* (adul– I mean non-kid movie). Gino assured me they were good quality and said I could come back to him if I wasn't satisfied. Of course, he did ask me first how long I would be in town, but I was happy with my purchases.

That night the kids watched *The Robinson's*. Except for the occasional Russian subtitle, it was fine. Dan and I watched the movie *Shooter.* This was the movie we'd bought at the DVD store. The quality was awful. Someone had secretly taped the movie by sitting in the theater with a video camera. It started off well enough until someone sat down in front of the camera. For a few minutes, instead of us watching *Shooter,* we watched someone else watching *Shooter.* [*End blog*]

May 4, 2007 Man-O-War Cay, Abacos
(*from the blog of* Alegria)

Alright, Man-O-War Cay is really not that bad, it's just that its inhabitants are very uptight. There are a lot of rules. There is a small marina here and moorings because you really can't anchor in the small harbor. If you take a mooring (a floating ball to which you attach a rope from your boat; the ball is attached to a chain that is anchored to the sea floor) instead of docking in the marina, the dockmaster charges you $2 more per token for the laundry. Also, there is a big sign that states that ONLY those in the marina may use the pool, not those of us on moorings. Of course this made me mad after paying extra for the laundry, so we used the pool...after hours, when we thought no one was looking.

The people who run the main businesses are all part of one or two original families, white descendants of American colonists. I know this is going to sound mean, but they all look alike. Everyone says this. You'll see a woman running one shop and then go down the road, and you'll swear you see the same person at another store. They're not real receptive to tourists either, though there are a lot of tourist places to shop.

The descendents of the original families live in the center

of the village, and expatriates live on the outskirts. There is no liquor on the island, though an American who lives there told me that the restaurants will let you discreetly bring wine in as long as the bottle is kept on the floor and covered. There is no dancing, card playing, or taking the Lord's name in vain. One islander told me a story about a captain who was filling up his boat at the fuel dock. In a moment of indiscretion, something upset him, and he said "Jesus!" The fuel-dock owner shut off the fuel and refused to serve the blasphemer any more gas, saying he would not tolerate anyone taking the Lord's name in vain. The captain apologized profusely and was granted a reprieve.

Another interesting twist is that, until recently, no blacks were allowed to spend the night on the island. When the sun went down, they had to be on the last ferry out.

On the positive side, the island is pretty and has a reputation as a good hurricane hole. Dan and I had considered it if we were caught in a hurricane while we were still in the Abacos. The harbor is well protected and churches double as shelters. However, knowing my luck, we would be hunkered down in the church, waiting out the storm, and I would look out the window and exclaim, "God, it's really blowing out there!" The next thing I'd know, I would be thrown outside on the church steps (me and the black man who missed the last ferry) with the words "We do not take the Lord's name in vain" ringing in my ears. I really don't think I can take that chance. If anyone has any suggestions for another good hurricane hole around here, please let us know. [*End blog*]

We continued to explore the islands of the Abacos, never tiring of the soft, white sand, the gin-colored shallow waters, and the abundance of marine life. The sailing between the islands was easy, and surprisingly, each island was somewhat unique. Of all the places we traveled over the several years of our adventure, Hope

Town Harbour on Elbow Cay, was Tessa's favorite.

As we entered the narrow, shallow inlet, the view was straight out of a painting. The famous red-and-white striped lighthouse, dating from 1863, regally stood watch at the entrance. Several wooden docks fronting small restaurants lined the harbor across from the lighthouse. Brightly painted turquoise, pink, and coral houses with teal shutters were perched on the top of a small hill. Just like New Plymouth on Green Turtle Cay, bicycles and golf carts were the rule. The entire town had a relaxed feel.

After we had secured *Alegria* to a mooring, our new friends from *Bella* came by to say hello. They told us Cap'n Jack's, a small dockside restaurant, was having a Cinco de Mayo party, and we agreed to meet them there. That night we were also reacquainted with Fred and Kathy on *Makai*, the cruising couple we had met briefly in Old Bahama Bay Marina. We shared a table, swapped stories of our trips so far, and watched the sun set behind the lighthouse. It was a great way to end the day and introduce us to our new community.

Community is an important part of the cruising world. A cruiser's net came on the VHF radio every morning, providing weather information, noting safety issues, and discussing whatever else was happening on the island. It also let cruisers know who was leaving and who was arriving. It was nice to have this sense of community, and we learned a lot from other sailors.

The VHF radio was how we communicated with our cruising friends, but it was far from private. Everyone was able to hear any conversation we had. It worked this way. We hailed a boat on one channel, the hailing channel, and then we and whoever we were hailing switched to another channel for a *private* conservation. The problem was that sometimes when we switched to a so-called private channel, half the harbor switched with us. How did we know? Shamelessly, the interlopers would let us know that they had eavesdropped on our conversation.

There is no such thing as privacy in a small harbor. In many of the anchorages, the boats are close together, so whatever you do outside the boat is usually entertainment to someone.

May 9, 2007 Hope Town, Elbow Cay, Abacos
(from the blog of Alegria)

It's a beautiful day in Hope Town, and I decide it is time for me to get the name on the side of the boat. We have *Alegria* on the back and one hull, but still have one more side to change. If I get it wrong or uneven, it will be very obvious. Tessa is on the bow. It's her job to hold the dinghy in place next to the hull while Tristan and I stand in the dinghy and measure down the side of the hull for the right location.

The word *Alegria* is about 20 inches tall and close to 5 feet long, printed in gray vinyl letters. The entire name pulls from the backing, like you would peel off a sticker; then you put the sticky side on the boat. Getting this unruly, 5-foot sticker on the boat correctly requires some skill. Basically there are two options. One way is to put a little soapy water on the back of the name and then press the name on the boat. You use a squeegee to get the water out and the name sticks. The water keeps the name from sticking too quickly, allowing you to move it around until you get it the way you want it. It's the easier way and the way I put the letters on the back of the boat. This time, thinking it will be faster, we try it the harder way, which is measure down from the top of the boat, rip the backing off, and stick it on.

It's very hot and starting to get windy. Tessa loses her grip on the front of the dinghy while I am standing in it, causing me to fall into Tristan, who is also standing. He drops the name in the water. This is not going well. After about twenty minutes and a lot of frustration, I realize this isn't going to work. I send Tessa inside to get some water so we can try the squeegee method. Another round of sweating and yelling, and the name is on the side of the boat. Now I just need to squeegee, slowly pull back the outer paper, and the name should stick.

Nope. More squeegee. No sticky. More squeegee. More squeegee. More sweaty. Still no sticky. I lie on my back in the dinghy, cursing myself for doing this.

"Hey!" Someone is yelling to me. I sit up and look around. It's the guy on the sailboat moored behind us.

"What?" I yell back.

"The guy on the boat down there," he points to a sailboat about 50 yards away with a guy sitting on the deck watching me. "He says to tell you the name would look better if it was closer to the front of the boat and higher up."

My mouth drops open. I can't believe it. Noticing the look on my face, he hooks his thumb in the other guy's direction and says, "He said it. Not me."

I am appalled. This busybody on the other sailboat got on the VHF radio and called the old guy on the boat behind me to tell me I am not doing it correctly! I am hot, I am tired, and I am in no mood to be messed with.

I yell back, "Well, you tell him I'm not moving it!"

I scowl at my critic across the water. Mike on *Dual Dreams* yells over to me, "I think it looks great!"

I thank him and go back to my squeegee. Life in a small-town harbor. [*End blog*]

Life was very easy in Hope Town. Our days unfolded with homeschooling in the morning, either on the boat or in the Hope Town Coffee Shop where we could use the internet. After school we went for a swim either in the pool at the Hope Town Harbour Lodge or the beautiful white beach behind it.

Slowly we began to shed the rules from our old life that

we had so acceptingly burdened ourselves with, and we began to examine what would work for us. We developed a good plan for homeschooling. Before we left the US, I had ordered an entire curriculum, first grade and fifth grade, from a well-respected homeschooling company. It was expensive, but very comprehensive; each grade level had over twenty books, including reading books, workbooks, and textbooks. When I called the company to see where I should start since the kids had already had half a year in their school back in North Carolina, the company representative said I should start at the beginning. Oh heck no! Are you kidding me? I wasn't a teacher by profession, and I was definitely not going to repeat lessons Tessa and Tristan should have already learned that year. Plus, there was so much material in those boxes; I doubted we would get through half of it.

Part of me wanted to chuck the boxes over the side and do the "unschooling" method, where basically your child learns all he or she needs to know from life's experiences. It was a proven theory, and as I gazed in frustration at the stack of textbooks, it was very tempting. I wasn't that brave, however. If my mom found out I wasn't giving my kids a standard education, I'm sure she would have called the Coast Guard to remove the children from my unfit care.

Still, I realized we had the unique opportunity to combine some pieces of a standard curriculum with having the kids learn from life experiences. We cut down on some of the "book learning" and embraced a life of perpetual field trips. Science was easily covered in our day-to-day activities. The marine life in the Bahamas was extensive. Our favorite snorkeling spot was the national park at Fowl Cay Reef.

June 11, 2007 Fowl Cay Reef, Abacos
(from the blog of Alegria)

The snorkeling at the first set of moorings was beyond our expectations for coral. The water was such a beautiful shade of blue, and once we looked below, we were just blown away. The underwater was transformed into an explosion of colors. Lush purple fans waved in the current, and the bright yellows from damsel and triggerfish and the brilliant blues from the surgeonfish kept us enthralled for hours. I'd never seen anything like it before.

At the next mooring, the water was colder and the coral less colorful. Because of the cold and the strong current, Tessa could only snorkel for a short time. As I was helping her back into the dinghy, I glanced up at the sky. Way off in the distance, I could see rain bands, and off to one side I noticed the start of a waterspout. It was well formed, with a big funnel at the top, spiraling down into a tight tail. It stopped about halfway to the water and then went back up. It came down again, broke into two distinct tails, and then retreated. It tried one more time to reach the water, and almost did, before it gave up and became a harmless cloud again.

We had one final spot to snorkel before we called it a day. It was even farther out. Tessa stayed in the dinghy, shivering under a towel. The water was just too cold for her. We watched a small southern stingray gracefully skim along the bottom below us, and then we swam into deeper water. Suddenly I spotted a grayish-brown shape, weaving in and out of the coral. Shark!

I grabbed Tristan, who was next to me, and pointed excitedly. Tristan got Dan's attention. The thought never occurred to me that I would be in the water with a shark, albeit a pretty harmless one, but here was a 4-foot-long nurse shark swimming less than 20 feet away. The shark would disappear for a bit, and I would quickly turn around to look behind me, making sure it wasn't sneaking up on us like barracudas like to do. A few seconds later, it would emerge, and we would follow along. Soon the shark got tired of us stalking him and left. We agreed you really couldn't top seeing a shark, so we swam back to the dinghy.

Once back, we got a surprise. About 6 feet away lurked a huge barracuda. His mouth was open, showing us his big teeth. Unlike sharks, barracudas don't have to move to breathe, so they can remain in one place for a long time. This one was trying to hide under our dinghy. I really wanted Tessa to see it. She was still shivering under the towel.

"Tessa, you need to jump in the water and see this barracuda," I said.

"No!"

"You'll regret not jumping in."

She thought about it for a moment then courageously donned her mask and jumped in. She went underwater and came up sputtering "Oh my God! Oh my God! Oh my God!" and shot into the dinghy.

I told her later she was very brave. It's one thing to already be in the water and see a big barracuda, but another thing to jump in when you know one is there. [*End blog*]

3

Seahorse, Stingrays and Visitors
ABACOS, BAHAMAS

W E REALLY LOVED THE BAHAMAS. It was a perfect first stop on our journey. Every day we swam with colorful fish and friendly rays. Every night we sat outside and gazed at the Milky Way. Every morning we woke up to white sand and crystal-clear water. We had the best backyard in the world.

Things were getting better and better on the boat. We were all learning to live together in a very small space; a shock coming from a 3,400-square-foot house. There were other issues we had to deal with too. Working in the corporate world had been stressful. We'd tried to maximize our time as a family when we weren't working; for example, instead of cooking during the week, most nights Dan or I would bring home take-out. And for the last thirteen years in North Carolina, we'd had a wonderful woman named Dolores clean our house. Unfortunately, Dolores wasn't with us anymore, so I constantly reminded Dan and the kids, "You had better pitch in!" They were trying.

Privacy was tough. On the negative side, Dan and I never went anywhere alone. That would change later on when the kids got older or when we were in a marina. On the positive side, I went from feeling like I never saw my children, or husband, to being with them 24/7. I loved it.

Homeschooling was getting easier every day. We were still working on putting together a schedule that would work. The hardest part was figuring out Tristan's and Tessa's learning styles. Tessa adapted to my "stuff scattered all over" approach and modeled it well. Though we had a cabinet with bookshelves solely for homeschooling supplies, Tessa's assignments, folders, pencils, books, and just about everything associated with school, somehow something disappeared nearly every...single...day. Tristan was much better organized. Sometimes he would get so involved in a lesson he loved, nothing would disturb him (which was a good thing). But if it was something he had no interest in, he could easily become distracted, like when I became frustrated with his sister, "How is it possible that you have lost all of your schoolwork again? The boat isn't that big!"

It was a learning process for us all and a guilt trip for me to think of all the years I possibly went cheap on Teacher's Appreciation Day. Those people were saints!

An interesting comment I would get from non-cruisers pertained to Dan and me. What did we talk about all day? They could almost understand being with the kids all the time (though when we told people we were going sailing for a few years, a majority asked if we were taking our kids), but they couldn't understand what spouses would find to talk about all the time. I thought that was really sad. Though we had our share of disagreements and drove each other crazy at times, Dan and I really enjoyed being together.

But the biggest question we got from people was "What do you do all day?" Coming from a life where multitasking was not only rewarded, it was expected, our new lifestyle was hard to understand. Living on a sailboat, you could honestly expect to handle one major issue a day. If it was laundry day, you did laundry. Needed a boat part? That was sure to take all day. Needed to get groceries? You had better clear the schedule.

June 23, 2007 Marsh Harbour, Great Abaco Island, Abacos
(from the blog of Alegria)

This is what a typical day of getting groceries looks like for us.

We walk into town, usually during the hottest part of the day, each of us carrying backpacks and large shopping totes. The grocery store is about seven long blocks from where we leave our dinghy, and we have to cross busy streets to get there. It seems it's always 90-plus degrees and rush hour when we go. There are no sidewalks, so we have to keep a constant vigil on the kids.

Groceries in the Bahamas are not cheap. You've heard of the CPI (consumer price index) used to keep track of food prices? Well, we use the SSS index (salsa, soda, spray cheese). We have found prices for these vary widely in the Abacos: salsa ranges from $6.99 at Green Turtle to $5.49 at Marsh Harbour; Diet Coke is always close to $6.00 for a six pack; and apparently the can of spray cheese is made of pure gold because it's $7.99!

But even worse than the prices is the fact that we have to carry it all back. We bring along bags and backpacks, but still, it's an ordeal. It's the same story every time we go. The Haitian bagger pushes our overloaded cart outside into the blazing heat, mystified about our intentions. Tristan complains that we bought too much. Tessa insists she can't carry the paper towels. Dan threatens next time to bring the duct tape and tape them to her body. I whine for a taxi. Captain Bligh (Dan) insists taxis are too expensive. We have never priced a taxi ride to the grocery store, but apparently, he is psychic. It's at this time, I choose to remind him of the fact that I didn't leave my job as senior vice president to schlep groceries across the surface of the sun. The bag boys enjoy the show.

Eventually we whittle down an entire cartload into four backpacks and several shoulder bags. The can of pineapple juice threatens the eggs. The outrageously expensive chips flatten into inedibility. The milk has somehow inverted itself and begins a rhythmic drip, which will of course seek out anything that needs to remain dry, and there was never any real hope for the bananas. But we pull through as a team, shoulder our groceries and begin our journey. I have to give the kids a lot of credit because after the initial complaints, they are great about carrying the bags. In fact, Tristan always tries to carry the heaviest bag for me. About two blocks into it, we start getting cocky.

We have to walk past the discount beer and liquor store. A six-pack of beer most places is $14, but here it is $10. We drop our bags, head into the store, and buy more. It's still a mystery how this new purchase makes it back to the dinghy, but somehow it does. Tessa and Tristan get into the dinghy first, and we stuff the bags around them, being careful to make sure nothing falls into the murky mixture of rain, saltwater, and possibly some engine oil or fuel that is forever accumulating in the bottom of the dinghy. Invariably, a bag always containing something we really don't want to get wet slides into the dinghy water, eliciting an outburst from Dan. Seriously, this happens almost every time.

When all of us and our packages are squished into our 10-foot dinghy, we motor back to *Alegria*. Our dinghy motor is really underpowered, so with all of us on board and loaded with beer, soda, and groceries, we are very slow. If there is any kind of wave in the harbor at all, instead of racing smoothly across the top, or planing as it's called in the boating world, we bounce hard, splashing more water into the dinghy, getting us and the formerly dry food soaked. This elicits an outburst from the kids and me. Seriously, this also happens almost every time.

When we arrive at the stern of *Alegria*, the grocery bags need to be carefully lifted up from the dinghy and placed onto the back platform without anything falling overboard into the water. We set up an assembly line. To keep bugs and roaches off the boat, everything must be taken from its packaging. Anything in cardboard (cereal, mac and cheese, etc.) has to come out of the box and into plastic bags or clear canisters.

I vacuum seal the meat in plastic bags. All the cold items are put together on the counter so that I only have to open the freezer once to get everything loaded. This keeps the freezer cold. Tristan places the fruit in the fruit hammock in the cockpit. Tessa puts away the canned goods and the remainder of the dry food. Dan stores the drinks and the paper products. It takes about an hour to get everything put away, and by then, we are all hungry for a meal. Think about that the next time you complain about grocery shopping! [*End blog*]

Some days it seemed there was little to do, and other days there was too much. One day, after a long day of provisioning, we still had to go back into town to run more errands. By the time we got to the boat the second time, it was 4 p.m. We were exhausted. But Fred and Kathy called us on the VHF and asked us to join them at Junkanoo, a Bahamian festival full of music, dancing, colorful costumes, and of course, delicious food. So, two hours later, we were back in town, for another long, long walk to the Junkanoo grounds.

The summer Junkanoo was held over several Fridays, June through August, in Marsh Harbour. We arrived at 7 p.m. and headed straight for the food. There was so much to choose from, but we settled on a dish of cracked lobster and Bahamian mac and cheese. Tristan and Tessa ate quickly then joined in the kids' activities: musical chairs, the three-legged race, and the potato-sack race.

We wandered around the parade grounds, looking at the beautiful Junkanoo costumes up close. The detail and time that was put into those costumes was very apparent. The base of the costumes was formed from cardboard and wire and then covered with crepe paper and silver or gold beads. Tessa talked to a girl her age, admiring the costume the girl was going to wear that night. It was a beautiful blue and white tunic with silver beads that fit over her shoulders, hung down in front and back, and looked very heavy. Tessa showed me a beautiful pink and white Junkanoo hat with silver beads she was holding. After admiring it, I asked her to please put it back carefully. The father of the little girl Tessa had been talking to said, "No. That is hers to keep. I gave it to her."

I was touched by his generosity. Of course, we all had to take turns trying on the hat and decided it looked the best on Tessa first and Fred second. At 8 p.m. the parade started. The music was loud and infectious. Cowbells, drums, whistles, the beat—all resonated throughout our bodies. We couldn't help but be moved by it. The parade made its way through the grounds then turned around. Everyone was welcome to participate. Tristan, I, and Tessa in her fabulous hat joined in. We had so much fun.

We stayed until about 9:30 p.m. After that we were just too tired. Instead of walking back, we got a taxi. Kathy asked the taxi driver if it was alright to have a beer in her taxi. "Go ahead," she said. "I'm having one."

As we left, the crowds started coming in. People with young children were just arriving. Even though the official start time was 6 p.m., the locals wouldn't come until about 10 p.m., and the party wouldn't really take off until around midnight. The taxi driver said we should stay longer as the main entertainment was the dancers and singers they brought in from Nassau. One performer was a famous glass eater. I was really sorry to miss that one! Maybe next year.

The next day we planned to stay on the boat the entire day. Tristan brought out the Dread Pirate game, and we spent over four hours involved in a high-stakes game of piracy on the high seas. Later that afternoon our friends on *Magnificat* called us on the VHF and invited us to the marina pool. They were sailing back to the US the next day. We grabbed some drinks and snacks and spent the rest of the day poolside.

June 27, 2007 Marsh Harbour, Abacos
(from the blog of Alegria)

We headed into town again, early in the morning, because I needed to get my hair cut. As I stepped into the dinghy, I noticed something small and gray floating in the water next to it. We were in a hurry, so I didn't pay too much attention, but suddenly Tessa pointed to it and yelled, "Seahorse! Mom, it's a seahorse!"

Sure enough, it was a seahorse floating on its side. I assumed it was dead as I couldn't imagine why else it would be on the surface. Actually I was thinking it was the dead seahorse that a guy on Great Guana Cay had given Tessa a few days ago. I was about to have a discussion with her about taking better care of her things, when I reached into the water and scooped it up. When it was in the palm of my hand, it started moving, stretching its head up and uncurling its tail. He was alive. And he was adorable.

"Can we keep him?" Always Tessa's first thought.

"No." But instinctively I knew he wasn't supposed to be floating on top of the water like that. Something must be wrong. I couldn't just drop him back in the harbor because I was sure he would die. "Quick. Get a bucket."

Tessa grabbed the nearest one, and I filled it with saltwater. She held the seahorse in her hand for a moment, then gently set him in the water. He swam a bit, then stopped but remained straight up; that was a good sign. We hated to leave him, but I was late for my hair appointment. Tessa set the bucket inside the cockpit where it would be safe, and we raced the dinghy toward the salon in town.

Last time Dan and Tristan had their hair cut at the black barbershop. This time they were joining me at the white beauty salon. A cruiser had recommended the salon to me. She had gotten a great haircut there, so I thought I would give them a try. The reservationist managed to squeeze all three of us in at the last minute.

The shop was like many discount hair salons in the US. It had two stylists cutting hair, while the owner managed the front desk. And like many salons in the US, it had all the elements of a soap opera.

As Mary, my stylist, was cutting my hair, her sister Liz came into the shop. Liz was trying to fill out some medical forms and needed help. It soon turned into a group effort for the entire beauty salon, and it become obvious that everyone in the shop knew more of her medical history than she did.

"Don't forget to put down...," said Mary.

"Remember you had...," added the other stylist.

"You've got to tell them about...," reminded a customer under the dryer. No one seemed to be worried about medical privacy.

"Tell them there are no more toys in the playpen," added her sister. Hmm. Toys? Playpen? This was a medical condition I was unfamiliar with.

"I don't have room to write that here." The word "here" came out "heeahh." White Bahamians have an accent that is very close to a New England accent.

"Make sure they know you still have the playpen."

Finally, and don't ask me how I figured it out from the clues, I realized they were talking about a hysterectomy. I found it surprising that this woman appeared to be in her thirties and had undergone a hysterectomy.

"Write hysterectomy," Mary instructed.

Liz started to write then stopped. "I don't know how to spell it."

"Ask Ginene. She knows."

Ginene, hiding under a dryer, was trying hard not to get involved in a spelling bee. When everyone in the salon, including me, looked at her expectantly, she simply shrugged her shoulders and went back to reading her magazine. When it seemed no one was going to come up with the correct spelling, I helped out.

"H Y S T...," I began.

She cut me off, "Wait. H... Y..."

I nodded and continued, "H Y."

She paused and gave me a blank stare. I think she was having trouble with my accent. I tried again, slower, "H... Y." Finally, we connected and got it right.

"Make sure you tell them it was only a pahtial [partial]," added Ginene.

"And it was experimental," came the voice from the other dryer.

I spent the next forty-five minutes learning more about medical procedures in the Bahamas than I ever cared to know. But my haircut was fantastic! Great day so far!

Back at the boat, our seahorse was settling in just fine. He'd found a spot to cling to on the side of the bucket. The bucket was yellow, and the seahorse appeared to be changing colors to better fit in. I picked him up gently. In my palm, he arched his back and stretched out his tail. As I held him, he let out a high-pitched clicking sound. We later learned they communicate by rubbing the sides of their head together. He had a small fin on either side of his head that he used to propel himself through the water. His head sloped down to a long, graceful snout designed to suck in food. His eyes were open, watching me. He was part miniature dragon, part miniature horse. He was truly magical.

The kids and I did some research on seahorses, trying to find the best place to release him. I was not about to put him back into Marsh Harbour because the water there wasn't that clean. I wanted to take him to a grassy spot near Mermaid Reef, but it was already getting dark. We would have to wait until the next day.

I was worried about our seahorse. I had heard that seahorses mate for life. If they lose a mate, it takes them a long time, maybe never, to find another one. It made me sad to think there was another seahorse waiting for him to come home; worried that maybe her mate had been eaten by a fish or met with some other disaster. Maybe we should go out in the dinghy and search the harbor? Where would I start? Tristan lost his sandal in the harbor the other day, and we couldn't find it. If I couldn't find a boy's sandal, I was sure I'd have no luck with a 4-inch-long seahorse.

Because they are so small, seahorses need to eat constantly. They eat by anchoring themselves to grass or coral and using their powerful snouts to suck in food as it goes by. It was now the next day, and at a minimum, he had not eaten in twenty-four hours. Our seahorse needed food. On the internet, we discovered they eat brine shrimp. I looked in our canned goods. No brine shrimp. I didn't think I would find any, but hey, we did have canned crab meat. I decided to try it. As I dropped the crabmeat into the bucket, I noticed that the seahorse was lying at an angle instead of straight up and down. He showed no interest in the crabmeat which had settled uselessly on the bottom of the bucket. Not good. I used Skype to call the local bait shops, looking for brine shrimp. No luck there either.

It was now after lunch, and there wasn't much time. We had hired a worker to climb up our mast and fix our antenna, and unfortunately, he wasn't finished. We couldn't leave the boat until he was done, and we all wanted a part in the seahorse's release. The kids and I waited nervously, watching our little friend valiantly cling to life. We whispered words of encouragement to him to hang on a little longer. Finally, we could leave the boat.

Tessa put the seahorse bucket into the dinghy. The rest of us piled in after. The seahorse looked lifeless. The plan was to get out of the harbor and around the corner to a grassy spot, about a mile and a half away. The wind had picked up, so we were in for a soggy, wet ride. As we motored along, the rough waves kicked up the water in the bucket, causing the bits of crabmeat that had settled on the bottom to move. Suddenly the seahorse started sucking up the crabmeat bits that were swirling around him. He ate them as fast as he could. Seahorses only eat live food and the bumpy boat ride had made the crab pieces swirl in the bucket, causing our hungry friend think they were alive. It was a seahorse miracle!

Excitedly, we stopped in a grassy area. It was low tide, so the water was less than a foot deep. Tessa had her goggles on, prepared to snorkel in 8 inches of water. I had our underwater camera ready so I could take pictures of our seahorse in his new home. We all said our goodbyes. As soon as I set him underwater, in the grass, he nearly disappeared, taking on the color of the surroundings. We caught one more glimpse of our friend, and I managed to snap a few photos. Then he disappeared, blending into the sea grass as if he had never been there. We missed him already. By the way, after more research on the internet, we discovered he was a *she*. [*End blog*]

In July we had our first visitors: Karon, Alan, and their two boys, Alec and Collin. It was regatta time in the Bahamas and Fourth of July, so there was much to do. We watched our friends, Anne and Steve race their catamaran, *Fine Line*, in the regatta. We ate all the free burgers and fries we could and washed them down with free margaritas at the Stranded Naked Party on Fiddle Cay. Despite it being an American holiday, we celebrated Fourth of July on Green Turtle with free beer and rum. And we made some new friends, Bob and Lisa, who were house-sitting on Manjack. They invited our kids to play with their kids, while Bob tried unsuccessfully to teach Dan about spear fishing. Bob even gave Dan a Hawaiian sling, a type of spear for spear fishing. I knew the fish would never be in any danger. It was a unique opportunity having our old friends meet our new friends and giving them a glimpse of what our life was now like. But all too soon it came to an end.

It was July, and July in the Bahamas and the rest of the Caribbean is hurricane season. Dan and I had discussed different options on where to go since the Abacos wasn't the safest place to be in a hurricane. We still hadn't made a decision when Fred and Kathy on *Makai* stopped by to say goodbye. *Makai, Fine Line, Sand Dollar,* and *Magnificat* were all leaving the next day to head back to Florida for hurricane season. I guess we should have expected this, but we were still shocked. What were we going to do?

We couldn't leave with them because our friends Karon and Alan were still visiting, and we also didn't like the idea of spending more time in Florida. We understood though that a weather window was a weather window, and in hurricane season you needed to get moving. Reluctantly, we said goodbye. Our friend Alan summed it up. "You meet these people, they become your friends, and then they leave and you never know if you'll see them again. It's sad." Exactly.

A few days later, we said goodbye to Karon, Alan, and the boys. That was hard. Now we were all alone with no idea where we were going and all the people we knew heading north. What were we going to do? I was sick to my stomach just thinking about it. A big part of me just wanted to go back home. I felt like I was homesick, but I couldn't exactly tell you what I was homesick for.

As I sat with it, I realized that what I was feeling was partially loneliness, but also a big part was fear. We started this trip alone, but we had gotten used to the idea of hanging out with other cruisers. Now we were back on our own again, in hurricane season, without a plan.

When we had originally thought about the trip, we agreed on sailing to the Bahamas and then southwest to Guatemala. Once we were on our trip and actually took an honest look at our capabilities, we realized we weren't those kind of sailors yet and decided against that. This left a big hole in our adventure plans.

One day while we were getting into our dinghy, which was tied near the marina in Marsh Harbour, we saw a large group of Boy Scouts file down the dock to one of the boats. We were curious as to where they were going, so we followed them. They boarded a large steel boat, and after talking to a few of the people standing around, we eventually met the owners, a very nice couple in their late thirties or early forties. They told us how they chartered to Boy Scout groups who went out on the ship for a week's adventure. The Scouts learned to snorkel and hone seamanship skills, in addition to performing chores like cleaning the boat. There had to be at least twenty-or-so Scouts boarding this boat, and I had no idea where they could all possibly sleep. The wife told me that they slept on deck. I asked what happened when it rained, and she said they just piled up somewhere below deck.

A delivery of several pizzas arrived, stopping our conversation briefly while one of the dads collected money for the food. I couldn't believe it. These Scouts paid several hundred dollars apiece to sleep on deck, clean toilets, scrub the boat, and eat pizza. What a great racket. I would feed them and let them stay on my boat for *free*, in a *bed*, if they would just clean it for me, especially the toilets. I had two kids who wouldn't know the first thing about cleaning a toilet. I wanted in on this. How could I get a

Boy Scout?

The couple told us they had a never-ending stream of Scouts coming down all summer. In late August, they'd sail to the Dominican Republic, which they loved. I cooled my jealously long enough to find out more information about the Dominican Republic. They told us the country, which shares the island of Hispaniola with Haiti, was safe, had good food, was cheap, and offered great hurricane protection. They strongly suggested we go there. That felt good to us. So in an instant, we changed our mind on Guatemala and solved our hurricane-hole dilemma. It was down the thorny path to the Dominican Republic, and fast.

Getting to the Dominican Republic (also known as the DR) and farther south wouldn't be easy. It is called the "thorny path" because it is a long trip directly into the waves and wind, and it is generally as hard on sailors as it is on their boats. In fact, about a year before our trip, I had read a book called *The Gentlemen's Guide to Passages South,* in which the author talked about the rough sailing down the island chain. He cited horror stories of weather and seas chewing up boats. In some places, you could only sail at night if you wanted to make any headway at all, and then you might have to sail close to shore with the risk of hitting rocks.

I still remember quite clearly reading that book. I'd been terrified and had told Dan there was no way I could do that, and we absolutely weren't going that way. That was why, back then, we had talked about going to Guatemala instead. But apparently the trip was taking on a life of its own because while talking to this couple, none of the fear of sailing to the DR came to mind. Seriously, I didn't remember any of the horrible sailing stories, and I have a very good memory. For some reason, unknown to me at that moment, our destiny lay south.

July 17, 2007 Marsh Harbour, Great Abaco Island, Abacos

(from the blog of Alegria)

We are trying to get everything done before we leave for Eleuthera, located within the next Bahamian-island grouping. Dan had to work on the boat insurance. Our current insurance company didn't want to renew our boat insurance because we were still in the hurricane belt. We had to scramble at the last minute to find a new company. While Dan worked on that, I took the kids with me to do laundry. We walked in the heat with four large bags, but the kids never complained.

The laundromat was crowded, and I wasn't sure if it was hotter inside the building or outside. Tessa quickly found some kids to play with, while Tristan helped me wash and fold. It didn't take long, but it was mind numbing. In most of the laundry places in the Bahamas (and the rest of the islands as we found out later), there was at least one TV set, and it seemed the only programs ever on were Law and Order or whatever was on the Lifetime channel. The episodes were always about an extremely violent crime taking place in the US. I couldn't imagine how people who watched those programs over and over ever thought about coming to America.

The laundry was finished. I was drenched in sweat. We gathered the bags and stepped outside. If possible, it had gotten even hotter. There was no breeze as we plodded to the dinghy. I wasn't sure I was going to make it. If I could just hang on until we got to the end of the block without my head exploding, I would be alright. It was after noon, and I knew I wouldn't feel like cooking lunch. When we got to the Bahamian mart that sold good deli sandwiches, I left Tristan, Tessa, and the laundry outside the store and went inside. I bought sandwiches, drinks, chips, and tomatoes. More stuff to carry. We made room and were back on our way.

We passed the discount liquor store. We were out of beer and soda, so we stopped. Again, the kids stayed outside. A guy sporting a distinctive mohawk cut in front of me in the line. "How rude," I thought to myself. I remembered this guy from the Junkanoo a few days ago, dancing by himself, lost in his own world. The day before, I saw him and another guy, sitting under the tree by the dinghy dock, smoking cigarettes, and sharing a beer. He bought something in the store and went outside. He came back in again as I was going out.

I now had two more heavy bags that I had no idea how we were going to carry. I set them down and looked at Tristan and Tessa. While I was tired and sweating, they were each enjoying a cold can of root beer.

"Where did you get that?"

"The guy with the mohawk bought them for us," said Tessa.

She explained that while I was inside, he walked up the steps to the store. Tessa called, "Good afternoon. How are you?" to him as he passed her. I am guessing this was something people hadn't said to him very often.

When he turned to see who it was, he said, "Princess!" Then he asked Tristan and Tessa if they wanted orange juice or root beer. They said root beer, and he bought it for them. I was a little shocked. A possibly homeless man, the man I'd earlier thought of as rude, had bought my kids a drink. There was an interesting turn of events.

When he came out of the store, I thanked him. He saw all my bags and asked if I needed help. I said yes as his friend rode up on a bicycle. The mohawk guy took two bags, the guy with the bicycle took the laundry bags, and we walked the last three blocks to the dinghy dock. I was lucky they helped us because we never would have made it ourselves. They refused a tip, so I bought some mangos from them instead.

As we left, Tessa waved to them from the dinghy. "I like that guy," she said. "He is so funny! I told him I liked

47

his hair."

Back at the boat, I asked Tristan to put the thermometer in the sun and see what the temperature was. It showed 110 degrees. That was without the humidity index, which made it feel even hotter. Dan said we couldn't put the thermometer in the sun because that wasn't accurate. I told him we walked in the sun, so it was accurate for us. [*End blog*]

The next day was the big day. We were leaving Marsh Harbour. I was nervous knowing we'd soon be sailing in the Atlantic Ocean to Eleuthera. We had been sailing in the protected waters of Abaco Sound since April, so it had been a few months since we had sailed in open water. As I pulled up the anchor, I heard a bird cry. Looking up, I saw a huge osprey circling low over our boat. He obviously wanted my attention because as soon as I looked at him, he stopped calling and headed off over land. It seemed to me it was a sign. Later I read about ospreys in my animal-totem book. It said the osprey teaches us that we need to move outside our comfort zone and take risks. We shouldn't be afraid of grasping opportunities just because they seem like they are out of our reach. The book went on to say that ospreys were messengers reminding us to pay attention to our intuition, and they would also help guide us back to a place of safety, security, or a feeling of being grounded.

Later that afternoon in Lynyard Cay, I looked for a place to anchor. We planned to leave early the next morning for Eleuthera. As we circled the harbor, I heard a bird cry again. There, perched on a dead tree near the water, was the osprey. It was as if he was telling us this was a good spot. I took his word and dropped our anchor in front of the tree. Little did I know then, but the osprey would be our guide over several islands, and I would constantly be reminded of his message. The next morning, bright and early, we hauled anchor and headed out of the Abacos.

4

Strange Days

EXUMAS, ELEUTHERA, BAHAMAS

THE TRIP ACROSS TO SPANISH Wells, on St George's Cay just off Eleuthera, was interesting. What little wind we had was on the nose, so we motored. (Yes, we could have executed an unending series of tacks and doubled our time for the crossing, but we had no interest in that. I wanted to be where I was going as soon as possible.) The trip was hot and long. Large swells lifted us up and down, causing Tristan and Tessa to become sea sick. I was feeling a little queasy too. To help with the nausea, I grated some fresh ginger into orange juice, and we all drank it. The kids slept and felt better when they woke up.

Alegria motored easily through the incredible, dark blue and very deep (between 2 and 3 miles deep) sea. As we got closer to Eleuthera, the wind died, the swells flattened out, and eventually the sea turned to glass. Dan pointed to something floating on the water off our starboard (right) side. At first we thought it might be dolphins, but as we got closer, we realized it was a pod of pilot whales. In calm seas, pilot whales will rest on the surface, usually in large groups. This pod was a group of eight. Tessa was over the moon. She wanted to see whales, and there they were, right off our starboard bow. The whales weren't overly big, maybe about 10 to 12 feet, and there were a couple of babies. As we passed as close as we dared, they quietly slipped beneath the surface.

It was after 4 p.m. when we dropped anchor at Spanish Wells and decided to explore the town. It was quite a shock compared to the other island settlements we had been to, feeling more like a small town in America than a Bahamian island. Several pickup trucks filled with young boys drove through town, stereos blasting. Spanish Wells was very small, less than a third of a mile wide and less than 2 miles long, so where they were driving to we couldn't guess.

This was a community of very wealthy lobster fishermen. Large satellite dishes were mounted to the roof of every house we saw. As we walked along the streets, occasionally we would see people sitting on their porches, but no one returned our hellos. We got the distinct impression we weren't wanted. Undeterred, I continued to wave at everyone, and undeterred, they continued to ignore me.

The inhabitants of Spanish Wells are direct descendants of a small religious group called the Eleutheran Adventurers; a group of English Puritans who left Bermuda, seeking religious freedom, warmer climates, and a chance to establish new territory. As a result of this small gene pool, almost every girl we saw had blonde hair and most looked very much alike. Also, as I alluded to earlier, they were severely lacking in the friendly gene.

According to our guidebook, the women and girls worked in the restaurants and the processing plants, while most of the boys left school at age fourteen and became lobster fishermen. It was a lucrative business, and they could earn a lot of money during a four-week trip. The kids generally remained on the island, with the boys buying houses before they were married. The guidebook said the marrying age for girls was between fifteen and nineteen, but an unmarried nineteen year old was considered an old maid.

I'm not sure how much of that was accurate, but there

was a very different vibe about that island. We came in on a Saturday afternoon, and by 5 p.m., except for the restaurants, the town was pretty well rolled up. Apparently even the crazy boys in the pickup trucks had grown tired of driving their short, rectangular path and had disappeared. The town boasted an internet café called Teen Planet and a movie house, but those were closed too. It was all a little too *Children of the Corn* for us.

We did find an open restaurant and stopped in for a sandwich. While we were there, I asked about the high-speed ferry we'd seen earlier. Our guidebook stated we could take it to Harbour Island for a reasonable rate. When I asked our waitress about it, what time it left the next day or what Harbour Island was like, she said she had no idea. She had never been there. Harbour Island was a twenty-minute trip by ferry, but neither she nor any of the other girls in the restaurant had ever been there. I asked her where she went when she left the island. She replied they went to Europe or the United States. Very strange.

To make sure we were still in the Bahamas we loved and hadn't passed through a portal into a Steven King novel, we took the high-speed ferry to Harbour Island the next day. It was a short walk from the ferry dock to the beach. Harbour Island proclaims itself famous for its beautiful, pink-sand beaches. The beaches were beautiful, with soft sand, but the pink was a bit of a stretch. There were some very fine, red coral pieces in the sand that if you looked close enough may have given the illusion of pink...Whatever the color, it was still pretty.

Dan had missed breakfast, so his priority was lunch. We decided to eat at Ma Ruby's for her famous cheeseburger. Ma Ruby held court by the door. She wished us a friendly "Welcome home!" as we entered her restaurant. She made us feel special from the moment we walked in. We spent the next two hours enjoying her delicious cooking and listening to the story of her life.

After lunch, we spent the rest of the day lazily wandering through town, taking in the beauty of the historic churches and houses. On our way back to the ferry, we passed a huge tree. Several local children were climbing its branches and swinging down from the vines. It looked like fun, so I encouraged Tristan and Tessa to join in. The other children made room and cheered them on as they stepped out on the limb and swung down like Tarzan and Jane, their faces lit up with huge grins.

We really liked Harbour Island. The beaches were beautiful, the people friendly, and the feeling was like an island paradise. I could have stayed there longer, but we knew we had to keep moving. Next up were the Exumas as we continued south among the numerous Bahamian islands.

July 24, 2007 Ship Channel Cay, Exumas
(from the blog of Alegria)

Goodbye Eleuthera, hello Exumas! We covered 55 miles today and decided to anchor off a small private island called Ship Channel Cay. The anchorage was empty except for a forlorn-looking houseboat with several lobster traps piled on top. Tied to the houseboat was a good-sized, open motor boat, or skiff. A man stood in the doorway of the houseboat, but we were too far away to see much else. We dropped anchor in what we hoped was good holding. Dan put on his snorkel gear to check the anchor, and our attention was immediately diverted by a helicopter hovering overhead. The pilot made a few low passes over our boat. I had no idea what he was doing.

Tessa asked if she could go with Dan. Usually we let her go, but this time I told her no. I just didn't feel good about it. Tristan had no interest in going either, which was unusual, so Dan swam off alone. It was a long swim because we were anchored in about 13 feet of water, and I had let out over 100 feet of chain. When he returned, Dan said the anchor was flipped, so he started the engine and backed down on it again. He hoped this would cause the anchor to flip over and dig in.

I was taking some fish out of the freezer for dinner when I heard yelling from the back of the boat. I ran into the cockpit and looked off the back of the boat. Just off our swim platform was the biggest barracuda I had ever seen. Just as Dan had jumped into the water to check the anchor, the barracuda had swum right underneath him. He'd almost landed right on top of it. It was huge. It had to be 5 feet long. Dan had yelled in surprise when he'd seen it and had hastily beat a retreat back onto *Alegria*.

The barracuda was waiting patiently for him. Dan didn't have much choice, he had to go back and check on the anchor. He grabbed his spear. I ran back inside to look for something to throw at the barracuda. I came back out with two kiwis.

"I'll try to chase him off," I yelled, throwing a kiwi.

When the kiwi hit the water, the barracuda retreated a bit, so I threw the second one. Note to self: kiwis float. They never went below the water and never hit the barracuda. He thought I was feeding him! He was distracted by my offering until he heard Dan splash back into the water. Dan swam around the port side of the boat. The barracuda followed. As I ran back into the galley to find something else to throw, a skiff pulled up from the starboard side, scaring the barracuda away. It was the guy from the houseboat.

"There are sharks in the water," he called out. I thought he was joking. He looked a bit like Crocodile Dundee—except, as Tristan pointed out, he wasn't wearing pants. (He was wearing a shirt over Speedos.)

"Yeah," I laughed. "We just saw a big barracuda."

I asked him about the helicopters.

"It was the DEA looking for drug runners. They were here all day yesterday too."

Great! I was now in an episode of "Cops, Bahamas." I

made a mental note to leave our sliding-glass door open that night so the DEA wouldn't have to break it down when they mistakenly raided us.

"Seriously," he said, looking toward Dan. "Tell him not to go back in the water. There are sharks."

I nodded thinking of the quaint sharks in the Abacos. We'd seen a lot of sharks. The nurse sharks are fairly docile. Nothing really to fear. No reason to panic.

"A hammerhead swam by me earlier," he said. "He was bigger than my boat." Did I mention his skiff was about 15 feet long? That was a perfectly good reason to panic!

My eyes widened as I realized Dan was still in the water. "He's checking the anchor. He took his spear gun," I offered meekly.

The Crocodile Dundee wannabe shook his head. "If that shark wants him, he'll get him. I'll go pick him up."

He put the engine to full throttle and sped to where Dan was, about 100 feet from the boat. I looked for more kiwi to throw. Wait! He said that shark was over 15 feet long. I was going to need bigger fruit! Mr. Dundee slid the skiff up next to Dan and said something I couldn't hear, but I could tell by Dan's mad scramble into the guy's boat what was said. Our hero without pants delivered Dan back to the safety of *Alegria*, then returned to his houseboat. He and another guy were fishing that night for jacks. Much later that evening, we saw their fishing lights in the far distance. Other than that, we were very alone in the anchorage. After a dinner of tilapia, the kids and I played a board game, and Dan worked on the port engine, changing the fuel filter. That night I slept like a baby under a blanket of stars. [*End blog*]

The farther south we went, the fewer boats we saw. We spent a few days enjoying ourselves at the Warderick Wells Exuma Land and Sea Park. We were the only boat there. That was fine with us. The kids had fun playing in the sand and watching the black-tip reef sharks swim near the docks at night. The park office had DVDs for rent and books to exchange, and except for not being able to buy food or groceries, it was perfect. Well, it was perfect until the butterfly incident.

At Warderick Wells you are not supposed to feed the animals; this included the fish. But we didn't listen. What harm could come from throwing bread crumbs to the fish hanging around our stern? The very large remora seemed especially hungry.

One morning during school, a huge, beautiful butterfly floated into the salon. It was the largest butterfly I had ever seen, and the kids and I were transfixed. This was one of those special moments that I liked to call a teaching moment.

"Kids look. See that butterfly? You don't see butterflies like that anymore in the US. This is the reason we came on this trip. To experience nature like this. I am so glad you are getting to see this." Dan was down in the bedroom. "Dan, come up here. You have got to see this butterfly."

The butterfly continued its aimless flight around the room. My heart was singing. The kids and I watched it playfully skip over our heads.

"What a great moment, kids. I am so happy we are able to experience this as a family." I was really laying it on thick, but I truly was caught up in the moment.

We have the standard fans on our boat. They are about 7 inches across, and the plastic blade is exposed on the back. Every so often, the fan gets turned so the blade is exposed to the front. Not a big deal for human fingers because the blade is plastic and designed to stop spinning if it hits an object like your finger, but unfortunately, not a butterfly.

"Dan, you have got to see this butterfly," I called to him again. Dan entered the salon.

"He's just flying around here. Oh wait," I said alarmed

as the butterfly suddenly drifted toward the fan. "Oh no Mr. Butterfly! Don't fly into the..." I jumped up from my seat, but it was too late. There was the distinctive sound of butterfly wings being ground by the fan blades. Bits of butterfly shot across the cabin.

"Turn off the fan!" I screamed to Dan.

Dan ran to the control panel and cut the power. The fan blades stopped nearly instantly. We all held our breath as we looked toward the fan. The silence was suddenly broken by a soft thud as the butterfly, released from the stopped fan blade, landed with a thud on the counter. We gazed in horror at what was left of this beautiful creature. He was still alive, but his wings were nearly all gone. I gently picked him up.

If there is any way to save an animal, I will do it. But what to do with this butterfly? I couldn't kill it, but its wings wouldn't grow back. I looked at the kids, who were staring at me, eyes wide, clearly shocked by the entire incident. Should I just keep it in a cup and feed it the rest of its life? Like I needed one more thing to look after. I decided to leave it up to fate.

I carried the butterfly into the cockpit. It still had half of a wing on one side and a quarter of a wing on the other. The kids followed me. I held it up over the stern of the boat.

"I think it has enough wing left to make it to shore," I said optimistically. The kids didn't look convinced. I held the butterfly up as high as I could before I let it go. He dropped quickly, but then there was a brief, sweet moment when it seemed he had found his way. Suddenly, out of nowhere, the remora we had been feeding leaped up and snatched the butterfly, chomping down on it with his greedy mouth before disappearing under the boat. The kids and I stood there, dumbfounded. Well, that was unexpected. Silently, head lowered in shame, I herded the kids back to school. Circle of life kids.

Our next stop south was Cambridge Cay, another remote anchorage in the Exuma Land and Sea Park. The Sea Aquarium was one of the best snorkeling spots we had been to, and we had been to some really great spots. There was even a sunken airplane, clearly visible in about 15 feet of water. We were about to jump into the water for a closer look when we noticed the wreckage was carefully guarded by three large barracudas, so we gave it a pass. The Sea Aquarium, though, was irresistible.

The Sea Aquarium is perfect snorkeling for kids, consisting of a miniature wall dive with plenty of fish and the most colorful coral we had seen yet. It was an explosion of color: bright yellow trumpet fish, yellow and black-striped sergeant majors, greenish-brown groupers, and purple damselfish all accentuated by the oranges, browns, purples, reds, and golds of the coral. A dark-green, netted barrel sponge that resembled a huge vase, smaller on the bottom flowing up and out to a larger opening, was a great hiding place for an angelfish. On the ocean floor, Tessa and I saw something with brown and cream markings with a snake-like body, and at first we thought it *was* a snake. Later when we got our reef-identification book, we discovered it was a tiger tail sea cucumber. We saw the biggest variety of sea life, and the best part? It was all free.

Early the next morning, as we were preparing to leave, the owner of the 60-foot motoryacht *Exit* came over in his dinghy with his two dogs. He seemed surprised we were heading south and not north during hurricane season. He asked us if we needed anything, like water or ice, and we said no. He gave us a great compliment when he told us we looked pretty self-sufficient. We really were. The solar panels did a great job of generating electricity, we had the generator if we wanted to run anything special that might drain our batteries, the watermaker made great water, the freezer kept food frozen, and the refrigerator made an excellent "cool" spot for the vegetables and our vitamins. With a big supply of books and DVDs and an incredible view out our windows every day, what more did we need?

While the Exumas were beautiful, they were also remote. There were no large grocery stores there or places to dump our trash. Our garbage threatened to overwhelm us. We needed to find a place to dump it and pick up some bread and milk. The Staniel Cay Yacht Club seemed as good a place as any, and we took a slip for the night. The yacht club was expensive for what we got, but we couldn't leave our garbage unless we stayed in the marina. They wanted to charge us $2.50 per bag for the first two small bags of trash and then $25.00 for every bag after that. We had three big trash bags, each containing two smaller bags. There was no way we were going to pay those fees. We dropped off one bag and resigned ourselves to traveling with the rest of our garbage farther south.

Once docked, we looked for a grocery store. The town wasn't that big, and it was incredibly hot, but we had our trusty map. The map got us lost as it had us looking for roads that didn't exist. There was a lot of construction on the island, so maybe the person who drew the map was being optimistic. A local walking down the road, not sweating nearly as much as we were, gave us the correct directions to two stores. With hopes high, we entered the nearest one, enthusiastically called a "supermarket."

From the outside, the not so super market looked smaller than my garage back home. Inside, it wasn't any better. It was dark and it was hot. It was over 90 degrees outside, and inside the store, with no breeze, I am sure it was over 100 degrees. As she watched us enter, one of the ladies sitting outside shouted to the one in the store to "turn on the freezer." That wasn't a good sign.

I searched for bread but couldn't find any. The clerk showed me an old, hard loaf that someone had made. I passed. The Diet Coke cans were actually hot, not warm, but hot like they had been out in the sun all day. There was no fresh food, just some overpriced dishwashing soap, a few canned goods, and strangely, Evian water. Dan asked me, "Who drinks Evian water anymore? These must have been here since the eighties!"

There was nothing I wanted to buy, but Dan said we had to buy something since they made a point of "opening" for us. I didn't dare look in the just-turned-on freezer. Finally I settled on a can of pineapple juice, grossly overpriced at $6, and two small bags of chocolate chip cookies. We left the oven posing as a grocery store and headed back to the boat.

On our walk back to the marina, I examined my cookies and saw that one package had a hole chewed in it, and the other one was somehow opened. I sighed. I didn't want to think of what animal lived in that store and chewed holes in bags of cookies. Well, they were perfect for where we were headed next, Pig Beach, and I took them along with the leftovers from Tessa's lunch.

When we arrived at the island, properly known as Big Major Cay, the tender from the megayacht *Milk and Honey* was anchored close to shore. A man and a woman sat inside, staring at what we came to see: pigs on the beach. A large pink pig immediately came out to greet our dinghy as we pulled up on the sand. A brown pig sat by himself in the water looking a little dazed.

At first the kids were surprised and a little scared, but soon they were feeding the pink pig cookies and running with her on the beach. The brown one sauntered over, but the pink one was more aggressive with the food, so she kept him away. Eventually she left, leaving the brown one to get all the attention.

I had two slices of meat left over from Tessa's lunch. I gave one to the brown pig and then set the other slice on the floor of the dinghy. I walked over to talk to the couple from *Milk and Honey*. They were watching a shark swimming close to our dinghy. They said they had been on the beach awhile and had given the brown pig four beers. I'm not sure why you would do that, but okay. I started to ask them questions about the megayacht when I heard Dan desperately calling my name. I turned around, then froze in shock as I saw the brown pig in our dinghy.

You know, back in the US when I was thinking about all the things we needed to worry about on this trip, a drunken pig in my dinghy did not make the list. Yet here we were trying to evict an intoxicated pig from our boat. I would love to see that covered in one of the sailing magazines. I can even picture the headline: *Don't go offshore until you know the pig-out-of-the-dinghy drill!*

It wasn't easy evicting our oversized nemesis. His entire front body and legs were inside, and he was very close to getting his back legs in. Dan was inside the dinghy trying to push him out. I rushed over and grabbed the back of the pig's body, pulling while Dan pushed. He didn't go easily. He slammed his head into Dan, causing Dan to fall and cut open his palm on the edge of the dinghy seat. Dan's hand was now bleeding.

"Put your hand in the saltwater," the megayacht guy suggested after seeing the blood. Excuse me, but weren't you just watching a shark in the water? Now Dan should stick his bloody hand there?

We pushed and pulled some more. The guy who turned the pig into the drunken mess that he was offered us no help. Finally, with one final push from Dan, the pig was out of the dinghy, but he wasn't happy. I stood between him and our boat, holding my camera in my right hand. He thought it was food and chomped down on my arm, hard! I cursed loudly. Luckily he didn't break the skin, but he bit hard enough so that a huge lump instantly formed on the outside of my forearm. The inside of my forearm had gouges from his big ugly teeth. I was very lucky he hadn't bitten my hand or my wrist, or his powerful teeth would most likely have broken something.

"He bit me!"

The woman said, "He bit me too, yesterday. On the butt."

Seriously? He bit you on the butt, and you came back *and* gave him several beers? What is wrong with you people?

Though Dan warned me not to, I slapped the pig hard on the nose. In retaliation, the pig nipped me on the leg. I hated this pig. Even if he mistook my camera for food, he had now gone over the line. We had to get out of there before this turned into a cage fight. The other couple was leaving too.

"Get in the dinghy," we yelled to the kids, who, in terror, had distanced themselves down the beach, wondering how something so fun had turned bad so fast. Of course the pig thought he was coming too and swam after us. At this point, it was every man, woman, and child for themselves. Dan pushed the dinghy out and I dove inside. The kids were racing down the beach, and I was screaming, "Get in! Get in!"

Dan fumbled with the motor while Tristan and Tessa splashed through the water. There was going to be some tough love if they couldn't outswim the pig. I held out my hand and Tristan grabbed it. I pulled him, then Tessa to safety. The motor roared to life. As I examined the lump on my arm, the guy from *Milk and Honey* yelled to me.

"Put your arm in saltwater."

I yelled back, "It isn't bleeding."

"Put it in saltwater anyway. It will help."

Thank you, doctor. Never take advice from someone who thinks it's funny to get huge, hungry, and aggressive pigs drunk.

Back in the safety of *Alegria,* I asked Dan to get me

some ice from the freezer. The ice was at the very bottom, and you have to lift nearly everything out to get to it. He couldn't find it, or simply lost interest, and instead handed me a bag of cold water and said (this is, unfortunately a direct quote), "Here use this. It's colder than ice."

I stared at him a while before I replied. "If it's colder than ice, wouldn't it be ice?" So much for good medical help on the high seas.

5

Strange Spirits

OUT ISLANDS, BAHAMAS

W E MADE OUR WAY STEADILY down the Bahamian chain, with brief stops at Little Farmer's Cay and George Town on Great Exuma Island before stopping for what we thought would be an overnight at the island of Rum Cay. We were getting used to the fact that we were the only boat crazy enough to be sailing in the Bahamas during hurricane season, but we were keeping an eye on the weather as best we could.

What the islands lacked in other cruisers, they more than made up for in beauty and friendly local people. The only downside to the out islands, once we passed George Town, was the lack of fresh food. Meghan, on Little Farmer's Cay, told us the supply boat hadn't been in for three weeks. It was just as bad when we arrived at Rum Cay.

We made it to Rum Cay without any problems. We were hoping to go farther, but with the wind on our nose (again), we decided to pull into the Rum Cay Marina and see if we could get better sailing weather in a few days. Tristan and I were on coral-head watch the last part of the trip due to the many reefs in this area. The water was the clearest we had seen. The depth finder showed 40 feet, and we could easily see the bottom.

The entrance to Rum Cay Marina was pretty well

marked even though we missed the last marker. There were tall white poles to guide you in, and George from the marina had told us to keep them to our right. I was at the front of the boat looking for reefs as we passed by the poles. We heard George calling a boat. First he called *Stardust,* then realized that was the wrong boat and started shouting "Catamaran!"

I was up front, so I couldn't hear what he was saying, and Dan couldn't leave the wheel. I finally ran back and answered his call on the VHF.

"Didn't you see the green ball?" George asked.

We were supposed to go between the green ball and the pole, and we'd gone to the outside of the green ball. In fairness to Dan and me, the green ball was about the size of a soccer ball and painted so dark we couldn't see it.

"Are we going to be okay?" I asked.

"Well, if you haven't hit anything," said George, "you are okay." Welcome to Rum Cay.

We were desperate for groceries, so after checking into the marina, we began the long hot trek into the settlement, a good fifteen-minute walk down a long dirt road in the middle of nowhere. In fact, we were just about to give up when we saw flags hanging above the road, designating the middle of the settlement.

Just past the center of the settlement, we found a small store prophetically named The Last Chance grocery store. The sign outside the store boasted vegetables, fruits, and ice cream. I was giddy with the possibilities. Inside the store, I found a large glass cooler containing several cartons of eggs. I opened the first carton, all but five of the eggs were cracked. I opened the next carton. This one was even worse, with only three unbroken eggs. There was one carton left, and I hoped that between the three of these I could make my own dozen. As I took it out of the cooler, it dripped egg yolk on my hand. Defeated, I gave up. There was no fresh bread, no Diet Coke, no cereal, and no bottled water. I found a small section of canned goods, some frozen chicken, and curiously, several boxes of cake mixes. Disappointed, I bought lettuce, baloney, and Gatorade.

Back at the marina, two sport-fishing boat captains were cleaning their catch. Tristan and Tessa ran down to watch. Later Dan checked on the kids and found Tessa hanging off the dock, holding a fish head in her hand, trying to get a nurse shark's attention. Spotting Tessa dangling over the dock, Glen, the captain of the *Jolly Rodgers*, warned Dan, "The nurse sharks are pretty tame, but a bull shark will jump out of the water." A few minutes after Dan made Tessa give up this game, a bull shark casually swam under the dock.

Our family settled easily into life on this remote piece of paradise in the middle of really nowhere. Though not much happens on the island, there is a thriving community of Americans, and very soon we became part of an extended family of expats, locals, and sport fishermen.

While it was very hard to buy groceries on Rum Cay, we didn't starve. In fact, we ate very well. *Jolly Rodgers*, one of the large sport-fishing boats that brought clients to Rum Cay to fish, hosted a dock cookout every night, and the crew invited us and several other Americans living on the island to join them. We feasted on whatever was caught during the day. If the catch was light, Captain Glen would grill the thick steaks he pulled from his large freezer. If the mosquitoes weren't bad, we all sat on the docks and talked until late in the evening. Some nights, we played late games of poker in the restaurants. Thanks to Glen and his wife, Melanie, we were living the good life in Rum Cay.

August 12, 2007 Rum Cay, Bahamas
(from the blog of Alegria)

We had planned to spend, at most, just one or two nights here while we waited for wind to sail to Crooked Island, which had lousy anchorages, or tried to make it to Mayaguana, 130 miles away. Dan is adamant about not motoring thirty hours straight to Mayaguana, however, so we've decided to wait for the wind. In the meantime, we enjoy another night of friendship and really good food as we join the dock cookout. Once again, we are spoiled with fresh grouper, conch, and prime rib. We could get used to this! Tristan and Tessa agree. After eating, the kids pile onto the fishing boat *Jolly Rodgers* to enjoy air conditioning, play games, and watch movies.

Tessa spends a lot of time with Chance, the son of the captain of *Jolly Rodgers,* who is her age, and Tristan has found a new friend in Will, a boy his age who just arrived for a fishing charter. The kids are having such a great time. During the day, they are off exploring around the marina.

Bobby, the guy who originally built and owned the marina before selling it to a real estate development group, really added some nice touches to the grounds and restaurant. Near one of the rental cabins, he built a tree house that the kids love to play in. Outside of the restaurant are rock gardens and beautiful limestone carvings that Bobby did himself. Inside the restaurant is a mosaic countertop and more of his artwork. Everything is designed to give off a very peaceful feeling.

We love to eat breakfast in the restaurant, especially since our breakfast supply on the boat is depleted. Ordering was a bit difficult at first because there is no menu. The first morning, Erica came to our table as soon as we sat down and asked what we wanted. I asked her what was available. She told me she could fix anything. Okay. I looked at the kids and asked them what they wanted. Their response? "What do they have?"

"You can have anything," I said. "How about some eggs?"

Erica jumped in, "How do you want them cooked?"

I paused. I told her I wasn't sure we really wanted eggs. We were just throwing out a suggestion.

Tessa asked, "Do they have pancakes?"

Erica: "What do you want with your pancakes?"

Me: "I'm not sure she really wants pancakes. Again, I think that was merely a question."

Tristan: "Do they have omelets and bacon?"

Erica: "Omelet, bacon. Do you want toast?"

Me: "Wait. I'm not sure that's what he wants. I think he is just asking."

This went on a few minutes more, and finally as my head was ready to explode, I told her we needed a few minutes. We couldn't seem to grasp the idea that they were willing to make us anything we wanted. Finally, we decided. We ordered pancakes, omelets, and scrambled eggs. A few minutes later, Erica came back to the table. She told me it would be awhile as they were out of eggs, and the cook was going to the grocery store for some more. My mouth dropped open. I'd seen those eggs at the grocery store (see previous entry) and wasn't sure I want anything to do with them. I decided to close my mouth and live dangerously. The breakfast turned out to be very good.

The next morning I was ready for her. Erica came to the table and told us she had grits. I thanked her for the information. I am not a grits fan and ordered an omelet for Tristan and scrambled eggs for me. I was so proud of myself that I was on top of things. As I started to say that Tessa would have French toast, Erica interrupted me, "We have grits."

"Yes, thanks. We don't really like grits. I think the omelet will be fine."

"We have grits."

"Okay. I heard that, but as I said, we aren't fans of

grits, so we'll have some eggs."

"We don't have eggs," she said. "We have grits."

So much for pre-planning. [*End blog*]

A week later we were still waiting for good weather. The wait wouldn't have been too bad if it hadn't been for the heat and the mosquitoes. When the wind died down, the insects were unbearable. We had screens for our hatches, but the screens attached on the inside. If we wanted to close the hatch, we had to remove the screen first. It seemed that every night we put the screens in, it would rain. We would have to wake up, take out the screens, and shut the hatches. With the hatches shut, the heat was unbearable. When the brief rain stopped, we had to open the hatches again and replace the screens. At Rum Cay, it might rain briefly several times per night, forcing us to keep removing and replacing the screens. So we stopped using them.

Finally, driven out by the heat and mosquitoes and enticed by the best weather window we were going to get, we left Rum Cay very early one morning for Mayaguana, the last out island before leaving the Bahamas for the Turks and Caicos. The wind was coming straight at us, and we had a short weather window, so we would be motoring the whole way. Dan wasn't happy, but we couldn't wait any longer, we were getting deeper and deeper into hurricane season. We departed with the idea that we would try to make it to Mayaguana, but if the weather deteriorated, we would stop at another island.

August 24, 2007 Overnight Passage to Mayaguana
(*from the blog of* Alegria)

The day started out well. The swells were 6 to 7 feet and about nine seconds apart, so it was fairly smooth. The kids had a little motion sickness but got better with some fresh ginger in a Sprite. One cargo ship passed by us, but that was the only other boat we saw. Again, we had the ocean to ourselves. Later that afternoon, thunderstorms appeared on the radar. Our Furuno radar was top notch. It displayed the intensity of the rain and storms in color, so we could easily decide which ones we could head into and which ones to steer a wide path around. As we passed Samana Cay, the storm activity increased. By 9 p.m. there was lightning encircling us and a strange electrical feeling in the air. The lightning came down in bright, jagged flashes, and the radar showed large clusters of storm activity all around us. It was going to be a long night.

Because it was hot inside the boat, the kids joined us in the cockpit. Everyone had their harnesses on and was securely attached. Tristan didn't like the lightning, but it didn't seem to bother Tessa. I decided this would be a great time to take their minds off the storm with a movie. We huddled together while the lightning flashed around us and watched *The Mummy Returns,* for about the tenth time, on our portable DVD player. I only lasted the first thirty minutes, and then I lay down to sleep before my watch. Since it was so rough, Dan and I decided we would sleep outside in the cockpit, and the kids would sleep inside in the salon. The harnesses were mandatory at all times.

I don't know if it was the storm that night or something else, but it was a very strange passage. We agreed on three- to four-hour watches. It was hard to sleep with the lightning because the air felt heavy and charged. I spent most of the time tossing and turning and having very intense dreams.

Something startled me, and as I groggily sat up and looked around, I had the strangest sensation of someone else being on the boat with us. It was weird. Dan, seeing that I was awake, pointed out a huge cargo ship passing close to us on our starboard side. I was looking at Dan standing at the helm, but behind him, I could clearly see another person looking a lot like Dan, standing on the seat at the back of the cockpit. This *person* was so real, I thought that he was the real Dan. They were even wearing the same clothes. This entity was looking so happy, so proud of the great job that Dan was doing. It was almost like he'd been sent from the spirit world to cheer us on.

The strangest part was that this *spirit* seemed more like the real Dan to me than the Dan at the helm. In fact, when my husband asked me if we should change course to get away from some of the storms, I replied, "That's fine with me, but you'd better ask Dan first," referring to the doppelganger at the back of the boat. Dan gave me a funny look, and I drifted back to sleep.

At eleven, I woke up again for my turn on watch. Our captain had done a great job of watching the radar and maneuvering us away from the storms. The seas were still high, but the radar looked clear as I took over. The lightning was gone and so was Dan's doppelganger. On all sides of us, the moon was hidden by clouds, but right above the top of the mast was a clear sky filled with stars.

I really thought I would be scared on this long, night passage, but I wasn't. We'd had a partial night sail as we crossed the Gulf Stream, but this was a true overnight. I loved it. The storms, the waves, the energy were incredible. I loved feeling that I had the ocean to myself for miles. In the wake of the boat, I saw sparks, like little sparkling diamonds in the water. It was bioluminescence churned up by the boat, and it was a great reward for standing watch on a night passage. I turned in my seat and admired it for a long time.

Halfway through my watch, I felt raindrops. I used the radar to weave *Alegria* away from the storm, and the system passed within a half mile. The wind picked up, but no more rain. Just as the storm slid past us and I was breathing a sigh of relief, the wind changed direction and pushed it back toward us. Luckily it missed us the second time too. Dan woke up at 3:15 a.m. and took over while I went to sleep.

When I woke up again, the lightning was back, and the air had that same heavy feel. I had the same sensation of someone else being on the boat. Sure enough, when I looked around, Dan's doppelganger was back. Whoever or whatever it was seemed to come with the lightning. Since it didn't seem it was there to do us harm, I drifted back to sleep.

I was treated to a beautiful sunrise on my early-morning watch. I am more of a night person and very rarely see the sunrise, so this was a treat. It was a pretty red sky that morning. In keeping with the old mariner's rhyme, "Red sky at night, sailor's delight. Red sky at morning, sailor's take warning," I was prepared for more storms that day. We hit our last storm late morning as we neared Mayaguana. Dan was again able to maneuver us around the weather. Fortunately the sky then cleared because we needed bright sunlight to enter Abraham's Bay off Mayaguana.

On the charts, Abraham's Bay is a minefield of coral heads—coral heads sharp enough to put a hole in a boat. Tristan and I were on bow watch, and we guided Dan through the worst of it. Finally after about an hour, we made it through. We dropped anchor with 6 feet of crystal-clear water beneath the hulls. Our long passage was over, and we breathed a sigh of relief.

Our reward? A huge bay, surrounded by white sand, and we were the only boat around to enjoy it. The water was so enticing that even though I was exhausted, I eagerly jumped in after Tessa. Within moments she was diving for sand dollars. She even dove down and startled a ray when she touched its back. She is becoming a little too familiar with the wildlife. [End blog]

We stayed in the water most of that day and the next, but made sure we were out by 4:30 p.m., or what we referred to as "shark time." Sure enough, right on schedule, we saw two large reef sharks swim by one evening. Later we learned that makos, tiger, lemon, bull, and nurse sharks were all common in the bay in the late afternoon.

By Sunday we were pretty much out of fresh food, so after making water, we dinghied to the dock near town in search of a grocery store. Because it was Sunday, the stores were closed, so we ate lunch at Paradise Villas. Smokey, the owner, cooked us a delicious lunch of fried conch and fried grouper. We made reservations for a lobster dinner the next night.

We were tired and happy as we motored our dinghy back to *Alegria*. Because it was so shallow close to shore, she was anchored about a mile offshore. She looked beautiful anchored all alone, surrounded by the lightest blue water you could imagine. We were talking and laughing as we puttered alongside her in the dinghy.

From the direction we were coming, we couldn't see the back of our boat. I pointed to a small boat far off in the distance. I assumed it must be a very small fishing boat. As we turned the dinghy around the stern of *Alegria*, we were surprised to see a large Bahamian man sitting on our platform steps, holding a spear gun.

At first I was startled. It's not every day you come home to find a big man with a spear gun sitting on your back porch! I think we startled him too.

"Hello," he quickly called out.

"Hello. You scared me!" I replied.

He apologized and explained that his boat, the small boat I'd noticed way out in the bay, had run out of fuel. He'd swum to *Alegria* for help close to "shark time," so had brought his spear gun for protection. It was a long, long swim to our boat, and I could tell he was exhausted. Dan asked him how we could help. He needed gas. His buddy was still on the boat—a large man on a small boat about to be carried by the current into a big sea.

Tessa and I boarded *Alegria,* while Dan grabbed our

72

extra gas can and then helped our visitor into the dinghy. Tristan went with Dan. It was a long ride. When they arrived at the fishing boat, the marooned friend was, needless to say, overjoyed. Both men were very grateful and offered Dan some conch, but he declined, saying he was happy to help. When Dan told me that, I told him *I* would have liked some conch. Dan diplomatically replied that he hadn't wanted the men to think he was helping them to get something back. Maybe, but if they had offered him lobsters? Hmm.

The next morning the kids and I took a break from school and went swimming. Smokey from Paradise Villas stopped by to show and offer us what he and his partner had caught in the bay. We were thrilled to buy lobster and grouper for our freezer. Fish was not going to be a problem, but other food we needed like fresh milk and vegetables was nonexistent at the grocery store in town. I was able to get some cereal and evaporated milk to tide us over, but it looked like we would need to do some serious shopping when we arrived at Turks and Caicos.

Before we could leave Mayaguana, we needed to get a weather report. Our satellite phone wasn't doing a good job sending us a signal, so we couldn't use it to download our weather. We asked for help at the Mayaguana Batelco office, and an employee there graciously allowed Dan to use her computer. Two days later, we pulled up anchor, sad to leave this piece of paradise. I had a setting full moon in front of me and a rising sun behind me as we left Abraham's Bay on the way to Turks and Caicos. After nearly five full months, we were leaving the Bahamas.

6

A Long Rough Passage
TURKS AND CAICOS TO DOMINICAN REPUBLIC

I T WAS A LONG DAY, with 50 miles to travel after we picked our way back out through the coral heads around Abraham's Bay. We needed to get to Turks and Caicos before Turtle Cove Marina closed at 6 p.m.

About two hours outside of Providenciales, better known as Provo, Tristan spotted a spray of water, and we were treated to the sight of a huge sperm whale. Dan brought *Alegria* as close to the whale as he dared. Boats and whales don't mix. A large sperm whale could have easily taken down our boat, so while we wanted to get as close as possible, we knew we had to keep a respectful distance. The whale stayed near the surface for awhile, giving us a pretty good look. We could now add sperm whale to the list of the most amazing things we had seen on the trip so far.

An hour out, the waves started hitting on the front quarter of the hull, and everything started getting tossed inside the boat. It was a rough last hour, and we cut it close, arriving at 5:45 pm. A guide brought us into Turtle Cove Marina, and thank goodness we had one because it was terribly confusing trying to follow the channel markers that were located dangerously close to the reef. Dan and crew had stayed there the previous year when they brought

Alegria to Charleston from the BVI. He said the marina hadn't changed at all, but the island had. Provo was really built up with hotels and houses. What a shock. It was hard to come from sleepy Mayaguana to this.

September 3, 2007 Providenciales, Turks and Caicos
(from the blog of Alegria)

It is really hard to get a good feel for Turks and Caicos from Provo. While the island is undeniably beautiful, with its white beaches and crystal-clear water, it's very commercialized. It's hard to find a native. I'm not sure if I've even met one. The town has a very diverse mix of Dominicans, Haitians, Filipinos, Asians, Canadians, and Americans—lots of Americans. I think this is all driven by the rampant construction here. Provo does have some good shopping, such as an IGA grocery store, a big home-improvement store, and something we haven't seen since Florida...a bookstore! [*End blog*]

We rented a car after we ended up walking 2 miles the first time we went to the IGA and the bookstore. When someone tells you something is ten minutes down the road, make sure you know if they mean ten minutes by car or ten minutes by walking. We were walking. We found out later, it was ten minutes by car. The walk was brutal. We had to walk on the shoulder of a major roadway with two lanes of traffic on each side separated by a median. It was hot and dangerous. We didn't give up though, and we eventually found the shopping center.

When we were done shopping, we didn't have the energy to make the walk back, so I asked the clerk if there was a taxi service. She said no, but there was a van service that ran along the highway. She told us to go up to the bus-stop shelter on the main road. A white van should be along soon. The van would beep its horn, and we should wave at it if we wanted a ride. The cost was $2 per person. She also said that we could ride with anyone who pulled over. It was perfectly safe.

Really? Perfectly safe to just hop into a car with anyone? Well, that sounded like fun. Warily, we made our way to the bus stop, and within minutes a small white van stopped and two women disembarked. It was the official public transportation, but it was too crowded. We motioned for the driver to go on without us. I guess that motion was mistaken for a wave because when the van pulled away, a horn honked and a small car pulled up to offer us a ride. The windows were dark tinted, and it was hard to see inside. When the driver rolled down his window, a cloud of smoke was released from inside the car. After coughing and waving the smoke away from my face, I could see that, thankfully, the car appeared already full. There was clearly no room for four more, and I definitely did not want my children inhaling whatever was coming from inside the car. The driver was Haitian, and we couldn't communicate anyway, so we waved him on.

As soon as he pulled away, a huge semi truck pulled up and honked. Was this some kind of joke? Were we on hidden camera? Tristan was, of course, all in favor of riding in a big rig. Dan and I looked at each other. No way were we getting into that. My thought was that we needed to get off the road, regroup, and really think this thing through. I started to walk away, but the next thing I knew Dan had another questionable car pulled over and was motioning for us to get in. It was only a two door, so the kids and I had to squeeze behind the seat to get into the back. This car reeked of cigarette smoke too.

Dan told the driver we needed to go to the marina. Our driver didn't appear to understand English, so Dan spoke slower and louder. It didn't work. Finally Dan pulled out a slip of paper that showed the name of Turtle Cove Marina. Now our driver knew where we wanted to go, but he had no idea how to get there, so Dan had to give him turn-by-turn directions. Meanwhile, I was in the backseat going over the list of life rules with Tristan and Tessa.

"Remember kids, don't smoke, don't do drugs, and don't hitchhike."

A short time later, we were delivered safe and sound to the marina. Dan paid the driver $8, and we had ourselves a story. The next day, as soon as they opened, we were at Scooter Bob's renting a car. The car worked fine for the first two hours before stranding us in the middle of a busy intersection. A good Samaritan helped Dan push it off the road then let us use his cell phone to call and ask Scooter Bob to bring us a new car. Once again the simple act of provisioning was turning into an all-day affair. On the bright side, the prices there weren't bad, so we stocked up.

While the island had some beautiful beaches, we didn't linger. As soon as we could, we made our way to Ambergris Cay, a private residential island at the southeastern end of the Caicos bank. There, we anchored in such isolation that for the first time we could clearly see the Milky Way.

September 5, 2007 Ambergris Cay, Turks and Caicos
(from the blog of Alegria)

We anchored in 9 feet of water, surrounded by coral, pretty far from shore, and as usual, we are the only ones here. A few local fishing boats passed by us on their way to who knows where, and except for the few construction workers on the island, we are all alone.

We enjoyed a great steak dinner last night and watched a movie. After the movie, I stepped into the cockpit. There was no moon, and it was pitch-black outside. I looked up and caught my breath. I believed I could see every star ever created. In the Abacos we saw a good bit of the Milky Way, but here I could see it stretching from nearly one end of the sky to the other. The stars were set in easy-to-see shapes like triangles, circles, and lines, in patterns I had only seen in star-gazing books. They were all here. And they twinkled. They really did twinkle.

There wasn't a clear-cut distinction between the water and the sky, just varying shades of dark blue from overhead, down to a hazy lighter blue where I presumed the water started. The light around me was so flat, I could only see out about 5 feet from the boat. It was hard to look at as my eyes tried to focus on something that wasn't there, only nothingness. It made me dizzy and forced me to keep looking up at the awesome show overhead. I was shocked to think that when we were back in Charlotte, North Carolina these same stars were there, we just couldn't see them. It's incredible how much beauty we miss in this world. [*End blog*]

September 6, 2007 Big Sand Cay, Turks and Caicos
(*from the blog of* Alegria)

Big Sand Cay, a tiny deserted island and bird sanctuary, was our last stop before the Dominican Republic. The water surrounding the island was crystal clear and extremely flat as we set anchor in 16 feet of water. We had the entire island to ourselves.

Leaving Ambergis Cay that morning was a little touch and go when we decided to take a short cut and wound up in the midst of some very menacing coral heads. About twenty minutes into it, we'd had enough. Fortunately we were able to turn around and pick our way back out. We took a longer, but much safer, route and were rewarded by seeing four large, spotted eagle rays, swimming under the water in a V-formation. They were so graceful to watch. We also saw the mast of a sunken sailboat, possibly from someone who decided to take the shortcut and wound up on the coral, sinking his boat.

Other than that, the day was quiet. We walked on the

beach, snorkeled, pretended we were the only ones in the world, and enjoyed another night of stargazing. We will be leaving late tomorrow, about 2 p.m., for the Dominican Republic and will be motoring again. We will give ourselves plenty of leeway, figuring if we get there too early, say before sunrise, we will just circle offshore. [*End blog*]

September 8, 2007 Overnight Passage to Dominican Republic
(from the blog of Alegria)

I don't think any of us had a great feeling about this passage. Not that we thought it would be hard or scary, just a feeling that it was going to be long and uncomfortable. It was shorter, mileage-wise than our previous overnight to Mayaguana, but we would be crossing rougher waters.

The Passages South guidebook said not to be fooled by strong winds when you leave Big Sand Cay. You should get out about 5 miles before you make up your mind to continue, but never leave in winds over 20 knots. At 5 miles out, the wind was about 16 knots, on the nose of course, so we were motoring. The waves were short and choppy, about 4 feet high. No big deal, so we kept going.

At this point our biggest concern was the bathroom. Dan walked into the cockpit, holding a small roll of toilet paper. "This is all we have, and the passage will take a minimum of fifteen hours," he said.

God be with us.

We left in daylight, at two in the afternoon. Later, when the sun sank below the horizon, the sky transitioned from red to purple then blue, and a feeling of melancholy settled over us.

It was Tristan's job to get the harnesses ready. He sat inside the salon, and from the back of the boat I watched him carefully take the harnesses from their bags, matching up the piece that went over the shoulders with the proper safety line that would then be attached to the boat. Tristan worked meticulously, and I knew he knew how important this job was. Our life could depend on staying on the boat. He was nervous, maybe even scared about the passage, but he was trying not to show it. Instead he focused on controlling what he could control, getting the safety harnesses ready. My heart went out to him. Part of me wanted to reassure him, but the other part wanted me to allow him to find his courage. It's a rare thing when a parent actually sees their child internally build character. I remained where I was, allowing him to be brave.

Dan took the first watch. The kids and I snuggled in the corner of the cockpit and watched a movie. I took over the watch three hours later. I was prepared for this overnight passage. I had all the snacks in resealable plastic bags on the galley counter. Everyone's favorite can of soup was there, along with the pans for cooking. I had my Diet Coke and Snickers bar. Dan had his coffee and snack crackers. Everything was secure and within easy reach.

I again suggested going to Ocean World Marina instead of the anchorage in Luperon, but Dan wouldn't listen. We had a brochure on Ocean World, and the marina looked amazing. It had a casino, plus an adventure park with sharks, dolphins, birds, and tigers; you could interact with all of them. Luperon had swimming rats. I was sure there was no avoiding interacting with them.

Dan was determined to go to Luperon though. It was where all the cruisers went for hurricane season. I told him it needed to be a joint decision, but he was adamant. I let the subject drop for the moment. We had a long night ahead of us.

Just as darkness fell, the lights of a cargo ship appeared. It looked like it was on a path right for us. Dan eventually made radio contact with the ship's captain, telling him our heading. The captain replied that he was aware of us, so we relaxed. As usual, there was lightning in the distance.

The winds picked up to 20 knots and the waves increased. There was no moon, only the sporadic lightning to give me a glimpse of the building waves in front of me.

Dan was feeling sick, so I stayed on watch longer. The waves were really confused. They slammed against *Alegria's* hulls. Whitecaps surrounded us. The wind speed increased to 26 knots. Every once in awhile, I heard a loud *whoosh* as a large wave broke beside the boat. The wind slowly built all night until it peaked at 30 knots, making for high seas, especially in the open area we were crossing. I was thankful for the darkness because I didn't want to see the waves.

Tristan was asleep in the cockpit next to Dan, and Tessa was sleeping inside on the salon cushions. I was worried about her because the waves pounding the boat were causing things inside to shift. I envisioned Tessa digging herself out from a pile of books and magazines that had fallen on top of her from the shelf above, but she slept fine. So did Tristan. I was all alone. I tightened my harness as the waves really rocked *Alegria*. Every so often, a large wave hit the boat and caused me to sway nearly out of my seat. Without the harness, if I went over in the dark, no one would ever find me.

To pass the time and keep awake, I listened to my iPod or Sirius radio, or I sang. Fortunately the sound of the engines blocked out most of the noise from the waves, and my singing. I wasn't scared. Not that I am that brave, but I was in the middle of nowhere and there was nothing I could do to make the trip any better.

I talked to *Alegria*, telling her she was doing a great job. I didn't know how to sail in these conditions, but I was confident that *Alegria* knew how to handle the waves. She was solidly built, and I trusted her with my life, with all our lives. I attached the safety line to the metal bar inside the cockpit, turned sideways in my seat so I was facing the open ocean, and resigned myself to a long night.

We missed the storm itself, but it continued to be an uncomfortable night. We weren't making good time. With high waves and winds of close to 30 knots on your boat's nose, you don't go anywhere fast. When Dan turned off one engine to give it a rest, the boat went slower and the ride was smoother, but our speed dropped down to under 3 knots. We had to turn the engine back on, or we would never make Luperon by 10 a.m. We heard from several sources that if you didn't arrive early, you wouldn't be able to get into the harbor because of the strong winds coming off the tall mountains on the north coast. At this speed, it would be very close. On a positive note, we didn't have to worry about the toilet-paper shortage because no one was going inside the boat anymore than they had to.

About 30 miles from the island of Hispaniola, true to what the guidebooks said, we could smell the Dominican Republic. It was a wonderful, rich, earthy smell that wrapped you in a blanket of comfort. Dan was feeling better, and he took over the watch; I was drained. A windy night passage will really make you dehydrated. I drank some Gatorade and lay back down. Before I drifted back to sleep, I heard the words I had been waiting for. "We may have to go to Ocean World." Yes! My night was getting better. [*End blog*]

7

Celebrations and Sadness
DOMINICAN REPUBLIC

WHEN I WOKE AGAIN, THE sun was up. The waves had actually gotten bigger. They were huge, coming up on our side. But what a view. In the distance were tall, lush, green mountains. They were gorgeous!

We pulled into Ocean World Marina after 11 a.m. With the wind and those waves, there was no way we could have gotten into Luperon. As we entered the marina, I tried to clean up inside the boat as best as I could. The rough passage had really created a mess. As soon as we docked though, the customs and immigration officials were immediately at our boat to check us in. Only one of them spoke English. I was embarrassed to have them see our boat in this condition, and I tried to explain we hit bad weather, but they just smiled. The whole process took about fifteen minutes; no bribes, no having to wait for customs or trying to track them down. Everything was very easy.

The marina was beautiful, with a casino, two restaurants, and a bar on the fourth floor, allowing a panoramic view of the boats and the mountains. Most importantly, the surrounding water was clean. Included in our marina stay was unlimited access to the Ocean World Adventure Park. *Actually, I don't think it was supposed to be unlimited access. I think it was supposed to be for only one day, but we kept our wristbands on and used them over and over. I think the staff was too polite to tell us any different.* The kids were beside themselves when they could see the sea-lion show from our dock. Dan and I thought we would settle in for a nap, but how were we going to keep Tessa and Tristan on the boat when they knew there was a dolphin and tiger show in their backyard?

We visited the marine park, and except for the annoying salesmen pitching timeshare opportunities as we walked in, it was great. After a few hours of seeing tigers, rays, sharks, birds, and tropical fish, we remembered the toilet-paper crisis. We needed to get to a grocery store. The marina had a taxi service, and Patrick, who worked at the marina, went along as our interpreter/guide. The *supermercado,* though small, was comparable to a US grocery store, and we found everything we needed. The prices were very reasonable, and they took US dollars.

On the way back to the marina, Patrick took us on a short tour of Puerto Plata. The city was crowded. Motorcycle taxis, known there as *motoconchos,* were everywhere barely making use of the lanes on the road. The traffic was chaotic, but we loved it. We couldn't wait to explore the country.

September 12, 2007 Puerto Plata, DR
(*from the blog of* Alegria)

Today was the day to leave the luxury of the compound and explore in our Ocean World taxi with Ramon, one of the marina workers who came along as our translator/guide. We didn't have an agenda, we just wanted to see as much as we could and get comfortable so we could later rent a car and go by ourselves.

I was glad we had a driver because traffic was crazy. It amazed me the way the *motoconchos* darted in and out of traffic. Even more amazing was seeing these motorbikes carrying sometimes four people and a baby. One time we saw three people on a *motoconcho,* and one of them was holding a washing machine. Another cruiser swears he saw a mother, child, and a donkey on a *motoconcho.* It was insane.

We needed some local money, pesos, so Ramon had the driver stop at a bank. While Dan got money, I saw a street vendor selling DVDs. Leaving the kids in the van with the driver, I looked through the selections. Some of the titles were in English and some in Spanish. As in the Bahamas, they had all the latest US movies, including the ones currently in theaters. I don't speak fluent Spanish, and the vendor didn't speak English, but he kept handing me movies. After I looked through the rack of DVDs and picked out three, he brought me to another pile. He handed a DVD to me, and I looked at the cover, and at first I was puzzled, not really sure what I was looking at. He filled me in with the one English word he knew, "Porn?"

Seriously? What is it with island people thinking I want porn? Is this what American's do as soon as they leave the US? Stop at the nearest DVD store and load up on porn? I politely declined as I handed him back the DVD.

Our next stop was the fruit market. I couldn't wait to stock up. The market was alive with colors and fresh smells. There were so many varieties of produce and many small farm animals: rice, beans, eggs, chickens, rabbits, pork, lettuce, grapefruit, onions, avocados (cheap!), oranges, plantains, lemons, potatoes, herbs, carrots, and much, much, more. It was endless! I bought bananas, garlic, tomatoes, cantaloupe, watermelon, limes, sour oranges, papayas, onions, eggs, and of course, avocados. There were so many vendors, we tried to spread our purchases around. The kids loved it. Two women shucking beans loved Tristan. They kept smiling and nodding at him. I think they loved his blonde hair and blue eyes. Meanwhile Tessa was concerned about the live chickens.

"Mom, what are the chickens for?"

I didn't want to lie to her, so I told her people were buying them to eat. While we were standing by the cages, a lady bought a chicken, and the vendor put the live chicken in a bag for her.

Tessa looked at me and said, "You're wrong Mom. She's buying it for the eggs." I wasn't going to correct her.

Cabarete, a beach town, was our final stop. Back in Palm Beach, Florida, Tristan read an article on kitesurfing in Cabarete and wanted to see the sport in person. The town was pretty, if not a bit too touristy, and of course, all the vendors on the beach were trying to sell us something. The kitesurfing was definitely impressive. There was no shortage of wind in Cabarete and that was what attracted a worldwide interest in the town for the sport.

After watching the kite surfers for awhile, we got hungry. We took a seat in a nearby restaurant and waited for our server, who was looking at a stack of DVDs, to acknowledge us. After our waiter finished his DVD shopping and took our order, the salesman came to our table. He spoke a little English, and as he set a pile of movies down on our table, he told us to wait as he walked over to another table. Instead of waiting, Dan and I grabbed a few. The titles were fairly new, but most were in Spanish. The fourth movie in my pile crossed all languages. PORN! Twice in one day—what were the odds? Dan and I looked at each other, then at Tristan, who was getting ready to grab a stack of DVDs. We lunged across the table and wrestled the DVDs from him just as the guy came back. He gave us a stern look as if *we* had done something wrong, then handed us the DVDs back after he filtered out the adult movies.

Another vendor approached our table with a case of jewelry. This was right up Tessa's alley. I waved him off, but he honed in on her, pulling out a necklace and putting it around her neck. Again I said no, but now Tessa was going through his case. I started to get annoyed, but then smiled to myself as I watched what was happening. Tessa was determined to try on everything in his case, and the guy, thinking that he was on track for a big sale, was happy to oblige. I read the entire menu while Tessa tried on necklaces. Dan and Tristan went to the restroom and came back, and Tessa was trying on bracelets. More time passed. The jewelry guy was getting antsy, but he didn't know how to get out of the situation. Tessa tried on the rings. When she was starting to make her way back to the necklaces, I figured he had learned his lesson and again told him we weren't buying anything. He unhappily snapped his case closed and left. I knew we wouldn't see him again. The best revenge on a jewelry salesman is a seven-year-old girl. [*End blog*]

September 20, 2007 Santiago, DR
(from the blog of Alegria)

Today we rented a car so we could run some errands. Dan asked about the insurance. The rental agent told him if we had minor dings in the car, it would be covered. If we had "car no more," it would be covered up to an amount she showed on the form. Dan and I were confused. Car no more? Hmm. That wasn't a term we were familiar with. It didn't sound good. Maybe we misunderstood. We asked her to repeat it.

"If you have minor damage," she explained in broken English, "you are covered. If car no more," and she did a dramatic slashing of her hands, "then it's covered here."

Yes, we heard correctly. Car no more wasn't good, but must happen often as they had a policy for it. She noticed us looking at her funny, and she started again, "Car no more..."

"Wait," we both broke in. "We don't want to think about car no more. Car no more sounds very bad. No more, car no more."

When we left with the car, we passed several vendors selling vegetables alongside the road. I asked Dan to stop. He hit the brakes. Two *motoconchos*, following too closely behind, nearly hit us and did end up bumping into each other. We nearly had "car no more," and we had barely gone a mile!

The next day we drove to Santiago, the second largest city in the Dominican Republic. Driving in Santiago is not for the faint of heart. The main road passing through Santiago has two lanes going each way, or that was how it was intended, but now it is more of a free-for-all. Cars and *motoconchos* drive everywhere. Two lanes of traffic quickly become five. We stopped at a traffic light, waiting for it to turn green. Our car was in the outside lane, and there was a row of cars to our right. Next to that row of cars, another row of cars was trying to merge in (they didn't have a lane). In the oncoming lane to our left, cars going the same way as us crowded in. Two lanes had now become five or six lanes.

Tristan brought our attention to the car backing up on the sidewalk. Not only did the driver back up, he picked up someone coming out of the store. It was madness, but we loved it!

It was like that the entire day, and the best part was that it worked. No one got angry, there was no road rage, no honking or yelling, everyone just made room for each other. Dan made a good observation on how this would never work in the US because Americans are too territorial. People would complain about someone being in "*my* lane," or think "I am not going to let them get in front of *me*," or "this is *my* side." In Santiago if someone needed to merge in, you let them. No big deal. There was plenty of road for everyone. My lane was your lane; my sidewalk was your lane too.

Dan needed a small hinge to replace one that had broke.

We found a hardware store similar to a Home Depot. It had everything. No one spoke English, but we weren't deterred. Nearly every day since we'd arrived in the Dominican Republic, we'd practiced Spanish. I'd have the kids think of something they might say that day, then I'd write it in Spanish on an index card for them. We had the basics down, "Hello," "How are you," "What's your name," and so on. I had several words and a few verbs covered, plus I carried the translation book. In the hardware store, Dan needed a hinge and the easiest thing to do was hold it up and inquire, "*Donde es?*" It worked for us.

Our favorite store was Jumbo, a large department store similar to a Super Target. It sold toys, clothes, food, everything we could want in a huge clean store. After the lean days of the Bahamian stores, we were in heaven. Tessa and Tristan made a dash for the toy section. Tessa found a toy she wanted, but she couldn't find the price. She asked me to find out how much it cost. I told her I couldn't because, at that time, I didn't know how to say "How much is that?" in Spanish.

"I'll find out myself," she informed me with her seven-year-old attitude and stalked off.

I maturely called after her, "Well good luck with that because they don't speak English!"

A moment later I found her talking to a man wearing a red shirt. I thought he worked there. She told him she needed to know how much the toy cost. He replied, in English, that the price should be on the shelf (leave it to her to find the only English-speaking person in the store). While she showed him it wasn't marked, I noticed he was pushing a cart full of groceries. He wasn't a clerk, he was a shopper.

"You can take the toy to the scanner," The man told me, pointing to it on the wall. He started to hand the toy to me, but mistaking my lack of interest (I'm not buying the toy) for misunderstanding, he instead said, "I'll do it for you."

He came back a few minutes later and said the scanner wasn't working. He asked me to watch his cart, and he would find out the price.

Minutes passed. The frozen food in his cart started to melt. I felt bad. I was astounded that he would go to all this trouble for us, but then it never ceased to amaze me what people would do for Tessa. Finally he came back with the price. I thanked him. Now, since he had gone through so much trouble, I felt obligated to buy the toy. I wanted to put it back on the shelf, but he was still close by, and I knew Tessa would put up a protest loud enough for him to hear. Sigh. She had outwitted me again. Luckily the toy was cheap.

I barely resisted the temptation to go on a shopping spree. I did give in though and bought a new tablecloth for the cockpit table, an artificial Christmas tree, some Christmas lights, and a few groceries. On the way home that night, we stopped at a roadside restaurant outside the town of El Mamon. The electricity went off twice while we were there, leaving us alone in the dark for awhile, but that was alright. It really bothered the chickens though. They ran around our feet, squawking crazily. Apparently they were afraid of the dark.

I forgot to mention one guilty pleasure we had while in the city: McDonald's. Yes, we gave in. We figured our kids had been good sports about all the less-than-attractive eating places we had dragged them to, and they had graciously eaten whatever was put in front of them, so they earned the right. [*End blog*]

September passed quickly. We loved the DR and were truly being spoiled by the staff at Ocean World. The kids and I loved the beautiful pool. Everyone was so friendly. All the staff knew us and watched out for the kids.

Dan and I celebrated our wedding anniversary by taking the kids out to eat at a local restaurant. Afterwards we settled Tristan and Tessa on the boat with a movie and went to have drinks at the Lighthouse, the bar on top of the Ocean World complex. It had great views, and we could look out the window and keep an eye on the kids as our boat was docked right below. They were more than happy to be on their own. The security guards were excellent and knew Tristan and Tessa, so we felt extremely comfortable. When we went into the casino, the casino manager recognized us. He asked about Tristan and Tessa, and when we told them they were on the boat, he said he would also keep an eye on them for us.

September 30, 2007 Ocean World Marina, DR
(from the blog of Alegria)

It's Patrick's birthday today. We love Patrick. He really makes Ocean World Marina special. He always has a smile and is always there with the golf cart to give us a ride wherever we need to go. Tessa and Tristan made him birthday cards. Tristan drew the Ocean World logo on his, and Tessa drew a picture of Patrick driving the golf cart on hers. They went up on their own to deliver the cards and said Patrick loved them. He laughed and laughed at the picture of him driving the golf cart and showed it to everyone. Another boater at the marina bought him a birthday cake, and people were calling him all day wishing him happy birthday.

Brooks, another boater here, introduced us to William, the owner of the rental-car company he used. William promised us a better car for the same price or less than the one we had now. Seeing as our old car had two flats and the driver's window wouldn't roll down, the decision seemed easy enough. Dan and Tristan went with William to look at the cars, and I stayed back to clean. Later, Patrick stopped by and brought me a piece of his birthday cake. He told me Dan and Tristan had already had a piece, and he wanted to make sure I got some too. [*End blog*]

October 2, 2007 Ocean World Marina, DR
(*from the blog of* Alegria)

Very sad day today. We had originally planned to leave early this morning for the mountains but couldn't get motivated. We were sitting in the cockpit when Ramon came by and told us about Patrick. Last night, not too long after he left work, Patrick had a heart attack and died. He was 46 years old.

We were in shock. We had to have Ramon repeat the news three times, thinking we must be missing something in the translation, but we weren't. The wake and funeral were that day, and the marina staff was offering to take us. We said of course. We just needed a few minutes to get ready.

I couldn't believe Patrick was dead. We hurriedly got dressed, not knowing how casual or formal to get. Wilfredo, the operations manager, went with us to be our translator. I was still not sure if we were going to a visitation, or the funeral, or what. I couldn't seem to grasp the fact of just seeing Patrick yesterday and him being buried today.

Our driver let us out at a small nondescript building in Puerto Plata. Except for the ambulance outside, there was nothing to indicate that this was a funeral home. I am not even sure it was a funeral home, per say, maybe just a place they have for the viewing. The small, gray-cement, one-story building had an open front to the street, with a door that rolled up. Directly inside were white plastic chairs, like patio chairs, that a few people were sitting on. As I looked around at the concrete floor, the plain walls, the plastic chairs, I couldn't help contrasting it to a funeral home in the US.

In the US most if not all funeral homes are relatively dark—dark carpet, dark lighting, dark wood. It's meant for containment: containment of emotions; containment of grief, until sometimes it becomes overwhelming, and you just want to get outside in the air. Here the air was all around us. We were right off a street, and while you may think that made it distracting, it really didn't. The warm air coming through the open front, the sounds of cars and people passing, the feel of outside was somehow comforting; as if life, like grief, didn't need to be contained here. They flowed together.

Pablo, the marina's dockmaster, led us into a room, almost like a hallway, with people sitting on either side. I assumed this was the immediate family. We made brief eye contact as we passed them, and Pablo led us through a door to the small viewing room. At the end of the room were three large wreaths of flowers with words of sympathy written in Spanish. A guest book for signing was near the door, and along the wall were benches for sitting. In the middle of the room lay Patrick's casket.

The casket seemed heavy, with an older, worn feel about it. A good feel. You knew this casket was made by hand, not churned out in a factory. It was hand varnished, and on the lid, near the bottom of the casket, was a gold cross and an engraved plate. The casket was closed, but built into the lid was a viewing window so you could see Patrick's face through a glass frame. Dan and I went up to the casket, but we had the kids stay on the benches. They could remember Patrick how they'd last seen him. It was strange to think that our children's first experience with the rituals of death would occur in a foreign country.

There was an older man sitting near the casket, and I asked Pablo if that was Patrick's father. He said no, Patrick's parents had passed away awhile back. Even though Patrick was born and raised in the Dominican Republic, he, like his brother and sister, had moved to the US for awhile. Patrick himself told me he had been married and lived in several cities in the US before getting divorced and moving back to the Dominican Republic. According to Pablo, Patrick's brother and sister would be flying in for the funeral, which was going to be late that afternoon.

Patrick's girlfriend came in briefly while we were in the room and then walked out again. Pablo told us she had been with Patrick when he died. Our Ocean World taxi driver came into the room and he was crying. Pablo was crying. We were crying. It was touching to see these men show so much emotion for a friend.

We finished our goodbyes to Patrick. I signed the guest book on the way out. As we passed by, I stopped to talk to Angie, Patrick's girlfriend. We'd never met, but she knew who we were from Tristan and Tessa. She told us how happy Patrick had been about the birthday cards the kids had made for him. She told us he had said, "They made these for me. Can you believe it?" He was so proud of them. She was keeping the cards as a memento.

Later that evening, we held our own version of a wake for Patrick, similar to the one we held for my uncle who had passed away a few days earlier. We went around the table, and each person said what they would remember most about him. Dan said he would remember how Patrick was always smiling. Tristan remembered how Patrick couldn't stop eating the brownies I'd made for him. Tessa remembered how much he loved the picture she drew of him driving the golf cart. What I will remember most about Patrick is how, after such a short time of knowing him, he inspired us to do nice things, to notice smiles, to make brownies, to draw pictures; in short, to enjoy life more. What a gift. [*End blog*]

8

Will We Ever Get Out of Here?

DOMINICAN REPUBLIC

OCTOBER PASSED SLOWLY. IT WAS hot and I was tired of being in the marina. We celebrated Dan's birthday with a last-minute party. Tristan, with the help of our neighbor Brooks, invited several boaters from the dock, and later that evening we had twelve people eating roasted pig, salad, and cake on *Alegria*. While I was happy to see everyone there, I was especially happy to see Deemian, the tiger trainer at Ocean World. I mean really, how often do you get to say you had a tiger trainer at your party?

Several cruisers and fishing yachts were beginning to leave the marina after having laid low for hurricane season. Dan wanted to stay until he was sure hurricane season was over. It was frustrating for me because I was anxious to get moving again and looking forward to exploring Puerto Rico. We ended up enduring a long month of rain and storms, but we did have a fun Halloween.

October 31, 2007 Ocean World, DR
(from the blog of Alegria)

We finally received the package my sister sent. Inside were the homeschooling books for the kids, reading books for Tristan and Tessa, and two books for Dan. I thought she had put in a book for me. Nope. I was so disappointed. I hadn't read a book in about a month and a half, and I was going mad.

We spent the rest of the day finishing Halloween projects, and before we knew it, it was time for trick-or-treating. I love Halloween. Dominicans don't officially celebrate Halloween, but I had a plan. I had Dan leave candy at the marina office and told him to give the staff explicit instructions. There was one bag of candy for them to give back to our kids, and the other bag they could keep for themselves. Simple right? Dan also left candy at the restaurant, and three other boaters in the marina told us to bring the kids by for treats. It seemed like my plan was foolproof.

When Dan came back from delivering the candy to the office and the restaurant, he looked worried.

"How'd it go?" I asked.

"I am not sure the restaurant workers understood."

"What does that mean?"

"Well," he said, "They were really excited about the candy."

"So what's the problem?"

"I mean they were *really* excited about the candy. I tried to explain that one bag of candy was for them and the other one was to be handed to our kids, but I am not sure they understood. They swarmed me. Maybe we should bring up some more chocolate."

Did I mention Dominicans love chocolate? Several times I have made brownies and given them to the workers in the office, the wait staff in the restaurant, and the security guards. In every instance, they were eaten in seconds. I put an extra bag of candy in my pocket, just in case, and we got off the boat.

The kids were wearing their Halloween costumes. Tessa was a duck, and Tristan was a dog. I know, not very scary, but they were the best (read easiest) costumes I could come up with. Before they were Halloween costumes, they were actually dirty-clothes hampers, which I'd bought at the last minute in Puerto Plata. I cut the bottom off each hamper, and the kids put them over their heads and stuck their arms out the sides, where I had also cut holes. What they lacked in scariness, they made up in being funny.

It started to rain as soon as we left the boat. Pablo showed up with a golf cart and a big bag of candy for the kids. He'd been worried the kids wouldn't have any treats, so had bought a lot. He had gum, suckers, candy bars, you name it. We really appreciated his gesture.

Pablo gave us a ride to our first stop, the marina office. Roberto was the only one on duty. The kids yelled, "Trick or treat!" Roberto stood there and smiled. They said it again. I was afraid he didn't get it.

"I want to see a trick," he said. Okay. He didn't get it. We all stood there, just looking at each other. Finally he went behind the desk, returned with the bag of candy and put it on the counter. Tristan and Tessa didn't take all of it, they left some for him. We left Roberto with big smiles and thank yous. Alright. One down, three to go. The security guard had a big laugh when he saw the kids in their costumes. I gave him some candy kisses on the way back to the golf cart. He was happy. Next stop, an apartment outside the marina.

A Dominican lady, a friend of Pablo, wanted to join in on Halloween too. When Tessa and Tristan yelled "Trick or treat!" she gave them full-sized, American candy bars. Now for those of you not acquainted with the Dominican Republic, American candy is expensive here. I'd bought a small bag of the fun-sized candy bars, and it was nearly double what I would have paid in the US. I was overwhelmed by her generosity, and Pablo's too.

We got back into the golf cart and headed to the restaurant. Everyone had big smiles when Tristan and Tessa walked in and yelled, "Trick or treat!" The manager walked over, grinning at their costumes. I didn't see any candy though. The kids looked at me. I looked at Dan. "Say it again," I whispered.

"Trick or treat!"

More smiles, but no candy. The kids looked uneasily at us. I whispered to Dan, "Who did you give the candy to?"

Dan motioned to the guy behind the bar. I quietly asked the bartender, "Did you get the candy?"

Big smile. "*Si,*" he said, giving me the thumbs up. So, they had gotten the candy, and they had eaten all the candy. Apparently "candy no more." Well, this was awkward. After a few more minutes of smiles and needless waiting, I said, "Okay then" and herded the kids back to the dock. They gave me a questioning look but said nothing. Out of view of the restaurant staff, I reached into my pocket and gave them some candy from the just-in-case stash. They were happy.

Our last stop was at our neighbors on *Life is Good*. The owner was Canadian, so I hoped this would go alright. The owner and the first mate met us with their dog, Amiga, dressed in her Halloween costume. She was an adorable-looking pirate. They had candy for the kids and books for Dan and me.

We talked to them for awhile, and then the crew of *Reel Easy* stopped by. They were supposed to leave that night to head to Florida, but an officer from the Dominican navy told them the weather was still too rough and wouldn't clear them to leave. The couple on *Life is Good* had tried to leave too, but they were also denied. We talked to the other cruisers until the kids were ready to die of impatience. They wanted to go to *Blue Heaven* for more candy. We relented and Amiga tagged along. The New York fishing boat had Snickers bars for the kids and beer for the adults.

Finally it was back to *Alegria* to check out the loot. What a haul! The kids were so happy and we were exhausted. While I sorted through the candy to find what I liked, Dan took the books we had finished reading over to *Life is Good*. What an evening. Due to the kindness of strangers, the kids had a great night of trick-or-treating, and we got new books to read. Where would we be without our community? [*End blog*]

November 8, 2007 The Good, The Bad, The Ugly, DR
(*from the blog of* Alegria)

THE GOOD
At 6 a.m. a naval official was at our boat with our *despacho* for Samana. A *despacho* is required in the Dominican Republic to go from port to port and to leave the country. Unlike the Bahamas where once you're in, you can go anywhere, this *despacho* is only good for the ports you specifically designate on the form, so you have to know where you're going ahead of time. The first likely spot to stop, according to our guidebook, was Rio San Juan, though we could take a short break at Escondido if we really needed it, with strict rules to never to try to enter Escondido Bay after 5 p.m. due to visibility. The last port was Samana.

"How long have you been here?" the guard asked.

I had to think. "Two months," I replied, a little shocked. A day short of two months exactly. Time flies.

The night watchman, who was Tristan and Tessa's friend, and the naval officer helped us cast off. A wind from the west greeted us as we left the marina, heading east. What a nice surprise. We knew it wouldn't last, but this was the first time, in a very long time, we didn't have wind on our nose. It wasn't a strong wind, but it was enough that we could put up the jib (front sail) and motorsail. The seas were forecasted to be 3 to 6 feet.

With the wind behind us, we were off to a great start, well over 7 knots. We would arrive at Rio San Juan very quickly. The wind from the west should have tipped us off that our weather was going to change, but we were so excited about finally leaving, we didn't think much about it. Our weather report indicated we had a good (though short) weather window, so we got a little greedy. At 10 a.m. we were talking about going straight to Samana. At noon we were thinking of heading overnight to Punta Cana, located on the east coast of the DR. How about just going on to Puerto Rico? Big mistake.

THE BAD

By the middle of the afternoon, storm clouds had built around us. This was expected, since it had rained nearly every day for the last three weeks. We had been very lucky on prior passages, using the radar to travel around most of the storms. But our luck had run out on this passage. I was sitting in the helm seat next to Dan. It was starting to get chilly. We could see lightning in the clouds.

"Should we go offshore more?" I asked.

"I can't be sure which way the storms are moving," he answered.

"Well, turn on the radar and find out."

A pause. "The radar isn't working."

I looked at him in surprise. "What? When did this happen? Didn't you check it before we left?" Dan was always very good about checking things before we left a port.

"It was working fine. Now it shuts off after a minute or so," he said.

This was the start of the bad. At some point, we'd have to sail at night to reach Puerto Rico. "It'll be fine. You are usually the calm one. Christopher Columbus didn't have radar when he came to America," he reminded me.

"Christopher Columbus didn't have to watch out for cargo ships," I reminded *him*. I guessed it would be fine. The radar would stay on for about a minute—enough time to give us a few complete rotations. Dan turned it on to look at the storm. The brief picture displayed showed rain all around us. We were going to have to suck it up.

Dan put on his foul-weather gear. The rain fell in a torrent. I stepped inside, determined to keep watch from there, but it was raining so hard I couldn't see 3 feet past the end of the bow. This was dangerous. We were motoring close to shore, and without the radar, we were traveling blind. I slid the cockpit door open and looked at Dan getting pummeled. "Do you need me out there?" I was hoping for a no.

"No, stay inside."

"I'm going to turn on the navigation lights."

"Don't turn them on," he warned. "The battery is low."

"What?"

"For some reason the batteries aren't recharging."

Okay. Strike two. I sat down in the salon and tried to read my book in the dim light while the kids watched a movie. The storm continued. A few waves slapped hard against the sides of the boat. It was getting late, and I hoped the storm would be gone before dark. It was still raining when Dan opened the door. "Carla, can you come out here?"

That tone. I knew that tone. Nothing good ever came from that tone. I took my time putting on my foul-weather gear. Reluctantly, I entered the cockpit.

MORE BAD

"The autopilot isn't working," Dan told me. "I have to hand steer. Can you help?"

I had never hand steered this boat in waves. No time like the present to learn. At first it was very disorienting. I had to accomplish three things at the same time: watch the GPS chartplotter, watch the land off our starboard side, and watch the dome of the compass so I could steer a compass course. Darkness fell. Dan was my lookout.

The waves were coming from the stern's port side (behind and from the left), and *Alegria* was surfing down the waves. At first it was hard to steer, but soon I got the feel of the boat, and everything was going fairly well. It was very tiring though, not something I wanted to do for a long time. The rain abated some, but it was cold. Our hopes of heading to Samana, or even Rio San Juan, were dashed. The new plan was to head to nearby Escondido Bay.

The good news was that our sometimes challenging port engine was doing great. Maybe we should keep going?

EVEN MORE BAD

Suddenly I heard a loud noise from the starboard engine. I looked over the side at the exhaust pipe. No water was coming out. I pulled back on the throttle and yelled out, "The engine!" just as Dan ran back into the cockpit. The lack of water coming out of the exhaust pipe was not a good sign. Dan shut the engine down. The most logical guess at that point was that the saltwater pump had failed.

For those of you keeping score, so far we had: radar problems; what seemed like battery problems, limiting our navigation-light usage; no autopilot; and only one engine. The good news was that the kids were listening to the *High School Musical* soundtrack and having a great time. The bad news was that I wasn't.

The waves, coming from the port side, combined with the lack of the starboard engine, kept pushing us closer to shore. In addition to worrying about the rocks onshore, we also had to worry about the small, local fishing boats. Occasionally a fisherman's light broke the heavy blackness of night, but we knew not every boat had a light. Without the radar, it would be very easy to smash into an unlit boat.

I was very nervous. Dan used the megawatt spotlight to spot the fishing boats around us. I concentrated on the chartplotter and my compass readings. With nightfall, I didn't have to concentrate on the land anymore. The dangers it held were still there, I just couldn't see them in the darkness. With the waves and only one engine, it was much harder to keep the boat on course. It took all I had mentally and physically, and we still had another hour or so to Escondido. I wasn't sure I could do it.

Dan was very calm. He skillfully navigated me through the web of fishing boats we seemed to have wandered into. As we came up on the entrance to the bay, he hesitantly asked, "Do you want to talk about what we will do if we lose the other engine?"

"No!" I shouted back. I really couldn't take any more bad news. It was bad enough it was a moonless night. We were going into the anchorage blind.

THE UGLY

Dan pulled out a paper chart. "According to these charts, three large rocks jut out from land near the entrance to Escondido Bay. They aren't showing up well on the chartplotter, so we have to watch for them."

Great! The guidebook gave the waypoint to the entrance of the bay and briefly mentioned the large rocks we must clear. You'll remember it also warned to get to the anchorage before 5 p.m. so you could see your way in. Don't go in after 5 p.m. We were well past that. I needed that radar. I scanned the chartplotter. One rock showed up, but there should be three. Where were the others?

I was scared now, so scared that my knees were literally shaking. I was going totally off the chartplotter since I couldn't see anything off the side of the boat. Dan couldn't see anything either, even with the spotlight. I needed to steer a compass course of 100 degrees to clear the rocks. With the storm, the waves, and the darkness, everything was disorienting. It was nearly impossible for me to hold course.

For some reason, my mind wandered, and for lack of a better phrase, I just "spaced out" for what seemed like several minutes. When I snapped out of it, I looked at the compass and realized I had been steering a course closer to 120 degrees. Oh my God! I had no idea now where the boat was or where the rocks were. For all I knew, I could be steering us right into them. All I could do now was pray.

Dan and I held our breath as we motored past where the rocks should have been. It seemed like an eternity had passed before we felt we cleared them and could breathe a sigh of relief. There was no time to celebrate though. Now I needed to focus on getting us into the bay. I took a deep breath, rubbed my leg to stop it from shaking, and headed toward the entrance to Escondido Bay.

It was so dark, we couldn't see into the harbor, so we had to rely on the waypoints. Dan wanted me to hit the waypoint before turning into the harbor. I was doing the best I could, but with the waves and the wind, I couldn't keep *Alegria* on course. I was beyond scared now.

We agreed I was as close to the waypoint as I was going to get, and I should turn in. The harbor was surrounded by tall cliffs, with a small beach area to one side. There were no lights coming from the shore to help guide us in. The depth as we entered the harbor was 60 feet but was expected to drop down to about 20 feet. That was where we could anchor. We had no idea where that would be though. We could hear the surf hitting the beach, and that was not a sound we wanted to hear. I motored around blindly, looking for a depth below 30 feet. The mountains felt so close. I was about out of my mind.

"You are too close to this side!" Dan yelled from the bow. I turned the boat. "I can hear the surf, go the other way," he yelled again. What other way?

Finally the depth finder showed 20 feet, and we agreed to anchor. Dan took the helm, and I went to the bow. In 20 feet of water, I would have to let out a minimum of 100 feet of chain, or a 5-to-1 scope. I preferred a 7-to-1 scope, or 140 feet of chain, but not knowing exactly where we were oriented in the bay, I couldn't risk letting out that much. Were we at least a 100 feet from everything? It was too dark to tell. Dan turned *Alegria* into the wind, and suddenly the back of the boat felt too close to the mountain. Intuitively I knew I shouldn't drop the anchor there.

"We're too close to the side." I could feel it. Dan motored out more until I said stop. I dropped the anchor in just under 30 feet of water.

I released 125 feet of chain, put on the bridle, and let out the rest. Dan backed down on the anchor, but with no visuals, it was hard to tell if we were really set or if we were dragging. The rain was still pounding, and the rapid current pushed against the boat. We collapsed exhausted into the salon, sleeping on the seat cushions so we could hear the anchor alarm if we dragged. Or the sound of us hitting the side of the mountain.

THE GOOD

The bright sunlight coming into the salon windows woke me up. I lay still for a few moments, staring at the ceiling, dreading the moment when I had to look out the window and see how close we were to the cliffs. Dan woke up about the same time I did. I took a deep breath, sat up, and surveyed the scene outside. I was shocked to find us anchored perfectly in the middle of the bay. How in the world had we managed that? That was just the first of the many surprises that day.

The starboard engine, located under Tristan's bunk, was the priority that morning. I expected the worst when Dan crawled out, but he said he didn't see any major problems. His best guess was an impeller blade on the saltwater pump had broken off and jammed. The errant blade was dislodged once Dan spun the impeller by hand. When he started the engine, it ran perfectly. Our good luck continued as Dan fixed our radar. It was only a loose wire. The autopilot still didn't work, but since we didn't have too far to travel, Dan planned to troubleshoot the problem at our next anchorage. The seas and wind were calm as we made our way to Samana. [*End blog*]

9

Meltdown in Samana

DOMINICAN REPUBLIC

W E MADE IT TO SAMANA without any more problems. No sooner had we dropped our anchor in the muddy harbor that afternoon than the harbor master, the commandant, and two other men came out to our boat. I was ready for them with brownies, fresh from the oven. It's funny how baked goods make the customs' process go smoother for everyone.

While the officials ate their brownies on *Alegria,* a sailboat and a powerboat both dragged their anchors and drifted aimlessly around the harbor. Reluctantly, two of the officials on our boat had to leave their brownies and chase after the other two boats. What was going on here? Samana was going to be an interesting harbor.

November 11, 2007 Samana, DR
(from the blog of Alegria)

Rain. We can't escape it. What is wrong with the weather in this country? It has rained hard since the middle of October, and I am sick of it.

When we finally got a break from the deluge, we headed to the Chinese restaurant for lunch and took a quick walk around the town. Samana is a stopping point for cruise ships, and whale watching is the big tourist attraction. Apparently we aren't seeing it at its best (or sadly, maybe we are.) Because of all the rain and the runoff from the hills surrounding us, the water in the harbor is a scary, brown color and filled with all kinds of debris. I've warned everyone to be careful not to fall in as we go back and forth in the dinghy.

The cruise ship companies recently built their own "mini town" within the town itself for its passengers. It contains a casino, restaurants, and a few souvenir shops all shiny and new and brightly painted, and all carefully designed to provide the illusion of a thriving, cheerful, affluent metropolis. Venture off a few blocks past the cruise-ship city, however, and you'll find starving dogs and desperately poor people. It's like being on a Hollywood movie set.

The night time is hopping though. From the park you can hear the sounds of *merengue* music all night. Street vendors pull their vans up to the light posts, illegally tap into the power, pull out tables and chairs, and blast the music, all while selling hamburgers and chicken. One night a van pulled up to the light post, tapped in, and the music started. Then we heard a loud boom. The lights went out in town and stayed out for about an hour.

This rain has to end soon. We are desperate for white, sandy beaches and long to jump off the back of the boat for a swim. We are all a little stir crazy. Good news, though. Dan fixed the autopilot. Like the radar, it was just a loose wire. The battery problem was due to a loose belt on the alternator which simply needed tightening. *Alegria* is back in business. [*End blog*]

November 14, 2007 Samana, DR, The Big Meltdown
(*from the blog of* Alegria)

It just won't stop raining here. I am so tired of it. I am tired of looking at the dirty water in the harbor. The flies are unbelievably bad here. I can't keep them out or kill them fast enough. Today was the worst.

We haven't been able to bring our trash up to the dock because of the rain, so three bags have been sitting on the back transom (back steps) for days. Today there was a break in the rain, so we decided to take them into town. I wasn't feeling well to begin with, and it didn't help when I noticed the dirty harbor water making a brown stain on our white hulls. I watched cans, logs, coconuts, and plastic bags float past *Alegria,* and then a huge dead frog. For some reason this just grossed me out.

"You're lucky you didn't see the maggots on the garbage bags!" said Tristan excitedly. Seeing my horrified face, he quickly added, "Dad washed them all off."

Those same maggot-filled garbage bags were now in the dinghy, waiting for me to sit next to them. This was my glamorous life.

We made it to the dock, and Dan took the garbage to the trash bin. We needed to find a grocery store to pick up a few things and an internet cafe to check the weather. The internet cafe was the closest. I had hoped we would be leaving the next day, but after checking the weather, Dan said we were trapped here for two more days. I was starting to feel sick.

The grocery store we found had a good selection, but it had dirt floors and no lights inside. I was scared to touch anything because I just knew a rat was waiting behind every box of cereal. Luckily we made it out of there unscathed. Dan wanted to get lunch, but I had reached my limit. I was tired of walking in the mud. I was tired of the heat and the flies. I was tired of seeing all the starving animals. I just wanted to go. So much negativity was really unusual for me. Normally I have no problem dealing with the worst conditions, taking it in stride, but today I just couldn't do it.

We passed a small, local cafe, and Dan suggested we eat

there, but I refused. I wanted to go into the nice restaurant in the new area the cruise line had built. Dan really wanted to eat local. I had a meltdown and informed him I was not walking through any more mud, nor would I be sitting outside on a dirty street waving off flies. I was going to the nice cafe with the white tablecloths.

We went to the nice cafe with the white tablecloths. It really wasn't much more expensive than the local place, and it was clean and bright. I was happy. Sadly it didn't last. I noticed Dan doing something with his foot. He looked at me sheepishly.

"There's a maggot in my sandal," he said in a low voice.

I gasped as it fell out of his shoe and onto the floor. Seriously? A maggot? The maggot was huge and was making a fast slippery trail for my purse. Could it get any worse? Oh, it did.

"Kill it!" I hissed.

Dan crushed it with his sandal. A white and red liquid trickled toward my feet. My stomach heaved.

"I need to get that picture out of my head," I said, holding my hands over my face.

"Think of ponies! Think of ponies!" cried Tristan.

We need to get out of here. [*End blog*]

I couldn't spend one more day in Samana waiting for a weather window to Puerto Rico. We decided to do the next best thing and venture southeast, hugging the coast, going as far as we could until the weather deteriorated. I didn't care where we ended up; I just wanted out of Samana.

With a new *despacho* in hand, we anchored overnight at nearby Cayo Levantado so we could get an early start. We knew that you weren't supposed to anchor there and soon found out why. After we dropped the anchor, an official onshore yelled to us that we couldn't anchor in that spot. I couldn't figure out what the big deal was until the anchor was almost up, and I realized we were pulling up a huge underwater cable at the same time. Fortunately, neither the official saw that nor did we cut power to the island. We untangled ourselves from the cable and anchored several yards away.

The next morning we had an early start and a beautiful day. It was the kind of day that made us think about not stopping at Punta Macao but continuing on to Punta Cana instead. But heck, why even stop there? It was such a great day, let's go all the way to Puerto Rico. On the VHF, we'd heard of other sailboats heading straight through, why not us? Obviously we hadn't learned our lesson.

A few hours of motorsailing later, we ran over a fishing net, wrapping it around the starboard prop and killing the engine. Dan had to dive over the side, in the middle of nowhere, and cut it loose. I made him tie a rope around his waist to keep track of him. The net removal wasn't an easy job. Dan had to swim under the boat and keep himself underwater while holding his breath and trying to cut away a strong net that was wrapped very tightly around the prop. All of this while not hitting his head on the hull, which was bashing up and down in the waves.

The water was rough, and I knew Dan was not entirely comfortable with this endeavor, which is why I'm sure he dropped two knives before finally holding onto one and cutting the line. It took some time, but eventually he cut it free without injuring himself, and we were underway again. Then, right on cue, the thunderstorms hit and we ducked into Punta Macao for the night.

The next day it was another early start for Punta Cana. Again the day started out great, and again we entertained the idea of going on to Puerto Rico; that is until the thunderstorms hit us again. We had a visitor on board with us this time. A small, exhausted bird rested on *Alegria* for about an hour after one of the storms. Even he was sick of the rain.

Our plan for Punta Cana was to spend one night in

the marina and get a weather report. They didn't have a slip that was wide enough for us, so we tied up to the fuel dock, which wasn't a great solution. The surge coming into the marina tested our lines and cleats, pushing *Alegria* forward until the lines became taut and then snapping her back with a loud creak as the water whooshed back out. This put tremendous pressure on the starboard cleat, and we knew we needed another option.

We thought about checking out Cap Cana Marina next door until we went in to prepay our bill. A price of US$16 for the slip, water, and electricity, plus unlimited use of the beautiful Punta Cana Resort, with its swimming pools and white beaches, was hard to pass up. Puerto Rico would have to wait. Unfortunately, as we would learn later, the cleat wouldn't.

November 22, 2007 Happy Thanksgiving, Punta Cana, DR

(from the blog of Alegria)

One of the interesting things about our travels has been how we deal with time. We don't use a calendar and very rarely use a watch. Time means nothing to us. As a result, sometimes important dates can sneak up on us. That's what happened with Thanksgiving. We had actually thought that Thanksgiving was next week and were surprised on Sunday when we learned it was this week.

We are still in the DR. We were set to leave Tuesday morning, but when we woke up, the wind was over 25 knots. Later that day it hit 30 knots, with the same forecast for Wednesday. The following week's weather report forecasted 10-foot seas and over 20-knot winds. We'll be stuck for awhile. It was such a disappointment. I wanted to be in Puerto Rico for Thanksgiving.

On Wednesday we rented a car and drove into Punta Cana to buy a turkey. We shopped at several stores, but the closest we came was deli-sliced turkey. We were totally unprepared for Thanksgiving. Thursday, Thanksgiving morning, we were still searching for food. Finally we gave up, bought the deli-sliced turkey, and went back to the boat. If I'd had any creative abilities, I could have, with the help of some mashed potatoes, molded the sliced meat into something resembling a turkey. Since I am artistically challenged, however, the meat lay flat and uninviting on the plate. We did have mashed potatoes, green beans, and gravy to liven the meal though. I used the good china (yes we do have good plates on board), and the kids lit the candles. Afterwards we took a walk along the beach under a nearly full moon. We didn't have Puerto Rico, or a real turkey, but we had each other. That's all we needed. [*End blog*]

Tessa couldn't understand why I was upset about nearly missing Thanksgiving. She loved not being locked into time. Her response to worrying about time was, "Why don't we just say what time it is?" She refused to be bound to a calendar. She's a very smart girl.

November 25, 2007 Cleat No More! Punta Cana, DR
(from the blog of Alegria*)*

The day started off simply enough, with the usual 20-knot wind, the boat jerking around in the swells, and the constant worry of breaking a line. Dan and I really thought about heading to Cap Cana Marina, but with the swells, the wind, and the untangling of about ten different lines, we weren't sure if moving would do more harm than good. That decision, however, was thrust upon us not too soon after breakfast.

The kids and I were just getting ready to head to the beach. Dan was worried about the boat and decided to stay on board. Suddenly a large swell hit our stern, causing

Alegria to jerk hard. POP! Dan instantly knew it was the cleat. Cleat no more! We looked at each other and said, "We've got to go."

Dan inspected the damage. I started the kids on battening down the hatches (literally!), putting the computer away, and stowing anything else that could move. It would be a short but bumpy ride.

We hadn't seen the dockmaster for a few days, and we didn't have time to officially check out. We could remedy that later. We were too busy trying to figure out how we were going to get out of there on our own. The wind, the waves, and the fact that we had at least ten lines to release made this a dangerous operation. I went to get help, while Dan worked on getting the lines untied from the dock.

Taking the broken cleat with me, I ran down the dock toward a group of men standing outside a fishing boat. Fortunately one of the men understood English. I told him our cleat broke, and we needed to get off the fuel dock immediately. He instructed one of the men to go with me. The newly appointed deckhand followed me back, and on the way, another one joined us. When I arrived back at the boat, I had three helpers.

The guys were a great help. They released the lines in perfect order. One extra spring line, the last one, was stuck. I couldn't get it off the remaining boat cleat; it was stretched too tight. The men couldn't release it from their side on the dock either. The wind was blowing *Alegria* away from the dock, hard, and this cleat was taking all the weight. I was afraid we didn't have much time before this one broke too. If it did, the surge would send us hurtling into the boats in front of us.

Dan used the engines to slide *Alegria* toward the dock, relieving the pressure, and I tried again to get enough slack to release the line. It wouldn't budge. The guys suggested cutting it, but it was such a thick line, I wasn't sure I'd be able to. I yelled for Tristan to get a knife, so he ran into the galley and ran back out with a giant butcher knife. That had disaster written all over it.

"Oh my God! Put that knife down!"

Confused, he took it back into the galley. Alright, if we couldn't cut the line, we had to try one more time to pull it off. All three of the men pulled hard on the line, then released it to give me a few seconds of slack. They kept yelling, "Lady! Lady!" They were afraid I was going to get my fingers caught or cut off when the rope went taut. This time though, I forced the line off half of the cleat. One more big pull and we were free.

Now the guys on the dock had a tough time getting it undone on *their* side. Dan slowly moved *Alegria* backwards, close enough for them to throw us the line when they got it loose. I really have to give Dan credit here as he did an excellent job of maneuvering our boat. Finally all our lines were freed, and we were ready to head out into the channel markers and into the waves. And what waves they were!

The forecast was for 8-foot waves, only six seconds apart, but this close to shore, they were much bigger than that. I stayed on the bow, making sure all the lines were secured as we motored out of Punta Cana Marina. Several times I had to hold on tight as a surging wave pounded *Alegria*.

The entrance to the Cap Cana Marina was right next door, but we needed to exit out and between the Punta Cana Marina markers, turn to the right, and then line up for the channel markers into the Cap Cana Marina. In between was a reef. Heading out into the channel, we buried the bow several times, causing water to shoot high into the air. If the engines had died, it would have been ugly, but they performed flawlessly.

Out in deeper water now, we needed to turn. The waves were still steep, but seemed to be a little farther apart. Right after coasting down the back of a big one, Dan turned the wheel, and then we were surfing down the waves instead of bashing into them. We had just started through the channel markers to Cap Cana Marina, when we noticed a boat coming out. This channel, in good weather, was not wide enough for two boats; with these waves it was almost impossible. Dan thought about turning around, but it was too dangerous to make a quick turn. Besides, the boat coming out was a 60-foot Lazzara motoryacht. They had a much more expensive boat, with a professional captain. They needed to watch out for *us*.

Dan motored a little outside the channel marker, closer to the reef, to give the other boat some room. They passed us, looking at us like we were crazy for being out there. Just when we thought we were in the clear, a dredger cut across outside the markers on a collision course with us. Not today my friend! Two guys in the small boat leading the dredger were calling us on the radio, in Spanish, I'm sure asking us to hold up, but we didn't. They had to wait for us. Dan guided our boat in flawlessly. I called the marina on the VHF to let them know we'd arrived.

Cap Cana Resort is a very expensive development, partially owned by Donald Trump. The marina, a part of the resort, is very upscale. Reminding everyone we were headed for the high-rent district, I told Tristan to get rid of all the makeshift bumpers we had out, including the garden hoses, the lifejackets, the deflated bumper, and the rolls of Charmin toilet paper (just kidding!). We (and the boat) were a mess as we got to our slip, trying to untangle lines and move them to the other side. The dockhands understood. They got us settled and even found us a new electrical cord to replace the one we had burned up in the Punta Cana Marina.

After all the drama, it was nice to sit in the cockpit, relax, take a look around at the beautiful marina, and give thanks for how great a job we all did. That was until I looked up and saw Dan's underwear hanging from the cockpit bimini for all the world, and the dockhands, to see. He had hung them there to dry the night before after washing them out by hand. I hung my head and gave a big sigh. We could really redneck up a place. [*End blog*]

When pulling Alegria *into a slip in windy challenging conditions like that, or any conditions, we always counted on the kids for help. Many cruisers made their children stay out of the way, but not us. We weren't parents taking our children on a sailing trip; Tristan and Tessa were part of our team. Even when she was a tiny six year old, I would give Tessa a fender and tell her it was her job to keep* Alegria *from smashing into the dock. She never let me down. Tristan was our line handler. He had the uncanny ability to know which line to pull on at which angle to get* Alegria *quickly secured to the dock. Both children earned the respect of the dockhands who watched them in action. It was a great feeling to know I could give them such important jobs and never have to think twice whether they were capable of handling them.*

It was December 4th and we were finally leaving the Dominican Republic. Nothing stood between us and Puerto Rico but the Mona Passage. The customs officer came to the boat to check us out of the country. We had just enough money to check out, or so we thought. The official didn't get to *Alegria* until after 5 p.m., which wasn't our fault, but he said he needed to charge us overtime. We didn't have enough pesos for overtime fees. We had exactly enough money for the normal check out. We didn't even have any US dollars.

I tore the boat upside down looking for any cash, but there was nothing. I told the customs officer we didn't have it. The best we could do was rent a car and head into town to an ATM machine. He looked at us and asked, "Do you like the Dominican Republic?"

"Yes, we really do."

"Will you come back some day?" he asked.

"We'd love to."

He shrugged. "You can pay me then." He gave us a big smile and left. And I didn't even have to make brownies.

10

Tropical Storm and a Homecoming for Alegria

VIRGIN ISLANDS

AFTER A REFRESHINGLY UNEVENTFUL MOTORSAIL, we arrived in Boqueron, Puerto Rico in the late afternoon. We needed to clear customs in Mayaguez, thirty minutes away. Raul, our cab driver, drove us the next morning. When he learned Tristan's birthday had been the day before, he took us to the mall to birthday shop at no extra charge. It was a shock to be in a busy mall after so much time in remote areas, especially one fully decorated for Christmas, complete with a Santa and elves. We had three goals: find a bookstore, buy Tristan a birthday present, and get an ice cream birthday cake. We spent three hours racing around the mall but less than fifteen minutes in the bookstore. The bookstore carried only Spanish-language books, so we were disappointed. We did find a large toy store and bought Tristan a game for his birthday present.

Surprisingly, there was a Baskin and Robbins in the mall, and Tristan picked out an ice cream cake. We carried the cake through the mall for an hour, then the half-hour taxi ride back to Boqueron, and finally in the dinghy back out to *Alegria*. An ice cream cake was the one thing Tristan wanted most, so even though it was somewhat melted by the time we were able to eat it, it was worth it.

The next day we left Boqueron. Our plan was to get to Ponce, check in to the marina, secure *Alegria*, and fly to Illinois for Christmas. The weather was good as we made our way from one remote anchorage to the next, heading east along Puerto Rico's southern coast. We didn't check the weather as often as we normally did. Maybe it was the upcoming holiday, maybe it was the excitement of our flying to Illinois, or maybe it was the fact that we were technically out of hurricane season, but whatever it was, we got complacent, and it came back on us.

As we motored into the harbor outside of the Ponce Yacht and Fishing Club, we heard a lot of chatter on the VHF radio about a tropical storm, recently named Olga, coming our way. How had we missed that?

We dropped anchor late in the afternoon, in the face of increasing winds. Our slip reservation wasn't for a few days, so we planned to stay at anchor in the harbor until then. We weren't thrilled with where we were anchored and even less thrilled about the fact that our anchor was going to have very little time to set before being tested, but the marina was closed, and it was too late in the day to go anywhere else.

Dan was worried about the storm, so he left our dinghy in the water. On our Voyage catamaran, the dinghy rode on a platform on the back of the boat. While this was great for traveling and kept the dinghy safe, it would not be a quick release if something happened, and we needed the dinghy in a hurry. It turned out to be a bad idea.

When the anchor set, *Alegria* faced east. By late evening the barometer dropped, and we had a wind reversal. The wind was now blowing from the west. When this occurs, one of two things will happen to the anchor: the boat pulling on the chain from the opposite direction will pull it out and set the boat free; or the anchor will pull from its position, reset, and everything will be fine. This would be our first time testing our Spade anchor this way.

The right anchor is one of the most important pieces of equipment on your boat. If ours ever failed us, in moments, we could lose our home and our family. I knew how much time Dan had put into researching this Spade anchor, so I was confident he'd made the right choice. I trusted Dan and I trusted our anchor.

That night the waves were the worst part. They slammed into *Alegria*. At times it felt like she was being lifted and dropped. The dinghy was hit hard. The wind, combined with the seas, picked it up, sending it almost airborne behind *Alegria*. I don't know how the line holding it didn't snap. Over the VHF radio, we heard that several boats in the harbor were dragging. This meant we also had to keep an eye out for boats dragging into us. They continued to drag all that night and into the next day, never getting their anchors to hold. Dan stayed up all night on anchor watch, but our anchor performed flawlessly. I would love to say I stayed up with him, but the storm, combined with the boat motion, was perfect sleeping weather for me. I went to bed and had the best sleep I'd had on the boat so far.

The next morning the wind and waves still hadn't improved, so we called the marina and arranged to pull into a slip earlier than planned. As we tried to maneuver *Alegria* into her slip, the wind worked against us, blowing hard against the boat, pushing her away from the dock. It took skill on Dan's part, plus the help of two strong marina workers, to get her side-tied to the dock.

The north shore of Puerto Rico got the brunt of the storm, while the south side, where we were, experienced strong winds and heavy rain all that day. All day the Coast Guard called over and over again for missing boats, and a rescue helicopter circled in the air. Tropical Storm Olga dumped over 11 inches of rain on us, but we were safe and dry inside *Alegria*. By the time, several days later, Olga met her end in Florida, she would go down as the worst December Atlantic tropical storm in history.

The facilities in the Ponce Yacht and Fishing Club were great. We felt very secure leaving *Alegria* there while we flew to Illinois to celebrate Christmas. It was tough leaving the warm weather and sunny skies to head to cold and snow, but with health issues affecting our families back in the US, we felt we needed to be there.

Though we left Puerto Rico with two suitcases, we flew back to the island in time for New Year's Eve with eight bags stuffed with school books, reading books, clothes, and anything we thought would make life a little better on *Alegria.*

We were tired from our trip, but it was good to be home. We spent a quiet New Year's Eve on the boat. I made a steak dinner, and we celebrated with music and fireworks coming from the marina. The next day we toured the city of Ponce. I fell in love with Ponce. I think we all did. The people were friendly, the colonial architecture was beautiful, and there was so much to do. You could visit one of the many museums, shop at the large Plaza del Caribe mall, or just walk around like we did, absorbing the city's charm. What really intrigued me was the mix of old and new. Old colonial buildings contrasted with new office buildings. Fancy cars lined well-maintained thoroughfares, but off a main street in town, you might see someone riding on a horse.

La Guancha, the recreational complex near the marina, was one of our favorite places. It was a very popular park, especially with families. Nearly every night, loud, but infectious, music was the norm, and we enjoyed watching couples dance the *merengue*. Small food stands in the complex sold our favorite foods, *empanadillas* (meat-filled pastries) and *tostones* (fried plantains). We ate there as often as we could. There were several really nice playgrounds across from the recreational complex, and they were always crowded with large extended families. Tristan and Tessa made many friends there. If I were ever to raise my kids in a city outside of the mainland US, Ponce would be my first choice.

After spending two more weeks in Ponce, exploring the city and enjoying the Three Kings Festival in nearby Juana Diaz, it was time for us to move on. We left Ponce and spent one night in Salinas, about 25 miles away. The next day we sailed to the Spanish Virgin Islands, east of and still part of Puerto Rico. The Spanish Virgin Islands are primarily made up of two islands, Vieques and Culebra. We stopped first at Vieques, anchoring off Green Beach. Vieques is the island where the US military used to hold bombing practice. That's over now, and what's left are white, sandy beaches and beautiful blue water. It is also a party island for Puerto Ricans. Our first night there, we were serenaded late into the night by a nearby boat full of revelers singing karaoke. I don't know who brings a karaoke machine on a boat, but they were having a great time, as most Puerto Ricans seem to do.

Our favorite anchorage on the island was, surprisingly for us, not by a beach, but in a beautiful mangrove in Ensenada Honda. That night we shared the anchorage with only the dolphins and an extremely large jellyfish. The kids were very happy, which surprised me. I thought they would have wanted to stay longer in Ponce where there was more to do, especially after having just coming back from the US with its unlimited opportunities for distractions, but they hadn't. They couldn't have been happier to get away from civilization again. Dan and I felt the same way. We spent a few more days on Vieques, enjoying the solitude, then moved on to the island of Culebra.

January 20, 2008 Culebra, Spanish Virgin Islands, Puerto Rico

(from the blog of Alegria)

We are staying on a mooring way outside of the town of Dewey, so a dinghy ride into the settlement leaves us soaked and me especially grumpy. Dan likes the town though. The people are friendly, and there are a few good restaurants. To me, the best part of Dewey is its proximity to Flamenco Beach.

I can't say enough good things about Flamenco Beach. The soft, white sand, the palm trees, the green hills, the horseshoe-shaped beach, and clear water make it one of the most beautiful beaches we have ever been on. They even have camping. Yesterday we took a cab to the beach. The kids loved swimming and playing in the sand. We ate lunch from a food stand in the park. For $2 we had barbecue chicken-on-a-stick, and of course, I had an order of *tostones.* I don't know how I will survive without them when we eventually leave here.

We went back for more beach fun today. This time we got caught in a downpour. It has rained or stormed every day that we have been here. Most days the rain has been light, but today it was a heavy rain and windy. Luckily we'd eaten our *tostones* and chicken before the sky fell. We cowered under a picnic shelter for 30 minutes before the sun returned and the beach fun was back on. We had about two hours to swim and play before the sky darkened again, and we took the taxi back into Dewey. The rain resumed as soon as we got out of the van, so instead of getting soaked in the dinghy, we went into Mamacita's restaurant and watched the football game with the locals. [*End blog*]

The next day another huge thunderstorm raged over the island. The rain came down in sheets, and the thunder was deafening. The worst part was the jagged lightning striking all around us. It was hitting very close, worrying Dan, but there was nothing we could do besides unplug the electronics and hope for the best. Lightning is one of a boater's worst enemies. In a single stroke, it can take out thousands of dollars in electronics, not to mention burn a hole in your boat. Even if it doesn't directly strike your boat, the electrical surges in the air can cause damage to your electrical system. Thankfully, the lightning storm was over quickly, but the wind and rain lasted all day. Throughout the day the Coast Guard was kept busy. It is sad and scary riding out a storm and hearing distress calls or hearing the Coast Guard calling for lost boats.

Finally in late January, we found a small break in the storms, mixed-up seas, and high winds that had kept us in Culebra. We left in the best of the sorry conditions and sailed the 20-mile passage through large, still confused seas to St. Thomas in the US Virgin Islands (USVI). We anchored just outside of Yacht Haven Grande Marina, home to some of the largest private yachts in the world. Next to the marina is the cruise-ship dock. Three or four cruise ships were docked there each day. If that didn't keep our interest, every few hours a seaplane would take off or land nearby. It couldn't get any better for the kids. Because the dock was full, one cruise ship had to anchor. He was anchored so close to us, we joked we could run a power cord to it for electricity. If we were in the Dominican Republic, ten people would have beaten us to it.

While in St. Thomas, we met up with our cruising friends Anne and Chris, from the sailboat *Blue Runner*. The last time we saw them was in October at Ocean World Marina in the Dominican Republic. They were now running the dive shop outside of Crown Bay Marina in St. Thomas. It was always nice to come to an island and reunite with cruising friends.

We spent the months of February through May sailing back and forth between the USVI and the BVI. Though we had chartered sailboats in the BVI many times over the years, we had never explored the USVI. We were pleasantly surprised.

February 12, 2008 Maho Bay, St. John, USVI
(from the blog of Alegria)

We arrived at Maho Bay, St. John after a particularly nasty 14-mile passage. The wind was from the east, so we motored the first part, into the wind. Anne had warned us that a weather system hanging over the island was making the seas outside the harbor at St. Thomas rough, but we were anxious to get moving, so we picked the best of the not-so-great forecasts. This one called for waves of 7 to 9 feet, but we were sure that meant out in the ocean, not right next to the coast. Boy, were we wrong. We were less than a mile offshore, and we took quite a pounding. Combine the waves with nearly 30-knot winds, and 14 miles is an awfully long way. The waves weren't only high, they were close together. Hitting them straight on wasn't as bad as having one of the hulls fall off the side of the wave, causing *Alegria* to pitch down, then up, then to the side as if she was riding a wild bronco.

I checked on Tristan and Tessa in the salon and noticed a hatch was open. Someone was watching over us because no sooner had I shut the hatch above the dining table, than a huge wave buried the bow, shooting water all the way back to the cockpit. There was so much saltwater going over the top and side windows that it reminded the kids and me of going through a car wash. If I hadn't shut the hatch when I did, all that saltwater would have flooded the salon.

Fortunately we only had to endure those conditions for less than two hours. As soon as we made the turn at the end of St. Thomas and headed north, the waves were blocked by the island of St. John, and all we had to deal with was the wind. We moored at Maho Bay, a protected harbor off the north shore of St. John.

The island is incredibly beautiful. The green mountains surrounding the white, sandy beach are breathtaking. It feels so good here; it will be hard to leave. [*End blog*]

It *was* hard to leave. There was so much to do. The USVI has a very impressive national parks system, and we really took advantage of it. We hiked the Reef Bay Trail with Deena the park ranger, who told us the history of the island. The 2-mile hike took us from high in the hills, down to the shore at Reef Bay, and past the remains of sugar mills, petroglyphs, and a former plantation. A few days later, Deena led a star watch, complete with telescope, on the white crescent beach of Cinnamon Bay.

When we needed food, we headed to the grocery store in Cruz Bay, or we would eat at either Cinnamon Bay Campground or Maho Bay Campground. Both had reasonable prices, and most importantly, a (cheap) steak night and prime-rib night. Both campgrounds had small grocery stores where we could buy unique items like Omaha Steaks and fresh, gourmet sandwiches.

On land, Maho Bay Campground was our favorite place in the USVI. We could seriously have lived in Maho Bay, on the boat, forever. The days unfolded easily there. In the morning the kids would take a quick swim before school. After school we would snorkel. While snorkeling close to shore, we often saw loggerhead turtles and an octopus or two. One day a mother dolphin and her baby swam nearby. After snorkeling Tristan would put our kayak in the water, and he and Tessa would play the rest of the day, paddling back and forth from the beach to our boat while Dan and I passed the afternoon reading or doing minimal boat chores.

At night we'd walk up the long flight of stairs to the top of the campground where we could watch a free movie, listen to a lecture on the environment, or see a glass-blowing demonstration. It was our little piece of paradise. The only thing it lacked was internet. Even that wasn't too bad. It required us to be more organized and creative (in general, skills we weren't known for) when it came to the homeschooling and checking on the weather.

One night on Maho Bay beach, an actual astronomer from the campground led a star watch lecture. She used a laser to point out the constellations. The beach was pitch-black, so it was easy to see the stars. While we waited for her to begin, the kids and I waded barefoot in the water, and we were delighted to find tiny bioluminescence sticking to our toes. They glowed as bright as diamonds.

It rained briefly during the astronomer's talk, and we were treated to a rare moonbow (a white rainbow). Well, all of us except Dan, who had to dinghy back to the boat because someone left a hatch open. That night we stayed up as late as we could and watched the lunar eclipse. Tessa fell asleep early, but we woke her up when the moon turned red.

The hardest part of being in the USVI was doing laundry. This required us to move the boat to Cruz Bay. The harbor was too crowded for us to anchor inside, so we had to pick up a mooring at Caneel Bay, a very rolly spot, and take a long dinghy ride around the corner into Cruz Bay. Doing laundry was one of my least favorite tasks, but since it had been a while since our clothes had a proper washing, we were due.

I had the kids bring their math to work on while I did laundry at the laundromat, but the TV volume was turned up full blast, making it impossible to concentrate. No surprise, it was turned to *Law and Order*. I am ashamed to say that Tessa and I watched back-to-back episodes of wives killing cheating husbands before the power went out. Dan and Tristan arrived back from the grocery store a few minutes later and said the power was out there too.

Now for the lesson in island patience.

Outside the building was a huge tree with an encircling bench. We took advantage of the shade, and Tristan did his math while Dan and I read our books. Tessa stayed inside talking to the lady who worked there. I have no idea what they could have talked about for all that time, but I had a feeling she was trying to avoid schoolwork. An hour later the power came back on.

It was actually nice having to wait for the power to return. After Christmas in the US, and then the hectic pace of Puerto Rico, it was good to remember things don't always go as you plan, and there's no sense getting upset. Just find a tree to sit under and wait.

In March we sailed to the BVI. There is nothing like the exhilarating feeling of a sailboat under sail; it feels like freedom. *Alegria* loved it as much as we did. The BVI has some of the best sailing conditions in the Caribbean and are our favorite islands. We had chartered boats there many, many times. Our first charter was on a catamaran with friends back in 1994. It was two weeks of paradise. From that moment, we were hooked. We returned very year after that, at least once, sometimes twice. Sometimes it was a monohull, and sometimes it was a catamaran. Tristan took his first trip to the BVI before the age of two. The same with Tessa. Our kids grew up in these islands.

This was a homecoming for *Alegria* as it was here that we first saw her for sale at Voyage Yacht Charters.

It was the summer of 2006, and we'd been looking for the perfect boat for some time. Our must haves for the boat were the following: it must be a catamaran, it must be well built, it must be at least 38 feet, it must be well maintained, and it must be in our price range because we didn't want to get a loan.

We worked with a broker in the BVI who had access to boats coming out of the charter-boat industry. Many potential boat owners frown on buying boats coming out of charter, thinking they are not well maintained and could be full of potential problems. We had chartered many times, and with the exception of one cheaper company we chartered through, the boats all seemed well maintained.

Eventually we found a boat for sale in the BVI that intrigued us. Our broker checked into it and said that it had just come out of charter. It needed some cosmetic touch-ups, but it seemed to fit what we were looking for.

Now our dilemma. Up until then, we had seen only two boats, both in the US, which we had driven to see. It would be a big commitment in time and money to fly to the BVI and look at a potential boat. Dan thought the idea was crazy at first. The only time we could get away was the next week, and last minute airfares to the Caribbean were outrageous, not to mention the hotel costs and trying to find someone to watch the kids. We had such a good feeling about it though. The pictures of the boat looked good, the price was right, and the name of the boat? It's About Time. I mean, was that the universe talking or what?

I left for a meeting, putting it in Dan's hands. If we were supposed to go, he'd find cheap airfare; if not, he wouldn't. That would be our sign, and I've always believed in signs. A few hours later, Dan called and said he found a last-minute airfare deal for under $300. He got the last two seats left. That was our sign. We arrived in Tortola, BVI the next week.

We saw It's About Time as soon as we arrived. The boat was sitting in the boatyard. I don't care how great a boat is, it never looks as good in a crowded boatyard as it does in the water. It had some dings, dents, scratches; normal things that would be easy to take care of. It needed cleaning, and there were tools left scattered about. A bigger problem was the kitchen. The stove was small, and there was a shortage of countertop and cabinet space. All in all, it didn't feel good to us.

We were disappointed. As we walked dejectedly back to the car, our broker showed us a picture of a catamaran that had just been listed. It was with a charter company in Soper's Hole, located on the south end of the island, and it met our criteria. Dan and I shrugged. What did we have to lose?

One of our favorite spots on Tortola is Soper's Hole. Here you will find shops painted in the tropical island colors of pink and blue with crisp white trim, steel-pan music floats out of open doors, and beautiful sailboats bob in the harbor. If you are hungry, you can eat at a table by the water. If you are thirsty, you can sit at the circular, dark-wood bar of Pusser's Landing, order their specialty rum drink, the Painkiller, and forget all your worries.

I have fond memories of being there on charter, taking Tristan to the ice cream shop, or sitting with Tessa, watching the colorful trigger fish dart underneath the docks. There is a great energy there too as vacationers get ready to head out on their week-long charters. They leave the dock quickly on their boats—the guests gathered happily in the cockpit, laughing excitedly as they apply sunscreen to their pale skin, shedding their scheduled lives as quickly as they shed their clothes. They motor excitedly past the slower moving sailboats returning to dock from their week in paradise. The mood on the returning boats is somber. Instead of gathering together, each person sits alone, lost in their own thoughts, reflecting on leaving a life of freedom to head back to a life of time, planning, obligations, and an endless longing to return again someday. It was a place of beginnings and dreams. It was the perfect place for our dream to come true.

We walked the dock in front of Pusser's Landing, and there in the prime spot for everyone to see, was the boat—a 38-foot Voyage catamaran named Calypso Quean, *and she was beautiful. When we stepped on board and walked into the well-maintained interior, Dan and I knew this was the boat. The galley was exactly what I was looking for: a four-burner stove, oven, two sinks, a front-opening refrigerator, and a separate, deep, drop-in freezer. Large, front windows allowed the sun to come in and reflect off the white walls, making the interior feel very bright and welcoming. The gray, leather salon seats were in great condition and were laid out in a horseshoe shape around a large, gray Corian table trimmed in teak. I could imagine us all gathered around it doing schoolwork, enjoying a meal together, or laughing as we played games.*

Steps on either side of the salon led down to the berths (bedrooms) and heads (bathrooms). The layout was a three cabin, Owner's version, exactly what we wanted and very hard to find in a charter boat. Tristan and Tessa's berths were to starboard (right) and they shared a bathroom conveniently located between their rooms. Dan and I had the entire port side, with lots of closet space and a huge bathroom.

The cockpit was large, and the outside table was more than big enough for our family. Another small detail that was important to me was that the captain's seat was actually a seat big enough for two people. I envisioned sitting next to Dan during passages, or one of the kids snuggling next to us. All in all, it was perfect.

Our broker submitted our offer the next day. Dan and I sat on the beach outside our hotel awaiting the verdict. As we waited, I noticed two women also sitting on the beach. One had a bandana on her head, and for some reason the thought occurred to me that she must be going through cancer treatment. They seemed as deep in conversation as we were, but instead of being happy, the one with the bandana was crying. As I watched them, our broker appeared over my shoulder and said, "They accepted your offer."

We were stunned. I jumped up and down screaming. I

couldn't believe it. Our broker left to start the paperwork, leaving Dan and me to celebrate. Seeing our excitement, the two women approached us. The one with the bandana asked, "Do you mind if I ask you what happened?"

"We just bought a boat," I told her excitedly. "We are going to quit our jobs and take our kids sailing for a few years!"

"Oh my gosh!" They looked as shocked as we were. "Congratulations!"

I saw her closer now and knew I was right about the cancer. After hearing our good news, she looked at her friend and smiled. A heavy weight seemed to be lifted from her shoulders. She turned to us and said, "Thank you for sharing that. I've been sitting here trying to make a decision, and now I have. That was my sign."

They walked away, chatting excitedly, then called back, "Congratulations!" I never found out what decision she made that day, but I know it was as life changing for her as it was for us.

I can't explain it, but even as I write this today, I become emotional. It was such a short moment, a chance encounter, but it really affected me. I don't know what her decision was or how she is doing now, but I know with all my heart, it was the right one. It's an amazing feeling to follow your dream, but it's just as amazing watching your dream influence someone else to follow theirs.

I Don't Think He's Wearing Pants

THE VIRGIN ISLANDS

S O NOW *ALEGRIA* WAS BACK where we found her, but unlike the mild weather we'd experienced with her that first summer, the weather in March was unpredictable. Our movements in the BVI were hampered by large northerly swells. Surfers were enjoying nearly 20-foot waves in Cane Garden Bay, Tortola. They hadn't seen conditions like that in years.

We eventually made it back to St. Thomas in time to retrieve Tessa's birthday gifts, mailed to us from our families in the US. We had established a mailbox at a mail-service business located at Crown Bay Marina. It came in handy for times like holidays and birthdays or when we needed small boat items sent to us. While on St. Thomas, we purchased a small, window air-conditioning unit; something that would become a lifesaver to us further on in our trip. A week later we were back in Maho Bay, St. John to pick up our friends Alan, Karon, and their boys, Alec and Collin, who came for another visit.

When our friends arrived, Dan and Tristan took the dinghy to shore to pick them up. On the first trip, they brought back the boys and the suitcases. As soon as Alec and Collin were on the boat, before I could even get a hug, the clothes were off and the suitcases were attacked.

Karon had packed their swimsuits in the outside pocket, and in less than five minutes, all the kids were yelling and jumping off the back of *Alegria*. It had been the longest they had gone without seeing each other, but you couldn't tell that from how quickly they all fell in together. It was wonderful to have them aboard. We played at the Maho Bay campground for a few days and then sailed over to the BVI.

April 6, 2008 Jost Van Dyke, BVI
(from the blog of Alegria)

We were enjoying a relaxing morning on Jost Van Dyke before preparing to haul the anchor and head to Cane Garden Bay, Tortola. The kids were playing in Tristan's room, a beautiful sun was shining, and the goats were calling on the hillside. All that was spoiled when Alan looked out the window and said, "I think those guys on the boat next to us are naked."

There was a moment's pause before we all raced to the window. Sure enough, in the cockpit of the monohull next to us, one man was totally nude, while the other had on a shirt but no pants. This harbor was small, with the boats and moorings very close together, so the men had to know everyone could see them, but they seemed very much at ease. At one point the totally naked guy went forward and stood by the mast for the entire harbor to see. What was he thinking?

Now, I'm not a prude, and if someone wants to go naked, by all means do, but not in a small harbor where everyone can see you. Couldn't you wait five minutes until you've cleared the harbor to strip?

After watching for awhile (and really, who could turn away?), we saw two women on board. There appeared to be two couples, but the women remained fully clothed. Our kids stayed downstairs and didn't see anything. For us, it was like watching a train wreck—we couldn't stop looking. The foursome was on a 36-foot monohull. Those are tight quarters for two couples. If they weren't wearing clothes on deck, they certainly weren't wearing them below. At minimum there was some naked bumping into each other. Ugh!

We all thought that one of the men seemed older than the other, leading to all kinds of speculation as to the relationship. The worst of all possible scenarios was "father-son." EEWW! Could you imagine going naked with your dad? It took us awhile to get that thought out of our heads. (No offense Dad!)

They were preparing to leave the harbor. The older guy, who was wearing only a shirt, was obviously worried about the sun because before he went to the bow of the boat, he put on a hat. A hat! Not pants like most people, but a hat. Oh, and shoes. He put on shoes because clearly he could stub his toe on something.

We all watched him walk to the bow to release the mooring lines. He checked the lines; we kept watching. He signaled back to the other naked guy; we kept watching. From the side, we saw him straining with the lines (naked straining is not pretty.) Suddenly their boat turned. Instead of a side view, we now had the full, naked-butt view. We kept watching as he bent over and *Dude! Not cool!*

We waited until they were well ahead of us before we left the harbor because as you know, "If you aren't the lead dog, the view never changes!"

The next day Karon and I shopped in Cane Garden Bay, while the men napped in hammocks, and the kids played on the beach. When we met up with the guys later, they had news.

"Those are the people who were naked on the boat," Dan said, indicating two dressed couples who were seated not far from him. Karon and I turned to look. They smiled and waved to us. We smiled and waved back.

Yes, the naked men were here. We had seen them earlier as we came into the harbor. A local had come to collect the mooring fee and the younger man had paid for it—naked. This was the first time we had a good look at their faces.

"How did you recognize them?" I asked Dan. "Did you follow them into the bathroom?"

They easily recognized the older man because he was wearing the same hat, shirt, and shoes we saw him in earlier. So they did have clothes. They just chose not to wear them. [*End blog*]

April 8, 2008 *Marina Cay, BVI*
(*from the blog of* Alegria)

Michael Beans, a self-proclaimed Caribbean pirate, singer, sailor, songwriter, and entertainer was playing on Marina Cay, and we took our friends to the show. Dan had been practicing his conch-blowing skills in preparation for the Conch Shell Blowing Contest. The winner would be crowned King Conch and win a liter bottle of Pusser's Rum. Not bad. Dan's personal best was forty-four seconds. We figured he had it wrapped up.

The show was fun. Michael sang songs, told jokes, and passed out free rum. Everyone had a good time. Dan and I won a shot of rum during the Name the Pirate contest. Tessa took my picture while I was drinking my shot; that was a mother-daughter bonding moment. Collin won a shot of rum for his pirate toast, but since he was only seven years old, he had to give the rum to Karon. Another Hallmark moment.

Soon it was time for the main event—the Conch Shell Blowing Contest. There was an adult and kids' contest. Tessa, Alec, and an older boy competed. The older boy won, but Tessa and Alec got a prize for participating. We were proud of them just for trying...*in a bar*. (Can you tell we have lowered our standards?)

The naked couples were there.

"Look kids! There are the people who were naked on their boat. They really have no decency. Collin! Win Mommy another shot of rum, son!" It's all relative in the islands.

There were seven contestants, including Dan, for the adult conch-blowing contest. The first one failed miserably, and our and Dan's confidence was high. Dan's turn. He picked up the conch, started to blow, and we settled in to what we thought would be a forty-second wait. But no. He choked. At twenty-nine seconds he was out. Would that be enough?

Two more contestants to go, a woman and a man. The woman went first. She took the conch and was strong. After fifteen seconds we started to worry, and at twenty seconds we were in a full sweat. At twenty-five seconds I knew I was going to have to cause a distraction, and I looked around for something to set on fire. Twenty-six seconds, twenty-seven seconds, twenty-eight seconds. She quit at twenty-eight seconds. That was too close!

Dan was worried. The last contestant grabbed the conch. He seemed calm, perhaps a little too calm, and we all wondered if he was a ringer. Could he be a professional? But no. After fifteen seconds, he was out too.

Dan won! The crowd cheered. Michael knighted him King Conch. He handed Dan his bottle of rum and yelled, "Do your victory dance!"

Dan had no dance. The look on his face was pure panic. He hastily did a move that was a cross between an Irish jig and something that was illegal in twenty states. But he had his bottle of rum and the love of his family, friends, the bar, and the naked couples. What more could you ask for? [*End blog*]

Our friends left a few days later, and we started on boat maintenance. *Alegria's* bottom needed to be painted, so we had her hauled at the Nanny Cay boatyard on Tortola.

It was too hot to stay on the boat, so we rented a hotel room nearby. It was worth it. The work went quickly, and less than a week later, we were back in the water. I was determined to lighten up the boat before we moved farther south, so I spent a few days cleaning out cabinets, under beds, and in lockers, getting rid of things we hadn't used in the last sixteen months. I am sorry to say, there were a lot of things we hadn't used. What were we thinking?

May 11, 2008 White Bay, Jost Van Dyke, BVI
(from the blog of Alegria)

I had a great Mother's Day on Jost Van Dyke. It was Reggae Sunday, and every bar and restaurant seemed to have someone singing, so we strolled the beach, listening to the music. We were moored outside of Ivan's Peace and Love Campground. The kids played on the tire swing and made castles in the sand while I read a book. Later we all snorkeled with the turtle family swimming around *Alegria*. The water here is such a clear, sparkling, beautiful light green, fading to dark blue, it's irresistible; you have to jump in. Ivan's bar, with its hundreds of seashells arranged into signs and pictures, is equally irresistible.

There is always something interesting happening on the beach at night at Ivan's. Last time we were there, about midnight, we were serenaded by drums being played by a group of young campers. This time Dan woke me up about 11:30 p.m. and told me to look toward Ivan's. There on the beach were the people from the catamaran moored next to us, juggling long, flaming sticks, accompanied by loud, techno music coming from the shore. It was quite a show. The person juggling was very good, but I couldn't understand why you would come on vacation and bring flaming sticks. I asked Dan, "Are they circus people?"

I mean, really, who brings that kind of stuff on vacation? I would have loved to have watched longer, but I was just too tired. I had another treat that night when I woke again later to see the Milky Way perfectly framed through the hatch above my bed. I went up on deck to get a better view. Tristan was awake, so I pulled him outside. We sat on the back of the boat, our legs dangling over the side. I put my arms around him, and we gazed at the stars.

I gave a silent prayer of gratitude for the last sixteen months and all the time I was able to spend with my family. I couldn't believe I even considered not doing this trip. Sure we had some trying moments in the beginning, but the freedom, the time we spent together exploring the world, was priceless. Unfortunately many people wait until an illness or a tragedy happens before they start really living their lives. We were fortunate that we weren't running away from our lives; we were running to them.

Tristan's eyes were getting heavy, so I gently lifted him up and helped him to his room. I checked on Tessa and gave her a kiss before I reluctantly drifted back to bed. It was a perfect ending to a perfect Mother's Day. [*End blog*]

If It's Thursday This Must Be Nevis

ST MARTIN TO GRENADA

FROM JUNE TO AUGUST, WE headed down the Caribbean island chain, ending at Grenada to wait out hurricane season. During hurricane season, lasting from June 1st through November 30th, many insurance companies demand cruisers be either north of Wilmington, North Carolina or south of 12 degrees north latitude, which is Grenada. With our insurance company, we could be anywhere, but we had to submit an acceptable hurricane preparedness plan every year, and if a named storm hit, our deductible would be doubled.

We were traveling again with our friends on *Makai, Fine Line, Salida,* and *Dawn Dancer.* They had caught up with us in the BVI. They all had more traditional insurance, so they were in a hurry to get to Grenada by August, which was when most cruisers felt hurricane season really began. It made for a fairly fast-paced trip though the islands.

Our first stop after leaving the BVI was St. Martin. We left late afternoon from Virgin Gorda and had a fast sail the 75 miles to Marigot Bay, on St. Martin's west coast. The island is actually split into two countries: French Saint Martin (north) and Dutch Sint Maarten (south). The advice most cruisers adhered to was eat on the French side, but shop on the Dutch side. We really enjoyed the laid-back island, especially the delicious food, but all of us will agree the highlight was a trip to the Sunset Beach Bar, next to the airport on the Dutch side. The airplanes fly over the beach next to the bar. When I say over, I mean right over, as in less than a 100 feet above the beach. The fun part wasn't being in the bar watching the plane land, it was being on the beach and having it fly over your head or have the plane engines propel you into the water. Tristan and Tessa had a blast.

The first time we stood behind a departing plane, it was small. Then the planes got bigger and we were *blown.* In the end we were covered with sand but otherwise unhurt. After lunch, the bigger planes were departing. A large American Airlines plane was on the runway, and Dan (even with all the warnings) thought he needed to experience it. As the plane revved its engines, Dan who had been standing on the curb, made the mistake of jumping back from the curb. That was all it took to get him airborne and carry him *all the way to the water,* where he was deposited harshly into the sea. Tessa and Tristan, who were already in the water, helped him out. He was covered, or rather embedded, in sand from head to toe.

After he cleaned himself up, we decided it was time to go. As we made our way past the runway, a huge, four-engine, Air France plane was getting ready to depart. Dan was close to the road. Tessa was next to him and farther back stood Tristan and me. The plane revved its engines. Dan's hat blew off and Tessa was blown to the ground. I grabbed Tristan and covered his head, trying to shield him. Dan was more concerned with his hat than with helping Tessa, who was being pummeled with sand. I watched in disbelief as my husband chased his hat while my precious eight-year-old daughter was rolled like a tumbleweed across the beach toward the sea. As she rolled past me, I reached out my hand, grabbed her, and pulled her into my arms. Dan was still chasing his hat. Luckily, none of us were hurt, just completely covered in sand. Next time, we will obey the sign.

From St. Martin we sailed down the chain. A beam reach (a strong wind from the east onto our sails as we headed south) gave us perfect conditions for *Alegria*. We stopped at the island of Saba. There is no beach or coastline, instead Saba seems to shoot straight up out of the sea. Most of the island is made up of Mount Scenery. People's homes, businesses, and the medical college are built on the side of this potentially-active volcano.

June 1, 2008 Saba
(from the blog of Alegria)

A hike to the top of the Mount Scenery volcano with Fred and Kathy from *Makai*? Sure! The peak is almost 3,000 feet high, and even though we had a taxi take us as far as he could, we still had 1,064 steps left. It was up, up, and more up. We took shelter from a sudden downpour under the giant leaves of the elephant ear plant. The foliage along the trail was beautiful—perfectly landscaped by nature. As we hiked higher into the rainforest, everywhere we looked was color, and the sound coming from the forest was a melodious mix of song birds and tree frogs.

We slipped, sweated, and huffed and puffed up the slick stairs in the humid heat. When we finally reached the top of the trail, we were disappointed. There was nothing to see. We had to take another trail, optimistically named Scenic Trail, if we wanted the view. So for another twenty minutes, we hiked in mud, crawled over rocks, shimmied through a rock tunnel, and walked onto an overgrown path of ferns and greenery, all while being surrounded by clouds. It was like being in a fairy tale.

Eventually we crawled up the last rock and found the end. Our dramatic conclusion? A cement post. There was no view due to the thick clouds, so our only reward was our own personal exhaustion, satisfaction, and a picture of a cement post. [*End blog*]

There was plenty of hiking and sightseeing to do at our next stop, St. Eustatius, also known as simply Statia. In the harbor, we snorkeled over cannons from the 1700s. We didn't stay long, but we found it to be, without a doubt, one of the friendliest of any of the islands we visited during our travels. From there we hurried on to the island of Nevis.

I wasn't very happy with how fast we were moving through the islands. The rough anchorages were part of the reason, but our friends were also anxious to get to Grenada. While I liked traveling with them, I was getting tired of the fast pace. We decided to venture out on our own, so when the other boats chose to go to Antigua, we sailed off alone to Montserrat. We couldn't pass up an island with an active volcano.

Only two sailboats sat at anchor when we entered the small harbor of Little Bay, off Montserrat. Patrick from catamaran *Passage* stopped by and introduced himself. He and his wife, Sylvie, both from France, had arrived earlier. Patrick asked if we wanted to share a taxi for a tour of the island. Of course. The tour consisted of a ride to the volcano observatory and then a drive around the island. Patrick and Sylvie gave us some time to get ready, and then we all met our taxi driver Christian on the dock.

Our first stop on the tour was the Montserrat Volcano Observatory. Here, we watched a video on the history of the island and the volcanic eruptions. The volcano had been dormant for hundreds of years, until July 1995 when it started spitting out small amounts of ash. This led to a major eruption in 1997, which buried the capital city of Plymouth in over 39 feet of ash and killed 19 people. Since then, it has been fairly active.

After the video, we stood on the observation deck. This was our first time up close and personal to a live volcano, and we were in awe. The volcano was putting on a show while we were there. Steam was streaming out of the side vent. Christian pointed out that the dome was building up again. That wasn't a good sign because it meant the potential for an eruption was increasing. We all piled uneasily back into the van.

Our driver took us into the exclusion zone to see the ash flow. Rocks the size of houses had exploded from the dome and buried portions of Plymouth. Christian drove on the ash "river" where the ash was up to 58 feet thick. He stopped the van, and we tentatively walked on the ash and volcanic debris. It was like being on the moon. Large gray rocks sat on top of gray dust, and there wasn't a person or animal in sight. Tristan felt the ash and then "knocked" on the road. It sounded hollow. It was an uneasy feeling. I had no idea what was under all that ash.

Christian drove us up to Garibaldi Hill in Isles Bay as far as the van could go. Then we walked to the top where we had an unobstructed view of the devastation. It was unbelievable. Everything was gray and desolate. The buildings in the town were still there, but the ash filled the interiors to the second floor or higher.

We drove through the country club and onto the golf course. Expensive homes still fully intact, including lights hanging from the ceiling and glass still in some windows, were filled with ash. And it was quiet. There wasn't a sound. The quiet was what really got to me. Nothing living was there, not even a bird.

You would have thought that, over time, looters would have come into these houses and helped themselves to whatever was left, but they hadn't. I had the feeling that they were afraid to—not afraid of the owners, but afraid of the volcano. We stopped by a hotel in the exclusion zone. There were curtains in the windows, glasses on the counter, and an open magazine next to a chair. Everything was just as the occupants had left it after the last explosion. It was eerie.

The volcano had damaged more than just the island. It seemed to have put a pall over the people. The islanders seemed tired, a little wary, as if waiting for the other shoe to drop. Many have left the island and relocated to England. The schoolchildren, usually the most animated on other islands, passed us with small smiles. The people here have seen it all: death of friends to the volcano, loss of property, and the pain of family members who have chosen to leave and start anew in another land. Every day they live with uncertainty, including the uncertainty that Britain could shutter the island and force them all to leave. It's sad.

Christian stopped alongside the road where a freshwater stream was cascading down the mountain. We all took a drink from the cool, refreshing water. Legend has it that if you drink from this stream, you will return to Montserrat. We hoped that would be true for us someday.

From Montserrat we sailed on to another of our favorite islands, Guadeloupe. We anchored just outside the marina, near the city of Basse-Terre and at the base of the beautiful mountains. Surprisingly, for a big city like Basse-Terre, there was little English spoken. Not to worry. Dan and I both had high-school French (a long time ago), and we were armed with our trusty *Cruiser's Guide to French*. How hard could it be?

Trying to find an ATM was tough. Guadeloupe uses the euro, and we had none. The customs agent said to try the post office, so we joined the long line, hoping we were in the right place. People did seem to be standing in line to get cash. I asked a woman in front of me about an ATM, but she didn't speak English. Luckily the woman in front of her understood me. She thought I could get cash here, but she wasn't sure. She said I could cut to the front of the line and ask the lady behind the counter. That would have been a great idea if I'd actually known how to say what I wanted to say. Instead I remained in line and practiced my French.

Trying to put together the sentences I needed involved flipping back and forth between several pages in the French phrase book, all while Dan kept making changes in the wording.

"Okay. Ask her if you can get money," he said.

Alright. I looked that up. *"C'est bien la queue pour le distributeur de billets?"* (Is this the line for the ATM machine?)

"How much do you think we should get?" Dan asked.

"I don't know."

"How about one hundred?"

That sounded good. I flipped through the book to find one hundred, while trying to keep my finger on the line I wanted to say. I couldn't find it.

"Excuse me," I said to the lady who helped me earlier. "How do I say one hundred?"

"Cent." (Sahn)

"Merci beaucoup," I replied. I practiced again. *"Je voudrais cent euro, s'il vous plait? Je voudrais cent euro, s'il vous plait?"* (I want to get one hundred euros, please.)

"Maybe that's not enough," Dan interrupted my practicing. "How about one hundred and fifty?"

I struggled with the pages again. "I can't find one fifty."

"We might need it."

"I can't find it."

"Okay. One hundred is probably enough anyway."

I kept practicing. He interrupted me again. "Two hundred. Do you think two hundred would be better?"

I sighed in frustration as I flipped through the pages in the phrase book, trying to find the French word for two hundred.

"You know, maybe two hundred and fifty would be better."

I was getting mad now. "I don't know how to say two hundred and fifty."

"Well," Dan said, "I think we may need two hundred and fifty."

I was done. I shoved the book at him and said, "Fine. You look it up."

He stared at me, then gently pushed back the book. "Okay. You know two hundred is probably okay. I was just thinking."

Finally it was my turn. I handed the clerk my ATM card and asked for two hundred euros (nearly flawlessly, I might add). She answered something back in French but didn't give me any euros which I interpreted to mean she couldn't accept my card. Great. That was a wasted effort. We walked dejectedly back to *Alegria*.

Later that afternoon in downtown Basse-Terre, a kind lady helped us find an ATM. We withdrew money, bought a few bananas (bananas are the number one export), hit the bakery, and did laundry. Later that evening I was able to use my limited French to buy fresh tuna from the fishermen at the marina, but not without some hostility on the part of the fishmongers.

There were two men and a woman, and they were unloading fish. Among their fresh catch, I saw a tuna I wanted. First I said hello and *bon jour* to cover all my bases. Then, in English, I asked how much for the fish. They just stared at me. I tried again, this time in French. Again the blank stare. So the third time, I tried a combination of both French and English (Frenglish?) and was rewarded with a hostile, "We speak French here." *It is notable that the woman said this in English.*

Well excuse me, but I thought I *was* speaking French. Apparently it wasn't the French she was familiar with.

Anyway, I got the tuna, and I am sure they overcharged me. So much for my public-school education.

While there, we needed a part for the engine, and Pointe-A-Pitre, a city in the middle of Guadeloupe, is well known for its yacht services, so we rented a car. It wasn't until I was behind the wheel that I realized it was a manual transmission. I hadn't driven a stick shift in at least fourteen years, but it soon came back to me, and we headed out for an adventure in the countryside.

What a beautiful island. The road wound through palm trees, banana plantations, up and down steep mountains, and around sharp curves that skirted cliffs leading to the ocean below. There was something better to see around every corner. It was a feast for the eyes. The parts' store was closed for lunch, so we headed to lunch ourselves. While in the restaurant in Pointe-A-Pitre, we were surprised to run into Sylvie and Patrick, who we last saw in Montserrat. We chatted with them until they had to leave for the airport to pick up a friend flying in from France. Once they left, we pondered the odds of running into them again. The cruising world is very small.

After nearly a week in Guadeloupe, it was time to move on. We set sail for the small set of islands known as Iles des Saintes, or Les Saintes for short. These irresistible islands are a part of Guadeloupe and have a strong link to the north of France. We anchored off Terre-de-Haut and found it clean, slow paced, and full of color. You can spend your mornings in one of the bakeries, picking up fresh baguettes for the day or munching on pastries as you watch the town unfold. In the afternoon, it's ti' punch (rum and sugar water) and *accras* (an appetizer of breaded fish. Excellent!).

We were walking through town, and to our surprise, ran into Sylvie and Patrick again. There was a much younger woman with them, and Sylvie introduced her as the friend they had picked up at the airport. They were planning to sail to Martinique after lunch. Later, when we were back on *Alegria*, I saw *Passage,* Sylvie and Patrick's boat, leaving the harbor. They had to pass by us, so Dan and I stood on the bow to wave goodbye.

"Tristan. Tessa," I called down into the open hatch in Tessa's bedroom. "Sylvie and Patrick are leaving. Come wave goodbye."

I knew the kids were playing a game, so it would take them some time to get up and out to the bow. Thank goodness, because as *Passages* came by our boat, the young woman on board was topless and waving enthusiastically at us. Surprised, we slowly waved back. Suddenly Tessa popped her head up out of her hatch. "Hey," she said. "She doesn't have a—."

"Never mind, Tessa," I interrupted. "Go back to your game."

I could hear her shocked voice relaying the story to her brother. "Tristan! That girl didn't have a top on!" I didn't wait to hear the rest of their conversation before moving on.

We spent over two weeks exploring the next island, Dominica, also known as "the nature island," and home to endless hiking, beautiful waterfalls, and friendly people. Dominica is a volcanic island, so we anticipated a wide assortment of fruits and vegetables. We weren't disappointed. As soon as we arrived, we booked a tour of the island with Martin. He would serve as what was known as our *boat boy*. During our time in Portsmouth, he would be our guide, our taxi driver, our water-taxi driver, and basically, our go-to guy if we needed anything.

For our first tour, Martin took us to the North Coast. He was very informative, always stopping along the way to educate us on all the fruits, vegetables, and herbs growing wild in the countryside. It was mindboggling to see the almonds, cashews, mangoes, avocados, bananas, pineapples, lemongrass, and coconuts, just to name a few, growing everywhere. Martin told us that as a boy out playing, he never went home for lunch; he just ate off the land. As he said, you could be poor in Dominica, but you would never be hungry.

We covered as much territory as possible in Dominica. We hiked to waterfalls hidden deep in thick, green forests, including the double waterfall at Trafalgar Falls. We jumped from high ledges into cold, sparkling, freshwater pools. We ate lunch overlooking a palm-tree-lined beach. We visited a few of the many volcanoes. Just when we got used to the lushness of the island, the landscape changed dramatically as we headed to Red Rocks. There, the tropical forest was overrun by volcanic runoff, leaving behind a red-colored landscape. The colors were spectacular.

We made friends with two new families also heading down the island chain: on *Wanderlust,* a family from Chicago with three older children; and on *Toucan,* a family from Colorado, also with three children, though closer to Tristan and Tessa's age. Our kids became fast friends.

One evening Tessa spent the night aboard *Toucan.* It was her first sleepover, ever. It's one thing to have your child sleep over at the house of someone you have known for a long time, but another to have her sleep overnight on a movable house, in a foreign country, with people you've just met. I told her to call me on the VHF before she went to bed.

It grew late and Tessa still hadn't called. I called *Toucan* a few times, but didn't get a reply. Our friends on *Fine Line* (who we had caught up with) heard me on the radio. Anne broke in and said someone was missing her baby. I was. It was strange not having Tessa there. I really missed her. I could see *Toucan* off in the distance. Their boat only had an anchor light on, so I assumed they must have gone to bed.

Dan said sympathetically, "I guess she forgot."

I shrugged and went downstairs to bed.

Later that night, I heard the softest whisper on the VHF, "*Alegria. Alegria.*"

I jumped out of bed, raced up the stairs and grabbed the microphone. "This is *Alegria.*"

"Hi Mom. It's Tessa. I forgot to tell you goodnight. I love you."

My heart melted. "I love you too, Little One."

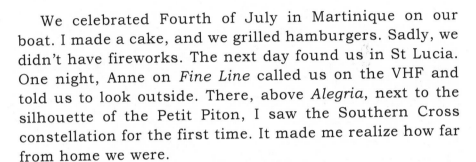

We celebrated Fourth of July in Martinique on our boat. I made a cake, and we grilled hamburgers. Sadly, we didn't have fireworks. The next day found us in St Lucia. One night, Anne on *Fine Line* called us on the VHF and told us to look outside. There, above *Alegria*, next to the silhouette of the Petit Piton, I saw the Southern Cross constellation for the first time. It made me realize how far from home we were.

Then we spent several days enjoying St. Vincent and the Grenadines, particularly the Tobago Cays. The water there was so clear and filled with marine life, it was like being back in our beloved Bahamas again, especially when the sharks came inside the reefs. Our mooring was near the sea grass, and we snorkeled with the sea turtles.

We relaxed on the island of Bequia for a week, then left the Grenadines and attended the local regatta in Carriacou. That island was full of surprises, from the excellent, cheap rotis we ate for lunch, to the archeological dig outside of town. A group of archeological students from North Carolina State University were working on a site that was a pre-Columbian settlement. The kids from *Toucan* and our kids visited the site, and the archeological group even let them get involved in the digging. It was fascinating to see the shards of pottery and get a glimpse of an important ancient culture. We stayed a few more days, through the regatta, before moving on to Grenada.

13

Island Time
GRENADA

T HERE WAS A LARGE CRUISING community already in place by the time we arrived in Grenada in early August. The Grenada carnival, called *Spice Mas,* was only a few days away. We anchored just off downtown St. Georges, in the heart of the carnival action. For the next week, from early morning to late at night, it was non-stop music blaring from huge speakers driven through the streets on the flatbeds of large trucks. Every day there was something to do. We attended as many events as we could, including the Panorama steel-pan competition at the National Stadium, but it was the parades we enjoyed the most.

On Monday morning at 5 a.m., we stood on the streets of St. Georges, watching the *J'ouvert* parade. During *J'ouvert,* participants called *Jab Jabs* cover their bodies in paint and parade through the streets, dancing to *calypso* and *soca* music blasted from huge DJ trucks. A *Jab Jab* is a devil that emerges from the darkness of night. In the past, the *Jab Jabs* painted their bodies black with tar, grease, and mud, and their purpose was to terrify onlookers as they danced through town. Some *Jab Jabs* today still keep that tradition, but the majority use colorful paints and aren't looking to scare anyone. Most prefer to gently dab paint on unsuspecting onlookers as they dance through town.

We were warned to wear old clothes, and we did, but the *Jab Jabs* were kind and always asked our permission before anointing us and the kids with paint. Consistently, the revelers thanked us for attending and for bringing the kids, but how could we have stayed on our boat? *J'ouvert* was an irresistible blend of music, dancing, and color that we wouldn't have missed for the world.

The parades were great to watch but even more fun to participate in. A cruiser told me that anyone could join in *Monday Night Mas*. All you needed to do was find which group you wanted to join and buy a ticket. The groups were sponsored by major businesses on the island, such as Carib, Heineken, and Digicel. I only bought two tickets at $50 EC (Eastern Caribbean dollar, or about US$18) because I wasn't sure if the kids could participate or not. Each ticket included a black Digicel t-shirt, a jester's-type cap that lit up and blinked on and off (how could anyone say no to that?), and a large red, plastic, reusable water bottle.

Monday night Dan, I, and the kids nervously gathered with the rest of the participants on the road outside of Port Louis Marina. We had no idea what to expect. I was under the impression other cruisers might join in, but we didn't see any. No one brought their kids either. We almost chickened out. But as soon the music started, we were caught up in the energy. All four of us excitedly joined our group.

I will try to describe it as best I can. Our Digicel group had at least a hundred participants, all wearing matching t-shirts and following behind our group's music truck. Multiply this by the same or more people per group, and by many groups, and you have a huge parade. Our truck would inch forward, and we would dance behind it, or rather we would move in a way the islanders call *chipping*. This was new to us, so we looked to our fellow *chippers* for help. It was easy—just stand with your legs apart and

153

shuffle your feet forward in time to the music.

The music was fast, but there were so many people, we covered very little ground. At different times during the night, the entire parade would stop, the music would change, and we would *jump up*, a dance which is exactly what it sounds like. We held our flashing hats high over our heads and jumped straight up and down in one place in time to the music. When the *jump up* was over, we would go back to *chipping* down the street.

Our t-shirts were thick and hot, and the night was incredibly humid. When we got thirsty, we danced up to the DJ truck and handed our red water bottles to someone on the truck who would fill it with our choice of coke, rum and coke, or just rum, as much and as many times as we wanted.

It's hard for me to put into words the exact feeling of dancing in the streets that night. The islanders danced in a celebration of life and freedom, and I felt it was my own dance of freedom—freedom from a life of someone I was no longer. I think we all felt that way. Tristan and Tessa were laughing and enjoying the music, and Dan had a huge smile on his face. I looked up at the moon high overhead, willing myself to remember that night and that feeling forever.

The parade began around 8 p.m. and at close to midnight, we had covered no more than a mile of the several-mile route. Along the way we saw our friends from *Makai* and *Fine Line* waving at us from the sidelines. At first I couldn't believe they saw us, but then I figured we were pretty easy to spot. We were hot and tired and couldn't *chip* one more step, so we reluctantly bid the *Monday night Mas* goodbye. Later, back on *Alegria,* we were too wired to sleep, so we sat on the trampolines in front and listened as the music slowly faded into the night.

After carnival, we moved *Alegria* to the anchorage at

Clarkes Court Bay, on the southern end of Grenada, and settled into the cruisers routine as we waited out hurricane season. The cruising group in Grenada is very social. Every morning the VHF-net is filled with ways to occupy your time: Mexican Train dominoes, hikes with the Hash House Harriers, burger nights, ladies' lunches, island tours, organized trips to the mall and grocery stores, and more. One of the more popular things to do is something called a hash...

August 24, 2008 Grenada
(from the blog of Alegria)

You know, most people would sit out a storm on their boats, but not us. We chose to join the hash and expose our kids to 45-knot winds, stinging rain, lightning on a mountaintop, and the dark of night during a nearly three-and-a-half hour *hike*.

First some background. All the way down the island chain, we had read with great interest this thing called a "hash," an activity sponsored by the running group The Hash House Harriers, which has chapters worldwide. A hash is basically a run or walk down a trail set up by the hasher, or hare, who volunteers to set it. The trail is marked with paper, with a few false trails along the way to keep you, the hounds, on your toes. The course can be set up through town or through countryside. Renee and Michael on *Jacumba* were regular participants, and we were eager to join.

Our first hash was a moonlight hash. Since it would be late, Dan graciously agreed to sit this one out with the kids. I joined both locals and cruisers on an easy moonlight walk along the streets, backyards, and across two creeks in the hour or so walk. It was a great time.

The next one however...

We took the kids this time. The hash started at St.

George's Medical University, and within the first ten minutes of the hash, it started raining. No problem. It rained almost every day in Grenada but just for a short time. This time it didn't stop, and the wind started blowing. We were walking with Anne and Steve from *Fine Line*. Renee and Michael were ahead of us, and we had lost sight of Fred and Kathy (*Makai*). We were nearly at the back of the group when Steve's cell phone rang. It was Jim on *Dawn Dancer*. We were all anchored together in the harbor. He was calling with an update. According to Jim, the wind was blowing 45 knots and there was a white-out. *Salida* was dragging, but all the other boats were fine for now.

We kept moving, and then Anne, Steve, and Dan stopped to call Jim and ask if he thought they should come back. Jim told them there was nothing they could do. First, they were at least twenty minutes by taxi from Clarkes Court Bay, where we were all anchored. Second, even if they made it back to the anchorage quickly, they wouldn't be able to make it back to the boats. Jim said the wind was so strong it was shearing the tops off the waves. There was no way a dinghy was going to make it through. He said he would keep an eye on the boats, and if any of them started dragging, he would take care of it. The group might as well keep going.

While this conversation went on, I and the kids had been walking with Renee, not realizing that Dan had stopped with Anne and Steve. When we reached the end of the field, the trail was not well marked and took a sharp turn off-road and up a ridge. I looked back for Dan, but he was nowhere to be seen. I waited a few moments, but I still didn't see him. I had a choice to make. Did I wait for him or keep up with the pack?

I learned a good rule of hashing the first moon-lit hike; stay with someone who knows where they are going. I perceived that to be Renee, who I was rapidly losing sight of. I grabbed Tessa and Tristan and raced after Renee. We didn't see Dan the rest of the hash.

We passed Fred and Kathy as we headed to the top of the first hill. They, too, had gotten a call from Jim on *Dawn Dancer*. Basically, he gave them the same news: stay put, you can't make it back anyway. On top of the hill, the conditions grew much worse. The wind was strong, driving the rain into us, and now we had thunder and lightning. I was worried. We had just started the hash, and we had a long way to go. How long was this storm going to last?

We pulled and pushed each other up the side of the slippery hill. The heavy rain made it almost impossible to keep our footing. Everyone was helping everyone else by lending a hand or giving each other a much needed boost. It was satisfying to reach the top of the ridge, until we realized that now we were even more exposed to the lightning. Now everyone wanted down the other side as fast as possible. But going down wasn't easy because the hill had turned into a mud bath. One cruiser was pulling needles out of himself after having slipped into a cactus.

Tessa was a little scared, and Tristan and I did our best to keep her calm. A young girl was crying as her parents tried to get her down the steep slope. Even the dogs were whining. The wind was blowing in strong gusts. The rain came down harder, and the darkened sky lit up with streaks of jagged lightning. We needed to get down and fast.

The safest way down was on our butts, trying to avoid the trees. With the rain and lightning cheering us on, that's exactly what we did. I followed Kathy down, showing the kids the best place to slide. Down slid Tessa and then Tristan. Actually, that part was a lot of fun, like a giant Slip 'N Slide. At the bottom of the hill, we were layered in mud. We wiped ourselves off the best we could and continued on...and on...and on.

The trail took many twists and turns, and I urged Tristan and Tessa to keep up and not lose sight of the group. I had lost sight of Fred and Kathy long ago; I was determined not to let Renee disappear from view. A few times I even had to make the kids run to keep up. I had given up any hope of finding Dan. He had the bag with the money and water, so if we got lost, I couldn't even pay for a bus to get us home. We were so thirsty our throats were burning. The hash was turning into a bad reality show.

We had walked a long time, and it was starting to get dark. Scratch that—it was very dark. Thankfully Tristan, who somehow was now leading the group, found the route down our last hill, and one of the girls in the group knew where we were. She took us on a shortcut. Well, since it still involved another mile or so hike, it wasn't really a shortcut, but we took it none-the-less.

The kids were wet, muddy, cold, and tired. I gave Tessa a piggyback ride the last half mile. They kept asking where their Dad was, and I kept telling them I thought he may have gone back to check on *Alegria*. The hash ended at the university, and we finally made it there over three hours later, well over the one-hour timeframe normally allotted for a hash. Inside the warm cafeteria, Tristan spotted Dan. We were so glad to see him. He had completed the hash with Anne and Steve, though he was suspiciously not muddy. Later we figured they missed the trail that we took over the muddy ridge and came down the road instead, finishing twenty minutes before us.

There were still several people out there. Fred and Kathy made it back later. We sat at the student union for awhile, eating pizza, swapping stories, trying to warm up, and waiting for the last of the storm to blow over. All in all, it was a long hike. We were all exhausted, but I was so proud of the kids for hanging in there the way they did.

By the way, this tropical storm that made our hash a nightmare, turned into Hurricane Gustav shortly after leaving Grenada. [*End blog*]

October 13, 2008 How We Roll in Grenada
(from the blog of Alegria)

Earlier I described what it was like to shop for food in the Bahamas. While Grenada had a much broader selection, it still had its challenges. It was a several-step process.

First, we took our dinghy to the rickety dinghy dock. The dock was located at the far end of the bay, close to the rum factory, which every so often would dump copious amounts of the foulest-smelling waste into the water, killing your sense of smell, and turning the water an unholy shade of brown. I had warned the kids that if they fell in, they were on their own.

Then, after Dan secured the dinghy, we made our way down the dock, which would be partially submerged during high tide. The dock also had the added excitement of swinging wildly, like a suspension bridge, when you walked on it, threatening to upend us all into the murky, rum-soaked water. After crossing the dock, we climbed a short, uphill trail, sandwiched between a fence and the side of a car, and walked through a chain-link gate. We'd then walk about a block to the main road where we waited in the sun for the public bus Number 2 (actually a large van) to barrel over the hill, the sound of its horn signaling its arrival before we ever saw it. If we were lucky, we got the bus with the good music and the entire busload would sing along. If we were really lucky, it wouldn't be full.

Once the bus took us into town, we had two choices: go all the way downtown to the bus station and get fresh fruits and vegetables from the nearby fresh market; or get off halfway to the bus station, walk a short distance, and catch the Number 1 bus going to Spice Island Mall and the IGA grocery store.

At the IGA we bought the basics such as paper products, canned goods, and meat. When we finished shopping, we caught the van that took us back to the bus station.

The huge, outdoor, fresh market was only a few blocks away. I had befriended one of the vendors who sold fresh vanilla, nutmeg, and other spices. We would talk about our daughters as she took me around to all the other vendors and made sure I got a good deal. I'd load up on lettuce, swiss chard, nutmeg, bananas, oranges, limes, and whatever other vegetables and spices we needed. The variety was endless. My favorite stop was the lady who sold green coconuts. She would slice off the top, hand me a straw, and I would drink fresh coconut juice from the coconut. Nothing beat it on a hot day, and really, every day was hot in Grenada.

We couldn't buy too much. There was simply no room to bring more than a backpack and a bag into the crowded van. If we needed a lot of provisions, we had to wait for the private bus sponsored by the grocery store to come to the different harbors, pick up cruisers, and take them to the store. But for small amounts, the van was fine.

If we were hungry, we might stop and have a street food called *doubles*. This was a small sandwich made with two pieces of Indian flat bread and chickpeas. It's very common in Trinidad and Tobago where the lady who sold them from her van was originally from. *Doubles* were cheap and delicious. We devoured them as we made our way back to the bus station to get in the line for the Number 2 van.

At the bus station, we were herded back into the vans. But the vans wouldn't leave half full. They didn't leave full either. Packed to the gills was the norm. A typical van had five rows, including the row in the very front with the driver. Normal seating would be as follows: one person plus the driver in the very front row, then four rows, each holding three passengers. Thirteen people, plus the driver, fit very comfortably. But comfortable was not what they were going for. The driver waited until the van had eighteen or nineteen minimum squeezed into the van, using the jump seats, plus the driver and the money man. The money man had the interesting job. We'd give him our money and he'd assess our size and then squeeze us in, rearranging everyone for maximum occupancy.

The van waited at the station until the driver deemed it full enough to leave. If you got on early, you waited and dripped sweat on whoever was unfortunate enough to sit next to you. (I should say the cruisers dripped sweat on the islanders. The islanders never seemed to sweat.) If you boarded late, you became the filler, the one used to squeeze in between people. You never wanted to be the filler. There was no air-conditioning in most of the vans, so you prayed you got a seat by the window. The driver would pick up more people along the way too, driving slowly as the money man yelled at everyone on the street, asking if they needed a ride.

When the bus passed close to our destination, we simply knocked on the ceiling. If the driver didn't hear us, the other passengers generally would, and they would repeat the signal. Getting out of the packed van was akin to being birthed. We squeezed our wet, slippery bodies between legs, thighs, and other personal body parts, always keeping our heads down and elbows in to avoid getting hung up on someone. We strained for the light of the open van door before finally being spit out onto the dusty road, our lungs, partially collapsed to save space, shrieking to be filled as the van sped away with more deliveries. It was what we had to do to live in paradise. [*End blog*]

The end of hurricane season was finally upon us, and Dan and I were having a tough time deciding what to do. Basically we had two options: sail north or sail west. Our friends and most of the cruisers had plans to sail north to either St. Martin or the Virgin Islands for the winter and then return to Grenada for hurricane season the following year. This was what many of them did every year.

Sailing west to Venezuela intrigued us. We attended a

cruiser's meeting led by seasoned travelers to Venezuela, and they professed their love of the beautiful anchorages, the friendliness of the people, and most importantly, the cheap prices. However, for every person who talked highly of Venezuela, there were equally as many, if not more, that preached how dangerous it was. Those who were selling the fear, had quite a vocal following. Though many had never personally been there (because of the pirates), they would hold cruisers meetings on the dangers of venturing west of Grenada, and how one should protect oneself from pirates by using firearms and other self-defense mechanisms, including Molotov cocktails. It made for interesting cruiser discussions.

We didn't take pirate attacks lightly and certainly would prepare for such a rare possibility, but we were more concerned about where to go once we left Venezuela. We could come back to Grenada and then up the chain again, but heading east against a strong current and with an easterly wind was a tough passage. The alternative was to head to Colombia, sailing the fifth-roughest sailing passage in the world. I didn't think I wasn't that kind of sailor yet; none of us were. Plus, most of the Venezuelan-bound boats had already left, and we didn't really want to go alone.

Everyone seemed to know exactly what they were doing, except us. During our two years sailing, though we didn't always agree on the exact weather conditions to leave an island, Dan and I were always in sync on when to leave and where to go. We had learned to *feel* our way through situations. When did it feel right to leave? Where did it feel right to go, versus what everyone else was doing? Leaving Grenada was hard because nothing felt right.

So we waited, for what we didn't know. As the last of the boats left for Venezuela, we resigned ourselves to heading north. Reluctantly, we told everyone we would be sailing to St. Martin and even had tentative plans to leave on Friday, October 25th. But, as I said before when we experienced the same indecisiveness in the Bahamas, this trip seemed to have a life of its own.

At the Wednesday burger night at Clarkes Court Bay Marina, we talked to Rennie and Denny of *Salt&Light,* another boating family. They had just returned from a trip to the US and heard we were undecided on where we were going next. "We're going to Venezuela," Rennie, the mom, said. "Then we're going to the ABC islands. Why don't you guys come too?"

Hmm. Venezuela, then Bonaire, Curacao, and Aruba? Why not? Aruba had a major international airport, and we could leave *Alegria* in a marina there and fly back to the US for Christmas. Suddenly it felt like a great decision. That following Sunday evening, we left Grenada for Los Testigos, a Venezuelan out island about 85 miles southwest.

14

Giving Thanks

OUT ISLANDS OF VENZUELA

IT WAS NEARLY MIDNIGHT WHEN we weighed anchor and slipped quietly out of Prickly Bay. With *Salt&Light* in the lead, we put Grenada behind us and motorsailed into the moonless night. The seas were calm and the winds light. Early the next morning, the crew of *Salt&Light* started fishing. Dan got out our new fishing pole too and put on our new Tuna Tamer lure. Within a short time, we caught our first fish ever: a tuna! It was absolutely beautiful, and we were so proud of ourselves. After a quick shot of rum to the gills to calm it down (then one for me as I watched Dan clean it), Dan quickly bled the fish and cut it up, and we looked forward to tuna for dinner.

We arrived in Los Testigos just after noon. Once we anchored in the turquoise bay, surrounded by green hills and white sand, Dan and Denny visited the *Guarda Costa*, the Venezuelan Coast Guard, to let them know we had arrived. We couldn't officially check in to Venezuela there, they weren't set up for that, but we needed their permission to stay.

The next day we all ate lunch at the small, blue restaurant on top of the hill. We asked the owner for directions to the sand dunes. Los Testigos is well known for its mammoth sand dunes that run east to west across the island. They were easy to find, but we wanted to know the best place to land our dinghies. Instead of trying to tell us in his limited English, the owner sent his six-year-old son, Miguel, with us to show us the way.

The hike up the sand dune was murder. The sand was thick and the hill was steep. The pain was worth it though, because the view on the other side was incredible. Steep, powerful waves crashed onto the expansive white beach. We were on the windward side of the island, but the beach was surprisingly free of the many plastic bottles we had found littering the windward beaches in the Bahamas. The surf was strong, so the kids couldn't swim, but they had a great time running into the waves and being tossed back to shore. They did this over and over until we knew they had to be exhausted. Miguel wanted to take us to another *playa* (beach), but it was getting late. We headed back to the restaurant and had a few cold beers, giving the kids more time to play. Soon we were all tired, and with many thanks to our host, we headed back to our boats. We left early the next morning for Isla Margarita.

Our fishing prowess continued. We caught a bonita and a mahi mahi during the next passage. Either we were becoming really good, or the fishing there was really easy. When we arrived at Isla Margarita, the harbor was packed with boats, and it took some time to find a good place to anchor. The sand dunes of Los Testigos had been replaced with the high-rise apartments and hotels of the city of Porlamar, a major, international tourist destination. It was too late to check in when we arrived, so we visited a beachside bar for cold beers, platters of oysters and shrimp, and a spicy *ceviche* that was surprisingly delicious. It was good to be in Venezuela.

Customs and immigration in Venezuela was different than what we'd experienced before. Instead of visiting these offices ourselves, we had to use an agent, such as Juan. For a fee, Juan took all our documentation, including our passports and cash, to pay the proper officials. This was supposed to make it easier, but it made me a little nervous to be without our passports.

We were low on food, so we needed to find a *supermercado* (supermarket), but first we needed to get bolivars. Converting dollars to bolivars, or "Bs" as they are also called, was a great economic lesson for our kids. Inflation in Venezuelan was high. Cruisers told us stories of having work done in Porlamar and paying for it with a briefcase full of bolivars. It was difficult to carry all those bills around, so in January 2008, the government declared, "We don't need those extra zeroes," lopped off the last three and 5,000 bolivars became 5 bolivar fuerte. It didn't make their currency more stable, only easier to carry.

Because of their unstable currency, many Venezuelans, especially business owners, wanted American dollars, so there was a thriving black-market business. When we arrived, the black market rate was 4.5 Bs to 1 US dollar. A few weeks earlier, the rate had been 7 to 1, then US dollars flooded the market and the rate dropped again. It was a great opportunity for us to show our kids the economic principle of supply and demand in action.

Juan could only exchange a small amount of money, so he sent us into town to an upscale clothing store where we discreetly asked the owner for an exchange. He wasn't able to give us as much as we wanted, but it was enough to get started. Fortified with our bolivars, we were ready to shop.

Porlamar is a duty-free zone for Venezuelan citizens, so there are several new malls, movie theaters, and of course, American fast food. We shopped first at an outdoor market that sold mostly clothes at great prices. We were looking for Halloween costume ideas. Tristan and Liam *(Salt&Light)* bought CIA and FBI hats, so their costumes were done. Tessa couldn't decide if she wanted to be a rock star or a genie, and she went back and forth so much my head hurt. Finally the shopping was finished, and we surprised the kids with lunch at McDonald's. I know we said no more after we ate there in the Dominican Republic, but it was nice to have a little bit of home so far away.

The next day we, our friends from *Salt&Light,* and several other cruisers boarded the free bus to the *supermercado.* Rumor had it that, unlike the smaller grocery stores we had been used to in the islands, we could get almost anything in the Venezuelan markets. The stories were true. The supermarket in Porlamar was the largest supermarket I had ever been in, anywhere. The fresh produce section was huge. There were aisles and aisles of canned goods. There were four extremely long aisles devoted solely to dried pasta. How many choices of pasta did one need? We were used to much smaller stores, with little to no variety. It was overwhelming. Should I choose spaghetti or rigatoni? Spiral pasta or linguini? Angel hair, fusilli, or fettucine? If I chose fusilli (because, quite frankly, it's fun to say), did I want whole wheat, gluten-free, or regular? All those choices had me frozen, and we rarely ever ate pasta!

Scientific studies have shown that more choices do not make you happier; they make you feel inadequate and unable to make a decision. That's what was happening to us. Over the last two years, we had existed quite happily with limited choices, and now that we had virtually unlimited choices, we couldn't make a decision. So what did we do? We grabbed a few items, like something from the toilet-paper section because that selection was much smaller, and left the store. Seriously. The next time we went grocery shopping, we were better prepared, but it was still stressful. We had no idea how we were going to cope when we went back to the US.

One new delicious item we discovered in the Venezuelan supermarket was *pan de tocino.* I was in the *panaderia* (bakery) when I smelled something amazing. Other customers smelled it too and waited eagerly for the source of that heavenly aroma to come out of the oven. It was some type of bread, and as soon as the baker took it from the oven and placed it in a bag on the shelf, the customers snatched it up. There was one left, and I grabbed it. The label said *pan de tocino*. I knew *pan* meant bread, but I had no idea what *tocino* meant. Tristan thought *tocino* meant bacon, but he wasn't sure. Back on *Alegria*, we cut into the bread and were thrilled to learn that Tristan was correct; *tocino* did mean bacon. There must have been a pound of bacon baked inside that loaf of bread. Jackpot!

It was Halloween, and the international cruising community in Margarita made sure the kids had a good time. The trick-or-treaters included: Tristan and Tessa; Michaela, Liam, and Ethan from *Salt&Light;* the two boys, Ben and Sam, from *Independence;* and a girl from *Our Luck*. They went from boat to boat by dinghy in the rough harbor waters. The strong winds and waves threatened to spoil their evening, but the kids had fun and ended up with a surprising amount of treats. Later the adults gathered for drinks on *Independence,* while the kids watched movies and ate candy on *Alegria*.

A few days later, the weather calmed down and we sailed out of Porlamar to explore the exceptionally beautiful out islands of Venezuela. Our first stop was Cubagua, once famous for its pearl beds until the pearls, and the Indians forced to collect them, were wiped out by the Spaniards. The next day we moved on to Isla la Tortuga, or simply Tortuga. The island was stunning. The water was unbelievably clear, the sand a blinding shade of white, and the fish camp on the island was painted the prettiest shade of turquoise, nearly the same color as the water. The best part? We had the place to ourselves, so we stayed a few days.

Cayo Herradura, on the island of Tortuga, was peaceful

on the Friday night we arrived. We celebrated my birthday with a potluck dinner and birthday cake provided by our friends from *Salt&Light*. This was what we came to the islands for: a nearly mile long, white sandy beach, and only four boats in the harbor. It was paradise.

While Friday was quiet, Saturday morning we were reminded just how close to the mainland we really were. This anchorage is very popular on the weekends. Nearly thirty powerboats arrived by mid-Saturday, including some small boats, a few expensive sport fishing boats, several luxury yachts, and one megayacht. A helicopter landed on the narrow strip of island and delivered guests to the luxury yacht *Drakkar*. That was the way to arrive in style.

The anchorage was soon hopping with jet skis, dinghies, people waterskiing, and kids playing on the beach. The *Salt&Light* kids got out their wakeboard, and Tristan and Tessa had their first experience wakeboarding. They loved it. That night the anchorage was filled with colorful lights from the fishing boats, and Latin music filled the air long after midnight. It was a clear night. The moon reflected off the white sand, causing it to glow, and the moon's rays off the water created a streak of white on a blue canvas. The water was so clear that even in the moonlight you could see the bottom. Dan and I sat on the bow for a long time that evening, taking it all in, and thanking ourselves for going west instead of north.

November 13, 2008 Los Roques, Venezuela
(from the blog of Alegria)

Our next passage was 85 miles overnight to Gran Roque, the biggest island in the archipelago of Los Roques. We left at 6 p.m., planning to arrive mid-morning, but at the start we were ahead of schedule, sailing over 7 knots. It was a great sail. Around 9 p.m. a large pod of dolphins surrounded our boat. At first, even with the moonlight, it was hard to make out what was causing the splashes. Then a dolphin leaped up high, next to the captain's seat where I was keeping watch. Another one did the same until nearly all of them were leaping high out of the water, wanting to see us as much as we wanted to see them.

Around midnight the rain started and didn't let up the rest of the trip. At times it was a whiteout, and I was again thankful for the radar. Since I couldn't visually see, I relied on the radar and the autopilot and sheltered myself in the cockpit.

We arrived mid-morning to clearing skies and warm weather, and Tristan and I dropped anchored outside of Gran Roque. While Tristan and Tessa stayed on the boat to do their schoolwork, Dan and I dinghied into town. We instantly fell in love with the place. The pace here is slow. The former vacation homes for wealthy Venezuelans are now quaint, colorful hotels lining streets made of sand. An airport for the small commuter planes that come from the mainland is located at the end of town. It does a good business because the island isn't easy to get to by any other means than airplane or boat.

As we started our search for a grocery store, a local named John asked if he could help. He took us to the *panaderia* and made suggestions on what to buy. Then he carried our groceries as he took us to the market for fresh fruit and vegetables. We bought a case of soda and a case of beer at another store, and somehow he managed to carry those too.

Our final stop was an internet café where we had our first internet access since leaving Margarita. It was nice to catch up on our email. When Dan checked the weather, the forecast showed squalls moving in, which meant we would have to move *Alegria* to a more sheltered location in the morning. That night we had sundowners on *Salt&Light* and were inundated with huge biting mosquitoes. The insects were so vicious, they even bit through our clothes. We sat on the bow hoping the wind would keep them in the cockpit, but they were determined to find us. Just when we thought this was paradise. [*End blog*]

November 18, 2008 Gran Roque, Venezuela
(*from the blog of* Alegria)

Okay, the constant rain was one thing, but last night was too much. When the rain and the wind finally stopped, it left us facing a new direction, closer to the mangroves. About 2:30 a.m. I was awakened by shouting and banging. The hatches were open, and we were invaded by hundreds (I do not exaggerate here!) of mosquitoes. It was worse than Rum Cay in the Bahamas. There were the sounds of whack, whack, whack, followed by an "Oh gross" when a mosquito full of blood was smashed. Tessa's room, with her side window located right next to the mangroves, was the worst.

The only sure way to kill the invaders was with the electronic zapper, which actually burned them up. This was preferable to having the walls, ceilings, and bed sheets covered with blood and dead carcasses. It took us more than an hour to kill the intruders, and we knew that we hadn't killed them all. Clean up this morning is bad. [*End blog*]

Thanksgiving found us in a small restaurant on the island of Crasqui in Los Roques. It wasn't a traditional Thanksgiving, but it was definitely our most memorable. We had made friends with Roberto, a very handsome Italian man whose father used to be the Italian ambassador to Venezuela. There was a small hotel on the island of Crasqui. Roberto told us the owners, Patricia and Felipe, would be happy to make us a Thanksgiving dinner. We said sure. We didn't get a dinner though; we got a feast.

Therese and Helge, a very young Norwegian couple on *Coquelicot*, Roberto, and the families on *Salt&Light*,

Independence, and *Uliad* joined us for an unforgettable dinner in an open-air restaurant on the beach. Thirteen adults, eight children, and four countries gathered as one on a tiny island, giving thanks for being together so far from our homes.

We didn't have turkey and mashed potatoes, but we did have nearly unlimited oysters, lobsters, two types of tuna prepared sushi style, grouper, tiny fried fish, and conch salad. We stuffed ourselves on an endless amount of delicious food. No one left the table hungry.

Later that evening Felipe turned on the music, using his surprisingly diverse iPod. He even let me play DJ. The mosquitoes arrived as usual at sundown, but we were having so much fun, no one wanted to leave. Patricia sprayed us and smoked the restaurant with some chemical I am sure shortened my lifespan. I nearly choked to death from whatever she sprayed, but it did make it relatively tolerable until about 7:30 p.m. when we couldn't stand it anymore. We dinghied to *Uliad* for dessert. Before we left the beach, I exchanged warm hugs with Patricia and Felipe, thanking them for their hospitality and the delicious meal. We finished out the night much too late on *Uliad,* talking and enjoying the night stars.

Everyone was tired the next day, but we pushed onward to Las Aves, the last Venezuelan out island before Bonaire. The island is uninhabited and is a bird lover's paradise. The stargazing was spectacular. Late one night Tessa and I were lying on her bed talking and looking at the night sky through her open hatch. Suddenly the sky was lit by a blue-red streak as a shooting star flashed by and seemed to drop on the island or in the ocean not too far from us. We both screamed excitedly like little girls.

The next morning we left early and had a very easy sail to the island of Bonaire. We celebrated Tristan's birthday the next day with a pizza and bowling party. We rented a car and toured the island and then did several loads of laundry before sailing off to Curacao, where we and our cruising friends would eventually go our separate ways.

Our friends continued on to Colombia, and we wished we were going with them, but we realized due to the continued poor health of some of our family back in the US, we needed to be home for Christmas. So while they sailed west, we found a boatyard in Curacao, put *Alegria* on the hard, and flew back to the US.

15

Craziness in Curacao
CURACAO, NETHERLANDS ANTILLES

February 12, 2009 Back in Curacao
(from the blog of Alegria)

We're back! After a seven-week hiatus to the States, we are finally back on our boat. We had a great time, but boy did we miss the warm weather and *Alegria*. Our trip back was surprisingly easy. We flew Air Jamaica, which allowed us to have two free checked bags per person; that's eight checked bags. We maxed out the weight too, with 50 pounds per bag for a total of 400 pounds. That's just the checked bags. Dan carried on a backpack, Tessa a rolling piece of luggage, Tristan had a big backpack inside a large shopping back holding other stuff, and I carried a small duffel bag and backpack. Our flight left on time from Chicago and early from our connection in Jamaica.

Dan was worried as we stood in line for customs in Curacao. The customs officers were going through people's bags with a fine-toothed comb. Dan was afraid they would charge us duty on all the things we brought, but not to worry. The customs official looked at us and all our bags and asked if we were on vacation. We answered yes, as if we always went on vacation with over five hundred pounds of luggage. He x-rayed our bags and waved us right through.

What did we bring back? The schoolbooks weighed the most, followed by small boat parts, and finally, new clothes. Our growing kids outgrew shoes and clothes like crazy. Thank goodness for the clearance racks! [*End blog*]

You know the saying, "It was the best of times; it was the worst of times"? Curacao was like that for us, except without the "best" part. Both times we were there, in 2009 and 2010, it was purely the worst of times. There really wasn't another place where I found the people so interesting (loony). In 2009 it was the people we met in the boatyard that drove us nuts.

Life in the boatyard was never easy, and this time we stayed on *Alegria* while we repainted the bottom, waxed the boat, and did minor repairs ourselves. The kids worked hard too, but since the paint was toxic, I kept their involvement to a minimum. Tristan helped scrape the barnacles off the hulls, and Tessa did some scraping too, but her main job was to entertain us by reading a book out loud. This was not an easy task as our work was hot, tiring, and frustrating.

The boatyard facilities were sketchy. The bathrooms and showers were unisex and were housed in the same small building, located right off the office. The three bathrooms, each with doors to allow some privacy, were too few for this big a boatyard and marina, and inevitably one or two of the three would be out of order. The showers were in the same building, and again, unisex. We at least had a very small, private dressing area attached to the shower, but it was very hard to dress in such a small spot. The side walls in the shower gave us privacy from shower to shower, but it wasn't that private.

There was always something besides personal hygiene going on in that building. One day I interrupted what I was pretty sure was a drug deal. Tristan and Tessa would often come back from their nightly showers and inform me that couples were showering together. The kids seemed to take everything in stride, but I was obviously too uptight for this boatyard.

February 23, 2009 Boatyard Blues, Curacao
(from the blog of Alegria)

Things got a bit ugly the other day regarding the bathrooms. One of the three toilets wasn't working, leaving only two. Not quite enough for everyone, but doable. A few days later, only one was working. This went on for a week, at least. Then Tristan used the last working toilet, and it wouldn't flush. Now there was no toilet, and of course, I needed one. The supermarket shuttle bus was about to arrive, and the supermarket didn't have a bathroom.

I was fed up. I stormed into the office and, in less than polite terms, told the woman behind the desk that the last remaining toilet was broken, we now had no toilets, they'd had plenty of time to fix them, and to call a plumber NOW! (Phew!)

When we returned from the supermarket, I sent the kids to check on the situation and guess what? Two toilets were fixed. Amazing! Later the boatyard manager knocked on our boat. He told Dan the toilets were fixed, but basically the clogs were Tristan's fault because he used too much toilet paper.

Alright. I tried to be calm. My dear son, as many of our friends can attest, does have a knack of unintentionally and occasionally clogging up a toilet or two. But how would the boatyard manager know how much toilet paper Tristan used? Well, according to the manager, in his own words, "Your son uses a lot of toilet paper. I know. I was in the stall next to him."

Okay. Despite the fact that something about that seemed morally wrong, or at the very least really creepy and possibly even illegal, the first two toilets had flushing mechanisms that had been broken for over a week. Tristan certainly didn't have anything to do with those, so why weren't they fixed? Anyway, all three bathrooms were now magically fixed, so we decided to let it go and concentrate on getting the boat painted. Between Dan and me, when it came to our boat and crew, we had our bottoms covered. [*End blog*]

March 9 2009 Bizarre Boatyard Banter, Part 1 Curacao
(*from the blog of* Alegria)

We now have a neighbor, Peter from Switzerland, on a Fountaine Pajot catamaran. He introduced himself while I was waxing *Alegria*. He and his wife are sailing the opposite way we are, having sailed from Colombia. Peter just flew back to Curacao from an emergency trip to Switzerland because of "all the things falling apart." I really wasn't sure what he was talking about until he said, "Don't you know about how bad the stock market is?"

Well...yeah! But that was kind of old, ongoing news, and right now my mind was preoccupied with the complexities of waxing and whether I could find a cheap, good quality pair of flip flops (we seem to be burning through our shoes). I looked at the news this morning; it was more of the same. The economy was bad, but that wasn't new. Flip flops were another story. We walked so much that they were constantly breaking or wearing out.

Peter told me more about his situation. The firm that had been managing his savings had lost a good chunk of it. He was afraid he was going to have to leave retirement and go back to work. I felt bad for him. Suddenly my flip-flop dilemma seemed very lame.

The next evening we were again scraping, waxing, and talking to Peter when we saw the Red Bull truck, the Amstel Bright beer truck, a boat getting ready to be put back into the water, and scantily clad women. That could only mean one thing. Party! The boat *Pegasus* was manned by two young men from the Netherlands. They planned to sail around the world in two years and report back on the condition of the ocean. Or, as us jaded cruisers would say, get paid to drink and party as they sailed around the world. Brilliant! This was their launch party.

The sponsors threw a great event: free beer, free whisky punch, good food, and my personal favorite, free champagne *in a glass*! Such decadence. Peter, Dan, I, and the kids joined the other boaters at the celebration. We sent Tessa to find our Brazilian friends, Sylvio and Lillian on *Matajusi*.

While waiting for the *Matajusi* couple, Dan introduced me to Bob and Mary, former North Carolinians who now lived on their sailboat, *Islands*. Dan had met them before and told me how intense they were, and I soon agreed. One of the first things Bob asked me was if we still kept money in the bank. When I said yes, he told me that was a big mistake; the banks were going under, there would be rioting in the streets, and people would be homeless. I told him I didn't believe that. He said I was uninformed, and even though we just came from the US and I hadn't seen any soccer moms beating their SUVs into swords, he was right because he spent eight hours a day reading stories on the internet. Back and forth we went in a spirited, friendly way, but the bottom line was Bob was convinced this was the end of the world as we knew it.

He informed me that I didn't have all the facts. He was probably right as I had been busy living my life rather than reading all those articles on the internet. Bob and his wife had sold their house in North Carolina and bought a place in Colorado. He said they bought it "as far in the hills as possible so the homeless won't be able to find us." What a humanitarian you are, sir!

I was through my glass of champagne and was desperate to end the conversation. I told him that even if what he said was true, there was nothing I could do about it. I wasn't going to live my life in fear, and he shouldn't either. He had no reply. I went to find more champagne.

Tristan, who had been standing next to me the entire time listening, said "Way to go, Mom."

On the way to find more champagne, I ran into Peter, who again lamented that he might have to go back to work. I told him that maybe the reason he would have to "leave" retirement was that he still had something to offer. Maybe there was some gift he still needed to share with the world. His face brightened, and he said he'd been thinking about writing a book. His friends told him his sailing story should be published (and after hearing all the drama and trauma he and his crew had gone through just sailing from Colombia to Curacao, including nearly sinking his boat, I absolutely agreed).

"See. Life isn't done with you," I said. He gave me a smile. It was gratifying to see him go from being down to upbeat. [*End blog*]

March 15, 2009 Bizarre Boatyard Banter Part 2, Curacao

(from the blog of Alegria)

You know, nothing makes the days fly here like teamwork and stimulating conversation. A few days ago Dan was standing on the ground, preparing to put the primer on the hulls. I was on top of the boat, buffing the topsides. The temperature was over 90 degrees, the humidity about 80 percent. We were all tired and cranky from lack of sleep due to the killer mosquitoes.

Suddenly I heard a yell, followed by, of course, cursing, which I, of course, chose to ignore. This led to more yelling and cursing. Apparently, Dan poured primer from the can into a smaller container. The container disintegrated and leaked yellow paint all over him and his new watch. He was desperately calling to me, even though I was desperately trying not to hear him. Finally I could fake it no more and had to see what he needed.

I leaned over the side of the boat. "What?"

"I need your help. Hurry! I have paint all over my watch. I need you to rinse it off before it dries!"

He was indeed covered in thick, yellow paint, but he was standing right next to the water hose. I would have to go to the back of the boat, climb down the ladder, and pick up the water hose that was *at his feet*. This made no sense to me.

"Why don't you just rinse it off with the hose? It's right next to you."

"I can't. I have paint all over my hands. Hurry! This dries in like five minutes!"

Really? That's odd. He'd been putting off painting for a few days because he was afraid it would rain (it didn't), and he said the paint would need to dry overnight. Now suddenly it would dry in five minutes? Curious.

I gazed calmly at his yellow-smeared appendages. "I thought you said the paint needed to dry overnight?"

"What?" He shook his head in disbelief. "Are you going to help me? My watch is getting ruined!"

He was a yellow time bomb waiting to explode. I decided I'd better help. I met him at the back of the boat, and he handed the watch to me. It was in dire shape. The face of the watch was fine, but paint had seeped into every nook and cranny on the band. I scrubbed it with a wet rag. The paint came off fairly easily, but it would take some time to get it all off, and I had wax drying on the topsides that needed to be buffed. More than five minutes had passed anyway, so what was another five (or ten)? I grabbed a plastic cup as Dan came up behind me.

"How's it going? Is it coming off?"

"Yeah, pretty well. I'm going to leave it soak in water while I finish buffing."

"What? You can't do that! The paint will dry and it'll ruin my watch!"

"Well, it's been more than five minutes and the paint hasn't dried like you said it would. Besides, the water will keep it from drying."

"No it won't," He's talking *loudly* now. "It'll dry in water!"

I looked at him, incredulous. "How can it dry in water?"

"It's made to!" He's approaching hysteria now. "I can't believe you're not helping me!"

"Well, I'm trying, but you're not making sense. First you say you can't paint because it has to dry overnight, but mysteriously it will dry in five minutes on your watch. You tell me you can't paint if it rains, and then you tell me the paint will dry in water. So which is it?" (Folks, this is the kind of witty repartee you can only get after being married over twenty years!)

Dan was about to lose his mind. "Are you going to help me or not?"

"I am trying to, but you're making it very confusing!"

I'll spare you from the rest of the dialogue, which deteriorated rapidly from there and ended with me resuming my buffing and Dan taking care of his own watch. When will the fun end? [*End blog*]

March 24, 2009 Bizarre Boatyard Behavior, Curacao
(*from the blog of* Alegria)

We are just going to blame the last few days on the spring equinox. There really is no other explanation.

It started Thursday night. Tristan and three friends were trying to use the internet. We were now in the water, on the dock, far from the office where the internet was strongest, so the boys sat outside the office playing a game online. A tall, rather rotund, Norwegian man was also using the internet, trying to Skype his wife back in Norway. I had seen this guy before in the boatyard. He was a taller, brown-haired version of the "Heat Miser" from the cartoon, *The Year Without a Santa Claus*. He always looked as if he was one second away from exploding in anger.

His call wouldn't go through and seeing the boys, in his words, "wasting the internet playing games" set him off. The boys said he called them "little ba#$@$%s" and "rich kids" and said they were using all the internet, so he couldn't get his call through. He wanted to know which boat they were on. They wouldn't say, which set him off even more. The boys wisely came back to *Alegria*.

This was where good parenting came in. I listened to their story and sympathized with them. Then I explained that when people get really mad like this, generally it wasn't because of the person on the receiving end. Something probably upset the ogre before they got there, and they just happened to be next in line. So while it was wrong for him to talk to them like that, they needed to have some understanding. Then I looked at Dan and said "Dan, you need to go kick some a**!" (I call it the yin yang of compassion.)

No, I didn't really say that to Dan, but I did say he needed to talk to the guy. So Dan and the boys went back to the office, and the boys got schooled in problem solving among grown men. After loud talking, finger pointing, name calling (the Norwegian called Dan "small," not sure why, but maybe in Norway that's a big insult), and nearly coming to blows, Dan was able to explain how the internet really worked. It was a lousy connection, and actually Skype takes up a good deal of bandwidth, so really the problem had just as much to do with him. In the end, Dan got the guy to apologize to the boys. Apparently he'd had a big fight over the phone with his wife back in Norway and that had started the whole thing.

The next morning we were sitting in the cockpit enjoying a relaxing breakfast when we saw the Norwegian stalking the docks, asking everyone, "Are you using the internet?"

He was trying to find out who was using all the bandwidth because I guess he needed to finish the argument with his wife. Craziness!

That night I came back from the shower and a Venezuelan had his truck parked a few feet from our boat. The truck engine was running, and its headlights were left on and shining into our cockpit, lighting us up like a Christmas tree. I looked around, and the owner of the truck and another guy were standing on a boat, talking. I asked him to turn off the lights. He looked at me like I was crazy. Maybe he doesn't understand English, I thought to myself.

I couldn't think of the term for lights in Spanish. I thought it might be luminaries, but then I thought that might mean a small votive candle, so I did the American thing of talking louder and using weird hand motions from the 1970s when you used to pull a knob in and out to turn on the car lights. I could be saying, "Turn off the lights" or "Let's play pinball." It was that close. Finally someone yelled back, "Yeah, just a minute."

He could have walked the few feet and shut the lights off, but no, he opted to talk for another ten minutes before moving the truck. I was about to reach inside the truck and shut them off myself, but with my luck I would have accidentally put the truck into drive and sent it barreling onto our boat. I didn't need that kind of international incident.

And finally, yesterday we had an absolutely frustrating day. Nothing was going smoothly. We tried to check out, but we missed immigration. Normally that wasn't a big deal, but Curacao has the worst customs and immigration location. The bus service didn't run to the boatyard, and even though immigration was across the inlet from the boatyard, we couldn't take the dinghy because there wasn't a dinghy dock or a safe place to leave it. So from the boatyard, we had to walk up a very steep road that dead ended into a parking lot at the top of the hill. Then we had to run across four lanes of traffic that were separated in the middle by a median. Because the cars were coming fast, and coming from around a curve, we could only make it to the median where we had to press ourselves flat to keep from getting hit.

After we made it across the road alive, we had to descend down a long staircase that deposited us in an iffy neighborhood. Now we had the pleasure of walking almost 2 miles to the footbridge which connected both sides of the city of Willemstad. The bridge opened for boat traffic, including barges and small cruise ships. If the bridge was closed, we could immediately walk across and then walk another half mile or so to immigration. If it was open, we had to wait. All this took place in the unending heat and humidity, which sucked the life out of us.

We were cutting it close on time yesterday, sidetracked by boat issues, but still thought we would make it to immigration on time. But when we got downtown, we had to wait for the bridge to reopen. Then customs was slow, so immigration closed for lunch before we got there. That meant we had to wait several hours downtown until they reopened. To kill time, we shopped for shoes for Tessa.

Tessa had been spending the last few days really pushing our buttons. From shoe problems to schoolwork, it seemed every day there was a new issue. For school on Thursday, I told her to sit on the back of the boat and observe the jellyfish. Later we would do some research. I was helping Tristan with his schoolwork when Dan asked, "What is Tessa supposed to be doing?"

"She's watching the jellyfish. Why?"

"She's got two jellyfish in a plastic container in the cockpit." While observing them, she decided to catch them in a small plastic box. Now she could observe them up close. Dan told me to make sure we never have her observe sharks.

Back in the marina that afternoon, after we finished with the check-out procedure, we stopped by *Tyee 111*, a Canadian boat, and introduced ourselves to John and Lucie. Tessa and Tristan were friends with their two boys.

We were having a beer and good conversation when Tessa burst into the cockpit of their boat.

"I lost my shoe in the water," she yelled. She was very upset.

"What shoe?" I asked.

"My shoe with the hump!"

Shoe with the hump? What was she talking about? Finally I realized she was talking about her new flip flops with the small heel—not a hump; the pair we had just purchased a few hours ago. Most people would say flip flop—no big deal, but it *was* a big deal. We had just spent hours shopping for flip flops for her that would last. Her last pair broke when we still had a long way to walk back to the boat. We had to carry her back. These were $20 flip flops and her only shoes besides her Heelys. Dan and I jumped up.

"Your new flip flop? We have to get it." We sprang into action.

Tessa tried to stop us. "It's gone! My shoe with the hump is under the dock!"

"It's not a hump, it's a heel!" I corrected her.

Dan and I scrambled out of the cockpit, calling back to a stunned Lucie and John, "Sorry!" and "We've gotta go," and lastly, "Flip flop! Flip flop!" like a crazed version of *Rain Man*. As we left, I heard Lucie asking about the shoe with the hump, and I yelled back, "It's not a hump, it's a heel!"

They were clearly bewildered by our sudden departure. I heard John calling faintly behind us in his heavy, Canadian accent, "It's only a flip flop, eh?"

We scurried back to the boat. I could barely make out a shoe floating under the dock. "Get the net!" I yelled. A few minutes later Tessa's shoe was safely back on *Alegria*. Dan asked if we could go back to *Tyee 111* now and finish our beers.

"Are you kidding me? We just ran out of there like crazy people, yelling 'Flip flop! Flip flop!' They think we're freaks! We're the freak family whose daughter wears shoes with humps!" [*End blog*]

16

Want to Go Somewhere?

ARUBA, NETHERLANDS ANTILLES

THE GODS BE PRAISED, WE finally made it out of Curacao and into Aruba, just in time for Tessa's ninth birthday. We anchored outside of Oranjestad in turquoise waters, off the beach and near the airport. The passage was rough, with confused seas, and we were all tired when we arrived. After securing the boat, we dinghied to the Renaissance marina and explored the Renaissance Resort. There was a casino, a movie theater, several restaurants, including the kids' favorites Dunkin' Donuts and Taco Bell, and an upscale mall across the street. The cruise-ship dock was very close. We were impressed.

What we didn't see nearby was a large grocery store. I planned to make Tessa's birthday cake. I had the cake mix and frosting, but no decorations. The larger grocery stores were outside of town. It was too far to walk, and I didn't feel well, so I needed a backup plan. Tessa, knowing I felt sick, graciously said she didn't need a cake. That was sweet of her, but no one in my family has a birthday without a cake. Tessa joked she could just have a donut from Dunkin' Donuts. That gave me an idea.

I bought a dozen Dunkin' Donuts. Back at the boat, I assembled them into something resembling a multilevel cake, complete with whipped-cream decorations. I put nine candles on top and it was perfect. She loved it. (*That birthday cake became a legend on* Alegria. *After that, even when we returned to land, only a Dunkin' Donut birthday cake would do.*)

While I assembled the cake, Dan and Tristan decorated Tessa's room and the boat with happy birthday streamers and balloons. A light rain fell, so we spent the rest of the afternoon opening gifts, playing games, and watching movies. Later, John from the French boat *Josie*, stopped by to see if we had the latest weather forecast. John was sailing with his family, and they had been in Aruba for a few months. They were heading to Colombia next.

He noticed the party decorations, and I told him it was Tessa's birthday. He left and returned with his wife, five-month-old son, two-year-old son, and five-year-old daughter, Noel. They brought presents for Tessa: a DVD and some hair bows. Tessa was thrilled. It never ceases to amaze me the friendliness and the generosity in the cruising community. Noel stayed on our boat and played with Tessa the rest of the afternoon. She spoke mainly French and Tessa only English, but they communicated just fine.

April 1, 2009 Oranjestad, Aruba
(*from the blog of* Alegria)

My husband is a very smart man. Our plan was to stay in Aruba merely to wait for a weather window to head to Colombia, but we've grown to love the island. The water is clear, and the anchorage near the airport has great holding. Tristan loves the anchorage. All the incoming planes fly low over our boat. He has his *Jane's Aircraft Recognition Guide* and can now name almost all the jets from their sound. We rented a four-wheel-drive Jeep and did some off-road exploring. Later that day, sitting on Eagle Beach, Dan said, "You know, this is a major vacation destination. Why are we leaving here so fast?"

Good question. First I had to overcome my ego which said, "You need to get going" and "Cruisers don't spend time in Aruba." I next had to overcome my fear of missing a weather window and possibly being *stuck* here for some time. Was that so bad? Everybody loves Aruba. Their motto is "One happy island," and it's absolutely true. We personally knew many families who spent thousands of dollars on a week's vacation in Aruba. We met several cruisers who had been here awhile, including those on *Denali Rose* who had been here a month, the French boat *Josie,* and *PR2* who had been here three months. The boat anchored behind us had also been here three months. They weren't here just waiting to go somewhere else, they loved Aruba, and so did we. Sitting in a lounge chair on the white sand at Eagle Beach, I agreed with Dan. Let's stay a little longer. [*End blog*]

We still had plans to head west, so we kept an eye on the weather and talked to other cruisers to see who might be sailing that way. Walking down the dock one day, we passed a middle-aged man with shoulder-length, white-blonde hair, working on his anchor. I stopped, said hello, and asked him if he was headed to Colombia. He said no; he and his wife had just returned from a trip to Chile and Argentina. They had been gone a month and had left their boat at the marina in Aruba. That stopped me short. You could do that from here? Dan and I had talked about doing a land tour from Colombia, but we had never thought about leaving from Aruba. We needed to hear more.

The man introduced himself as Mike from England. A few minutes later his Australian wife, Ineke, joined the conversation. She told us they both loved South America, and it was easy to travel there from Aruba. The year before, they had left their boat in Curacao and toured Peru and Chile. They had gotten the idea when they were in the boatyard (yes, that same crazy boatyard in Curacao). Ineke had asked Mike, "You want to go somewhere?" and off they'd gone.

I was dumbfounded. To leave the boat in Aruba and tour South America hadn't even occurred to me. Visiting Peru, actually seeing Machu Picchu, was a dream of mine. The wheels in my head started spinning.

Later, over drinks on their boat, Mike and Ineke told us about their adventure. They had no plans when they left on their trip. They traveled on buses and went when and where they wanted to. Sometimes they used suggestions in their guidebook, and sometimes they listened to advice from other travelers. The key was that by not having any pre-set plans, they left themselves open to all kinds of opportunities. Their enthusiasm was contagious, and they made it sound so easy. Could we really do that? When she described their adventure, my heart was already there. The pull was so strong, I couldn't imagine not going.

Later, when Dan and I were seriously discussing the trip, he asked me, "Why do you want to do this?"

I replied without hesitation, "Because I want to be like Ineke. Did you see her face light up when she talked about their trip? How out of the blue one day, she asked Mike, "Why don't we go somewhere?" I want to live my life like that, really living, not being afraid to say yes. I want to be her." I wanted it more than I had wanted anything in a long time.

Literally a few days later, we had decided on Peru and Chile. We had considered Bolivia, but the expense of their entry visa made Chile more attractive. We took Ineke's advice to fly into one country and fly out another, that way we wouldn't have to backtrack. The local travel agent in Aruba was very helpful in getting us cheap flights on Avianca Airlines. Tristan and Tessa even flew at reduced rates. Ineke gave me their travel guide for Chile, and Dan bought the *Lonely Planet Peru* travel guide in a bookstore in Aruba. There wasn't much time. We would need to pack for the trip and prepare the boat to be left for a month.

Preparing for this trip was totally different than anything we had done before. The old us would have had to have a plan, known exactly where and how we were going every step of the way, and I would have bought all new stuff to take with us. Instead we made flight reservations to fly into Lima, Peru, and arbitrarily picked flying back from Santiago, Chile a month later. The only other plan we made was to have a hotel waiting that first night because we'd be arriving in Lima at 1:30 a.m.

Once we made it official, we had less than a week to prepare. We moved *Alegria* into a slip at the Renaissance Marina. Sanders and Xiomara, the managers, agreed to watch over her. They would come onto the boat, air it out, and check the systems all free of charge. We appreciated that and knew *Alegria* would be in good hands.

For luggage, we would only take one backpack apiece and two very small rolling suitcases. While I prepared the boat to be left for a month, Dan and Tristan went shopping for comfort items.

We tried to buy as little as possible and instead use what we had on the boat. Everyone understood that it was important how and what they packed because they had to carry it. Each person's backpack, the same size as ones the kids used for school, was filled with: a blanket/sleeping bag tied to the bottom of the pack, earplugs (Mike's suggestion because the movies on the bus could get really loud), a blow-up neck roll (which really came in handy sleeping on the bus), wet wipes/antibacterial wipes, waterless soap, toilet paper, a towel, deodorant, toothpaste, toothbrush, books to read, a journal, electronics (such as iPods, Tristan's Sony PSP, or Tessa's Nintendo DS), cameras (I carried the underwater camera and video camera, and Dan carried his

Canon SLR), snacks (the peanut butter/jelly combo came in handy), aspirin, Band-Aids, a Spanish phrase book and a Spanish dictionary, a few garbage bags, and a bottle of water. Dan carried the disposable toilet-seat covers (a nice idea, but outside of the hotels, most toilets in Peru didn't have seats.)

Tristan put himself in charge of the travel guides. I put a complete change of clothes for each person inside a clear, resealable plastic bag. This bag went inside everyone's backpacks. Tristan and Tessa would also carry their pajamas this way, because we would sleep on the bus a few nights. We wore tennis shoes and carried flip flops in our backpacks. Nothing went into the kids' backpacks unless it was in a resealable plastic bag. That way if their backpack opened and tipped upside down, we wouldn't have stuff scattered all over. The two rolling suitcases held the rest of our clothes: six underwear each, one or two pairs of pants (Tristan and Dan had the zip-off pants that turn into shorts, which worked really well), one pair of shorts each, three pairs of socks per person, three short-sleeved shirts and two long-sleeved shirts each, and a small bottle of detergent so I could hand wash clothes in the hotel sink. This, with the help of a laundry service, would serve us for a month. Tristan and Tessa also had lightweight sweatshirts, and we planned on layering if it got really cold. After a brief set back of the head being plugged (Tristan!) and Dan having to run a new toilet hose (a task involving all of us pulling on a hose full of you-know-what at one point), we were ready to go.

PART 2

17

Making It Up as We Go

PERU

WE HAD A SHORT LAYOVER in Bogota, Colombia and landed in Lima, Peru about 1:30 a.m. After the initial excitement of actually being in Peru (I couldn't stop saying "I'm in Peru! I'm in Peru!"), a country I had wanted to visit for a long time, the first thing we noticed was the quietness. Sure it was early in the morning, but even at the baggage claim, everyone and everything was quiet. After getting our bags and quickly and easily clearing customs and immigration, we located the driver that the hotel was nice enough to have waiting for us and headed into the foggy night.

Hotel San Antonio Abad was actually in Mira Flores, an upscale district a short drive outside of Lima. It was an older hotel, built more in the style of a huge house, with a wide mahogany staircase winding up to our room on the third floor. Our accommodations were the first of what would become typical of our trip: a triple, which meant one double and two single beds, and breakfast.

Breakfast that morning was also typical of what we would later see: bread and jelly, maybe some fruit or fruit juice, and coffee. This hotel's morning spread also included eggs. After our late meal, Jose, our cabdriver from the previous night, offered to give us a tour of the

.or US$10. That was a no brainer.

Lima is a crowded city of over eight million people, located on the Pacific Coast. It's heavily congested and air pollution is a big problem. Driving in Lima reminded me of driving in Santiago, Dominican Republic. It was pandemonium, with cars driving erratically, including in oncoming lanes, and it seemed traffic lights were merely there for suggestions because no one paid them any mind. People stood in the middle of the road trying to sell things. We knew we were going to like it here.

But in the midst of all this chaos, traffic, and people, the one thing we noticed again was the quiet. No excessive horn honking, no music blasting, no one even talking loud; just quiet. It was weird. And it was hot; unexpectedly so for April. We were 12 degrees below the equator, so this was their fall, but it was warm.

Jose took us to the Plaza de Armas, the birthplace and the core of the city. Every Latin country has a plaza and that's where you want to be. It's generally a huge open square in the center of the city, with ornate fountains, ringed by park benches, and shaded by towering palm trees. It's an oasis of beauty and peace in a bustling city. At noon we sweated in the hot sun, watching the changing of the guard at the Palacio de Gobierno, the residence of the Peruvian President. Afterwards we walked and toured a few of the cathedrals, including the Monasterio de San Francisco where we wandered amid the damp, mostly creepy catacombs filled with skeletal remains.

Later Jose took us to a travel agency to see about a bus to our next stop. The agent spoke excellent English, was very helpful, and we were able to get tickets on a bus leaving the next morning to Nazca to see the Nazca Lines. We would arrive in the early afternoon, with plenty of time to fly over the lines. Instead of spending the night there, we would board an overnight bus that left at 10 p.m. and arrived in Arequipa early the next morning. Our guidebook warned of bus jackings, robberies, and kidnappings on the Nazca-to-Arequipa overnight leg (which, of course, Tristan had read about), so I was nervous. The ticket agent assured me those things were in the past, and this bus did not make any stops, so I felt better. Besides, Ineke and Mike had taken this route, and they had been fine. Cruz del Sur was a top-of-the-line bus service, so I was sure we'd be fine too.

On the way back to the hotel, we had Jose drop us off at the boardwalk in Mira Flores. We ate dinner on a cliff overlooking the Pacific Ocean, watching the surfers. Dan said the coast there was very typical of a California coast, with high cliffs overlooking the beach. We had a great view, but we had seen enough beaches for awhile. After a great meal topped off by our first Pisco Sour, the national drink of Peru, we headed back to the hotel for an early night.

The bus ride from Lima to Nazca seemed quick, though it was a little over seven hours. Dan and I sat in the very front seats so we had a bird's-eye view of the road ahead. That would have been pleasant, but our bus driver drove like a New York City cab driver, and after several heart-stopping moments, we closed the front curtain and only looked out the side window.

Tristan and Tessa sat one row back to our left. We were very impressed with the bus. Our seats were large, comfortable, and reclined almost fully, making it easy to sleep. We watched American movies, read books, slept a little, and enjoyed the views outside our windows. There was even an on-board game of bingo, in Spanish, and Tessa won. Don't ask me how she won a bingo game in Spanish, but she did. The prize was a bottle of Pisco, the famous alcohol of Peru. This was where our luggage started to expand.

Our bus traveled south on the Pan-American Highway.

Before the trip, all I really knew of the terrain in Peru was the towering, rocky peaks of the Andes, and of course, the lush greens of Machu Picchu. The view outside our window couldn't have been more different. The Pan-American Highway hugs the coast in Peru. Cities are few and far between in the countryside between Lima and Nazca. On our right side, we had unobstructed views of the Pacific Ocean; and on our left, unobstructed views of, really nothing, just brown-and-gray-colored desert.

As we drew closer to the small town of Ica, the tan-colored sand dunes grew to mammoth proportions. The most famous of these is Duna Grande, a sand dune nearly 2 kilometers high. It is one of the largest sand dunes in the world and is well known for the sport of sandboarding—a sport similar to snowboarding, but you slide down sand dunes instead of a snow-covered mountain.

Dan and I had read about sandboarding and were seriously thinking about trying it, but since we had never snowboarded before and hadn't skied in years, we decided we'd better pass.

Thank goodness we didn't try it. Later in our trip, we became friends with a young Canadian couple. They had tried sandboarding in Ica and hated it. Coming down the dune was fun the first time. They didn't have too much trouble with sand-in-the-pants. The huge drawback was that once they came down the dune, they had to walk back up. Anyone who has ever taken a sled down a tall hill knows the pain of having to drag that sled, through the snow, back to the top of the hill. To that, add the heat, thick, ankle-grabbing sand, and a dune over a mile high, and you'll wish you never heard of sandboarding. It is definitely a sport for the very-fit crowd, which did not include us.

Once we arrived in Nazca, we found a tourist agency, ironically called Alegria Tours, and purchased tickets for the flight over the Nazca Lines. We had all our luggage with us, and the agents graciously offered to hold our bags; no charge. The guidebook repeatedly warned to never let your bags out of your sight, but we couldn't take our heavy backpacks with us on the plane, so it was leave them with Alegria Tours in a locked room or leave them somewhere in the airport. We left them with the tour company, trusting that when we got back, all our things, including the kids' electronics, would still be there, and we boarded the van that took us to the airport.

Before our flight, we watched a short video on the history of the lines. Scientists think the lines were created sometime between 400 A.D. and 650 A.D., though some scientists claim as early as 200 B.C. One of the many unique facts about the lines is how they were made. The lines were formed by removing the reddish-colored rocks and exposing the white and gray ground underneath. The rocks were removed in such a way to create drawings of a condor, a monkey, and a spider, among others. The drawings are huge—so large that the pictures can't easily be seen at ground level. It's only by flying over them that you can see how the lines interconnect to form the pictures. Because the best view is from the air, even though the lines were first discovered in the 1920s, they weren't internationally known until the late 1930s when commercial flights began flying over the unique shapes.

Scientists are baffled as to why they were made. One of the many theories is that they were created as a large astrological map. Because the climate in Nazca is so dry with little rain to erode the drawings, the lines have remained well preserved.

When the video ended, we piled into a small six-seater plane. Tristan sat in front, Dan and Tessa sat in the middle, and I took the seat in the back. I was worried I would get airsick, and I hoped the ride wasn't going to be too rough. Oh, it was.

First, it was hot, extremely hot in the plane. My face was dripping-sweat hot. Second, there was turbulence, and the plane was small. Just sitting on the runway, the plane bounced around, buffeted by the wind. I had read the turbulence was worse in the late afternoon, which of course was when we were in the plane. Third, it was loud in the plane, so the pilot spoke through a microphone, and we listened on our large earphones. The noise was awful, so most of the time we had to strain to hear what he was saying. Fourth, the pilot had a unique flying style. He would fly level until we flew, for example, over the drawing of the whale. He would then yell "Whale!" with a heavy accent, then bank the plane sharply so we could see it. But our earphones didn't pick up his words very well, so by the time we figured out what he was saying, the plane was banking, and we would suddenly find our faces plastered against the side windows. The ride kind of went like this:

Fly level. Turbulence. Plane drops suddenly. Drip sweat. "Monkey!" Bank 90 degrees. Peel my face off the window. Fly level. Turbulence. Plane drops. Scared out of my mind. Sweat. "Monkey upside down!" Bank 90 degrees. Vomit a little in my mouth. Sweat. And so on.

You get the idea. Thank goodness we took the guidebook's advice and hadn't eaten before we flew.

At one point Dan said to me, "Tristan is getting sick." I watched as Tristan's head rolled back and then planted itself against the window. A few minutes later, he fell asleep. Tessa was asleep too. Dan and I stayed awake to see the Tree of Life, Astronaut (also called the Owl), Condor, Hummingbird, Spider, and a few others. We enjoyed it, but mercifully, it ended after forty minutes.

Bottom line, I'm glad we did it. If we would have passed it up, I would have felt like I missed something. But truly, this was one instance when we could have gotten just as much out of it by looking at the brochure while riding on a Tilt-A-Whirl.

After the flight, we took the taxi back to Alegria Tours to get our bags. Since we weren't leaving until later that evening, they said they would hold them for us as long as we needed. We walked into town, ate a late lunch, and then walked farther downtown to the small Plaza de Armas where we sat on the bench and people watched for awhile. Everyone smiled at us. It was a friendly town. They seemed very curious about the kids. I guess they hadn't seen many American families.

Night fell and we headed to a coffee shop for an espresso and ice cream. On the way, the kids played in a bouncy house set up off the square. Later at the coffee shop, we spent an hour talking to a Taiwanese couple who were going to hike the Inca Trail. Tessa sat outside talking to the coffee shop owner, playing with his dog and his new kitten. I'm not sure what they talked about because he spoke little English and she spoke as much Spanish. Then again, Tessa never did let a little thing like a language barrier prevent her from carrying on a conversation. Later we retrieved our bags from Alegria Tours (everything was there) and boarded our bus to Arequipa.

Sleeping on the bus was actually enjoyable. We felt very safe. Our backpacks were stored securely in a closed-in container under our seats and were only accessible by us. Our seats were large and comfortable, and they lay back like a recliner. The ride was smooth. We were able to relax, watch the American movie being played on the monitors in front of us, and get a fairly good night's sleep.

Tristan and Tessa acted like they had ridden overnight buses all their life. Without me telling them, they changed into the sweatpants they were using for pajamas, safely stored their backpacks, snuggled into their sleeping bags, and were fast asleep before the movie was over. They made traveling as a family so easy.

Early the next morning, we pulled into the bustling bus station at Arequipa. The first order of business was to find a hotel. We had a few ideas from the guidebook, but we stopped at the tourist information desk and asked the young man for help. He suggested the Posada de San Juan, near the plaza. It was a little more expensive than the hotels we'd been considering, but it included free transportation to the hotel and free use of computers and internet.

The Posada de San Juan was located on a busy street, but once we entered the three-story, adobe-style building, the outside world seemed far away. The hotel manager let us have a very early check-in. Our room was on the top floor and ended up being a suite with a double bed and a TV in one room and three single beds and a TV in another larger room. A door led to our own private patio giving us a great view of the Basilica Cathedral and the snow-covered peaks of Chachani, an inactive volcano to the east, towering nearly 20,000 feet. Another set of stairs led to a rooftop patio and views of the El Misti volcano. At 19,000 feet El Misti is a bit shorter than Chachini, but it is far from inactive, with its last eruption in 1985. Our guide later pointed out that El Misti had no snow on its peak, indicating that the volcano was heating up again.

We were hungry, so our first order of business was eating. We quickly showered, changed clothes, and found a chicken restaurant around the corner. Our bill for all four chicken dinners and drinks was under $5. Our hotel bill was $40. We loved Peru.

Mike and Ineke warned us about the altitude in Peru. They told us to make sure we had plenty of time to adjust. In Arequipa we were already above 7,000 feet. It would be uphill from there. We found a pharmacy across from the Plaza de Armas. I didn't have the name of the altitude sickness drug Ineke used (she couldn't remember the name of it), only that it was a red and white pill. Thankfully the pharmacist knew just what to give me when I asked. I also bought Dramamine. I was worried about getting motion sickness from how fast the bus drivers drove on the winding mountain roads, and Dan was worried about getting altitude sickness during our trip to Colca Canyon the next day. The passage would take us over 16,000 feet.

The pharmacy was housed in a *colonnades*, a stately building adorned with filigree and arches, flanking the plaza. On top of this white-stone building proudly flew the red and white flag of Peru. The plaza was packed. Children played near the fountains, families enjoyed lunch together under the towering palm trees, and young people walked by holding hands. I was especially fascinated by one park bench overcrowded with five elderly gentlemen. One man was holding an ancient typewriter on his lap. I felt like I went back in time.

Arequipa was undoubtedly one of the most beautiful cities I had ever visited. The city was founded in 1540 by the Spanish and is known as *Ciudad Blanca* (White City) due to its many temples, houses, convents, and palaces built from white ashlar stone. The clear blue sky and the energy from the people, the city, and the mountains in the distance—everything felt so good. There were so many places to see that we could have easily spent a week touring the city.

The Museo Santury was our first stop. This museum held the remains of the frozen bodies of Inca children left as sacrifices on the summit of Nevado Ampato over five hundred years ago. On display was a young girl encased in a sealed, glass freezer. Her body was frozen—not a mummy, but frozen with most of her skin and nearly all of her hair and nails intact. Small pieces of ice still clung to her hair and clothes. It was surreal to think we were looking at a girl, about the same age as Tristan, but from over five hundred years earlier.

The Incas made several sacrifices of female children to

the gods. The most beautiful girl in the village was chosen. The trip took over two months to climb to the top of the tall peaks. They used no special equipment, wore only woven sandals on their feet, and chewed coca leaves for nourishment and to prevent altitude sickness. What must have gone through the minds of those young girls, knowing they were climbing to their deaths? How had their parents felt? Yes, it was deemed an honor, but to knowingly send your child to death? And the reason for the sacrifices? The Incas had a premonition that something bad was coming. Sadly, their premonition came true despite their sacrifices. The Spanish arrived and wiped out their civilization—an entire civilization. We all left the museum deeply affected.

Later that afternoon I wasn't feeling well, and we walked back to the hotel. I was in for the night. The kids watched TV, while Dan sat on the rooftop terrace and talked to a young Canadian couple and an Australian woman named Linda who lived at the hotel. The kids were hungry, but I couldn't keep anything *in*, so Linda took Dan and the kids on a tour of downtown Arequipa in search of food. They came back with pizza and cheese cake, an interesting combination. They ate and I watched. I was worried that I would be sick for the tour the next day to Colca Canyon. Sure enough, I was.

18

The Kindness of Strangers

PERU

COLCA CANYON IS ONE OF the world's deepest canyons, nearly twice as deep as the Grand Canyon. The trip involved an overnight stay in the town of Chivay, as well as cutting through a very high mountain passage. It promised to be an exciting trip.

My primary interest in Colca Canyon was to see the condors. This was one of the few natural habitats left for them in Peru. These birds are legendary, living up to fifty years and having a wingspan up to 10 feet. Because they are so heavy, they need to live near canyons, counting on the updrafts to keep them aloft.

The bus picked us up at our hotel at 8:30 a.m. The price of the tour included roundtrip bus fare, a hotel room in Chivay with breakfast, a hike to the hot springs, and a local folk dance. The bus would return to Arequipa at six the following evening. We checked out of the hotel and brought our bags along. After the tour, we were going directly to the bus station to catch a night bus to Cusco.

Irene was our English-speaking guide. Our first stop was a roadside market where we bought snacks. Irene suggested buying a package of coca leaves to help us with the altitude sickness. The leaves, when chewed, act as a stimulant comparable to coffee and help relieve hunger, fatigue, and pain. They are a sacred part of the indigenous lifestyle of many South American cultures. We bought a package, and Irene showed us how to take a leaf, activate it by scratching it with a gray limestone rock (included in the package), and then tuck a few of these activated leaves into our cheeks. The limestone in the rock activates the alkaloids in the leaf. After a few minutes, our cheeks became numb.

The highway took us past an ever changing landscape, from desert, to *altiplano* (high plateau), to frozen tundra. The air was so clear we could see for miles. And for miles, it was simply nothingness; just open land. We made a few stops along the way to see the alpacas and llamas grazing near the highway.

I will never forget our first stop. The bus pulled over so we could get out, stretch our legs, and see a mother and baby llama in the near distance. I got off the bus, but knew I couldn't stand long without risking the activation of some dire bodily functions, so I quickly got back on and enjoyed the view from my window.

As I looked behind the bus, I noticed a woman running up the road toward us. On her back she carried a large blue bag. It looked like she'd taken a large blanket, put stuff inside, tied up the ends, and then carried it on her back like a Santa sack. When she reached the bus, she hurriedly put down her parcel. It was then I noticed she was also carrying a small child on a sling across her chest. She untied her bag to reveal what looked like knitted sweaters, gloves, and hats. She laid them all out carefully, all the while smiling this beautiful, energetic smile, hoping to catch someone's eye. She looked fairly young, and she had such a hopeful spirit. Everywhere around us was desolate. I couldn't imagine where she had come from, especially carrying such a load.

None of my fellow passengers seemed to be paying any attention, and the bus wasn't in a place it could stop for long, so no one ventured over to see what she had. Irene, oblivious to the young woman, herded everyone back onto the bus. As we drove away, I could still see her kneeling on her blanket by the roadside, slowly packing up her goods and her young baby. I watched her for as long as I could until she disappeared into the bleak landscape.

At the second stop, a refreshment stand in the middle of nowhere, I tried the coca tea, on the advice of Irene, hoping it would help settle my stomach. It didn't. By the third stop, there was no way I could get off of the bus. Irene asked me how I was feeling. I told her I thought it must be food poisoning. I had eaten raw spinach at the restaurant in Arequipa, and I thought maybe that was the culprit. I heeded the warning not to drink the water, but I had forgotten not to eat any fresh vegetables that may have been washed in water. Luckily a fellow traveler came to my rescue.

Graham, a nurse from England, asked me what was wrong. I told him my symptoms, and he said he had Ciprofloxacin, better known as Cipro, a strong antibiotic. He thought it might help. He pointed to his friend Tony, sitting next to him, and said he had food poisoning, had taken the Cipro, and had immediately felt better. He assured me it was safe and even tried to read to me the health information that came with the package of pills, but I stopped him. I knew about Cipro. If anything was going to help, Cipro would. I eagerly held out my hand, and he generously gave me several tablets. I couldn't thank him enough. Sure enough, about an hour later, problem solved. Graham was my hero. But now the altitude sickness kicked in.

Our bus stopped at an overlook, high in the mountains. Tristan ran across the road to see what Irene jokingly said was the world's highest bathroom, which I was sure Tristan would find a way to clog up. On his GPS he recorded an altitude of over 16,000 feet. He struggled to catch his breath when he ran back to the bus. Let the nausea and headaches from the altitude sickness begin.

We stopped for lunch and were offered a large buffet. I really wanted to try some authentic Peruvian dishes. I avoided the guinea pig, or *cuy* as it's locally known. I hate to admit it but I tried the alpaca served with a side of quinoa and loved it. But that was all I could eat. I waited outside while the rest of the group finished their lunch. After lunch, Dan felt sick too. When we got to the hostel, Irene said she would be leading a group hiking to the hot springs in an hour, but Dan and I were in no shape for it. They certainly didn't want whatever was coming out of my body polluting a natural spring.

The hostel in Chivay was our first hostel experience. I had never wanted to stay in a hostel, ever. Call me a snob, call me an elitist, but there was no way I wanted to sleep in a huge dormitory with ten or twelve people I didn't know. And share a bathroom with them? Are you crazy? Why wouldn't I just go to sleep in a prison? But we didn't have a choice. The tour included a night in the Chivay Hostel, so there we were. And it was fine, but to tell you the truth, I felt so bad from the altitude sickness I *could* have slept in a prison for all I cared.

We had a private room with our own bathroom, so that was surprise. Our room was clean, but small, just enough room for four single beds. The altitude sickness was growing worse. Our heads hurt so bad, all Dan and I wanted to do was sleep. There wasn't a TV in our room, or in the main part of the hostel, so it was up to Tristan and Tessa, who seemed to be unaffected by the altitude, to entertain themselves. Before I collapsed into bed, I told them if they were hungry, they needed to scrounge around in the backpacks and eat any snacks they may have brought with them. I felt like I was abandoning them, but I felt so awful.

There was no heat in the hostel and it was cold, but

the bed had four heavy blankets, so it was warm under the covers. I fell asleep even though it was only after 6 p.m. When I woke up later, the room was dark. Tristan was under his blankets, reading the guidebook with a flashlight, and Tessa was under her blankets with her iPod. Dan and I weren't getting any better.

I remembered I had the altitude sickness pills in my bag. In my delirium, I thought I had only bought a few, and I wanted to save them for our trip to Machu Picchu (which I later learned was much lower than where we were). Finally, I couldn't stand it any longer. I found the pills, and Dan and I each took one. That was when I noticed I had actually purchased ten pills. Within the next two hours, we started feeling better, and by morning, after a much needed hot shower, we took another pill and felt even better. We didn't have much of an appetite, but the breakfast was small anyway: biscuits, jelly, and juice or coffee. At least our headaches were gone. Those pills were miraculous. Thank goodness, because that day was all about the scenery.

Chivay is a unique town. Technically, it sits in a valley, but the valley is at an altitude of almost 12,000 feet. To put that in perspective, Chivay valley is higher than the mountain tops in Vail, Colorado. Just outside of town, we passed rings of terraces surrounding the valley and rippling up the mountains. The agriculture was unique. Peru grows over three thousand varieties of potatoes. Also growing on the hillsides were corn, quinoa, and onions. The terraces follow a plan that was designed over five hundred years ago by the Incas. Corn grows at the lower elevation, and farther up the mountain are the hardier vegetables, like potatoes. Even at the lower elevation, it's still cold at night for the corn, so the Incas came up with a great idea. They surrounded the square fields with thick fences of rock. During the day, the sun heats up the rocks, and at night the wind blows the heat off the rocks and keeps the crops warm. They created their own microclimate.

The scenery there was truly breathtaking. At certain vantage points, we could see Colca Canyon and the darkness of its depths, and then look up and see the snow-capped peaks of the Andes. Most importantly, we could feel the mountains; really feel them. It was a great feeling, like someone watching over you, protecting you. The mountains feel very much alive and they are. They are still growing, several centimeters each year. It's easy to see how the Inca's thought of them as gods. The mountains have an energy you can't forget.

Our bus arrived at Condor Crossing early in the morning. We stood on the overlook on the rim above the canyon, and within a few minutes of our arrival, a huge, male condor soared gracefully right over our heads. He circled around slowly for a moment, then dove down to glide next to the canyon walls. A few minutes later, the updrafts lifted him level with the rim. Soon he was joined by a female and a juvenile condor. They were easy to spot from their large size alone, but they also had the telltale white feathers on their wings. Watching these enormous birds glide so easily on the updrafts from the canyon, we could hardly believe they could weigh nearly thirty pounds. Not to be outdone, a few hawks came by and demonstrated their ability to hold themselves motionless in the air while their sharp eyes raked the mountainside for food. We had quite the show.

Before we headed back to the bus, Tessa and I did a little shopping with the ladies who had set up their crafts along the roadside. I bought us sweaters, gloves, and scarves. The sweaters were supposed to be hand-knit alpaca. I'm not sure if they were alpaca or wool, but at $8 for a sweater and $2 for the gloves, they were a bargain. Plus, they were so soft and warm. They turned out to be lifesavers over the next few weeks.

The tour bus was due in around six that evening, and we planned to catch our overnight bus to Cusco at nine. On the way back to Arequipa, our bus picked up Judy, another tour guide with the same company as Irene. She had been leading a group to the top of the El Misti volcano. She sat in the back of the bus with us, and I asked her questions about other sites in Peru. I told her we were taking the bus to Cusco that night. She asked if I had checked to make sure the bus was still going. Apparently there was a protest in the town of Juliaca, and the roads were blocked. The farmers, protesting water rights, had blocked the road to Machu Picchu with rocks. Judy said this happened all the time, and tourists didn't find out about it until it was too late. If their bus ran into a protest area, it wouldn't go on, and they were left on the roadside with no refund and no transportation.

According to Judy, if you asked at the bus station before leaving, "Hey, any protests anywhere I should know about?" the ticket agents had to tell you and give you a choice to rebook or take your chances. It was an "If they don't ask, we don't have to tell" policy. But our bus line, Cruz del Sur, was one of the more expensive ones in Peru and well researched by Tristan just so we wouldn't have these kinds of issues (or robberies, or buses going off cliffs, you get the idea). Tristan's research consisted of hours of reading the guidebook, internet searches, gut instinct, and deciding which bus looked the newest and coolest. Hey, it worked.

That night at the Cuz del Sur ticket counter, the ticket agent told us the bus was cancelled. We would have to go the next night instead. The really bad news? Our seats on the cancelled bus were the fully reclining VIP seats. Those same seats for the next night, and the night after that, were booked. We were back in the *semi cama*. At first the ticket agent wasn't going to refund the difference in the ticket price. She was as surprised that we expected her to refund the difference as we were that she thought it unnecessary. After she made a call to her supervisor, we got our refund.

We took a taxi back to our hotel, and they still had our room available. After settling in, we dashed across the street for a quick bite to eat. Dan had the *lomo saltado*, which was steak stir fried with vegetables and served over rice, with french fries (pure genius!). The kids and I split two fried-rice dishes. The portions were huge and we couldn't finish them. The total price for our meal was $3. Unbelievable, and no one was sick later.

It was actually good to spend another day in Arequipa. It gave us time to see more of the city. Linda, the Australian woman who had helped Dan find the pizza and cheesecake the last time we were at the hotel, helped us find a *lavanderia* to have our clothes washed. There was a laundry service at the hotel, but the clothes were line dried, and we were leaving that night. We couldn't risk them not drying in time. There was a laundry service across the street from the hotel, but Linda said that wasn't a good one, and she then proceeded to take us on a ten-block tour, trying to find one that was open. I didn't think Dan was going to make it.

She walked so fast that Dan, carrying the heavy bag of laundry at such a high altitude, nearly had a heart attack. Linda was trying to be helpful, but really she was taking us so far from the hotel. We seemingly wandered in circles, all while Linda told us horror stories about Cusco and how people there would "squirt mustard on us and steal our wallets" or "slash our backpacks," and that we should "watch our children" and "don't even think about wearing an expensive watch there!" Trying to keep track of the dos and don'ts of Cusco while keeping an eye on Dan's deteriorating physical condition and trying to remember how to get back to the hotel...well, it was a little overwhelming. Every time I would try to interject into the conversation that "Isn't there a laundry across the street from the hotel?" my words fell on deaf ears. Dan, staggering behind us by about 10 feet, was getting very testy. He stopped being subtle. "This is crazy! There's a laundry right across from the hotel!"

I shot him a look that told him to stop being rude. Linda just went on in her Australian accent, "You want to use one that doesn't wash your clothes with someone else's. That's a trick you know! They'll mess up your laundry. You don't want your clothes coming out a different color, eh?"

I turned to Dan. "Eh? Want your clothes a different color?"

We kept going. Every corner it was the same. "One more block this way."

Behind us Dan was getting louder. "This is a stupid idea. Why are we doing this?"

I was stuck listening to more of Linda's life story about everything negative that had happened to her, hoping she wouldn't hear Dan.

Dan: "This is stupid!"

Me: "Really, Linda? Your husband and your best friend took all of your money?"

Dan, getting louder: "I'm going back!"

Me: "Seriously! She stole your house and your husband? Incredible!"

Dan: "I mean it!"

Me: "You don't say? Just squirt mustard on your shirt and take your money? Fascinating!"

Dan: "Carla!"

Me: "Unbelievable! Your hair just caught on fire, huh?"

Finally we found the laundry, which, after all the circling around, ended up being only three blocks from the hotel.

The bus from Arequipa to Cusco was okay if you don't count me waking up in sheer terror when it seemed the bus was careening wildly down the mountain. A unique feature on the bus was a lighted sign that flashed a warning if the driver drove over the recommended safe speed. Ours flashed the entire trip. I closed my eyes and went back to sleep, thinking I would rather not know if we were going to sail off the side of a cliff. At least the wild driving took our mind off how cold it was on the bus. Mike and Ineke had warned us about that. I was so glad we had our sleeping bags to keep warm.

We would figure out many things about riding buses in Peru, but one thing we never got right was where the bus would drop us off. We always boarded at the bus station, but, except for the time in Arequipa, we were usually dropped off in seemingly random areas of the city and nearly always on a deserted street or back alley. That's what happened in Cusco. About 6 a.m. the bus pulled into a deserted parking lot in a questionable area. Half asleep, we wandered around getting our bags, not having a clue where we were.

We thought it was going to be like Arequipa, with a nice tourist information booth where perhaps we could get a free taxi to the hotel and maybe a refreshing beverage. Not a chance. Besides, technically, we didn't have a hotel. Before we left Arequipa, Dan found a great hotel on Trip Advisor, called Hotel Torre Dorada. He sent an email to Peggy, the hotel owner, inquiring about reservations. She replied she thought she had space, but we didn't actually make a reservation. Undeterred, and since we had no idea where else to go, we grabbed the last cab and showed up, unannounced, on Peggy's doorstep.

Peggy was very gracious. She didn't have a room for all of us together, but she put us in two very nice rooms next to each other and gave us a family discount. She did admonish us for not letting her know we were coming, not because she didn't like us showing up without reservations, but because she didn't feel that bus stop was very safe.

She told us that if she'd known we were coming, she would have had a car waiting for us. That was Peggy. Her guests were very important to her.

Peggy could tell we were hungry, so even though technically we weren't entitled to it until the next morning, she told us to please help ourselves to the free breakfast. She didn't even have us officially check in. She was more concerned about getting us fed and settled. We loved her. We sat in the bright dining room, stuffing ourselves on fresh juice, fruit, and delicious fluffy omelets.

Hotel Torre Dorado is located a little outside the center of town. Peggy always provided free taxi service to anywhere in the city we wanted to go. The first day we took it easy, had a good lunch, and toured some of the museums and cathedrals. Afterwards, we went shopping for a sweater for Tristan. He'd been wearing his sweatshirt, but I was afraid the farther south we went, the colder he would get. Unfortunately, in all the stores we shopped, the sweaters were too big.

We went to the *supermercado* to call the Torre Dorada taxi to pick us up. As we waited on the steps outside for our ride, a constant stream of Peruvian ladies passed by, trying to entice us into buying their goods. The good news? One of them had a sweater that fit Tristan perfectly. Matching gloves? Why not? How about making me a deal on the hat? Sure. Dan wants a hat and gloves too. One-stop shopping. That was fun.

We spent a day touring Cusco, and later we left Tristan and Tessa at the hotel while Dan and I went to the train station to buy our tickets from Ollantaytambo to Aguas Calientes, part of the trip to Machu Picchu. Most tourist groups try to do Machu Picchu in one day, leaving Cusco early morning, taking a bus to Ollantaytambo, a train to Aguas Calientes, then a bus to Machu Picchu. These crowded groups usually get to Machu Picchu late morning and only stay about two hours.

With Peggy's help, we made our own bus and train plans. Peggy knew we wanted to tour the Sacred Valley, which consists of several Inca sites, including Ollantaytambo and Pisac. She suggested instead of taking a bus to Ollantaytambo, we could hire Richard, the hotel taxi driver, to take us, and we could stop at all the sites we wanted. Great idea.

She suggested a hotel in Aguas Calientes and made our reservations for us. We would return to Torre Dorada after Machu Picchu, so we left our suitcases there, along with most of our clothes, and took only our backpacks and daypacks. We packed carefully: sweaters, gloves, hats, cameras, toilet paper, and at least two changes of clothes. We would leave our backpacks at the hotel in Aguas Calientes and then take only our daypack to Machu Picchu. Packing lightly and being organized were not skills that came naturally to the BeDell clan, but we were learning fast.

The next morning, after another great breakfast, Richard was waiting for us. Dan tried to pay for the nights we had stayed, but Danny told him not to worry about it; we could settle up when we returned. We spent two nights in their hotel, ate free breakfasts, and they didn't even ask for a copy of our credit card. I guess our dirty clothes were enough collateral.

Richard drove us to our first stop: a rehabilitation center for injured wild animals. After admiring the condors from outside their enclosure, the young man who became our guide allowed us to go inside the pen. The condors were huge. When I knelt next to one of the adults, his head was over mine! The condors were surprisingly docile; of course, they only eat dead animals, so we weren't in any danger. The male condor was a showoff. He allowed me to touch his back, and then he spread his wings wide so we could admire his black and white feathers. Tristan and Tessa had an interesting face off with a juvenile condor which was bigger than them. I wasn't sure who was the more curious, the condor or my kids.

Our guide was very enthusiastic, and you could tell he really loved his job. He walked us through the center, pointing out the different animals. I was very excited to see an ocelot. An ocelot is a type of cat, about double the size of a really big house cat, with spots like a leopard. They are endangered. This one was rescued from the jungles of Peru and was deceptively adorable. I wanted to pick it up, forgetting it was a wild animal with sharp fangs. It was kept in a small building with a glass window. I asked our guide if it was possible to get a better look. He said he needed to get some protection, miming that he needed gloves so the ocelot wouldn't claw him. He came back a few minutes later and said he couldn't find any. He knew I was disappointed, so he opened the door a crack so I could snap a quick photo. Here's where a good deed went bad.

The ocelot was at the door in a flash, claws wrapped around the edge of it, trying desperately to get his head out. The guide was trying just as desperately to keep him in. Our guide would pry the ocelot's claws off the door, only to have to wrestle with the cat's head. He'd push the head back in and then out came the paw. He did all of this while trying not to get clawed. It was quite a moment. All I could envision was this ocelot breaking loose and eating the other endangered animals while my terrified children watched.

At last, the ocelot was safely in his closed cage. We thanked our guide profusely before he left to seek medical attention. On our way out, we left a large donation to the center.

Also on our way out of the rehabilitation center, I stopped to use the bathroom. While I was minding my own business, doing my business, a large aggressive parrot walked under the stall door and began nipping at my legs and clothes. I screamed. From over the stall door, I could hear my family dissolving into laughter. They saw the parrot follow me into the bathroom and were now enjoying my predicament.

I tried to shoo the bird away while putting my clothes back on, but I wasn't successful. The parrot was mean. I couldn't scare him.

Suddenly a large wooden stick swept under the stall. Through a crack in the door, I saw a robust, older woman, bent over, looking under my door while wildly swinging a thick, wooden stick at the parrot, aggressively trying to get him out. The parrot was unfazed. The more the woman swung the stick, the more aggressive the bird became. She yelled at the parrot, and the parrot screeched back. That was unpleasant. It appeared these two had tangled before and shared a mutual history of dislike.

The woman was determined to get the bird, and the bird was equally determined that she wouldn't. My "savior" was now on her hands and knees, her head under the door, looking up at me. Awkward! As we made eye contact, the parrot, the woman, and me, a thought occurred to me that surely I must be on *Candid Camera Peru*. If so, I'd better get my clothes on. So while trying to pull up my pants, I had to avoid being bitten by a parrot, avoid being whacked by a large stick, and stop a Peruvian woman from crawling under my bathroom door. It was really a lot to ask, but I was up to the task. The bird, sensing the end was near, wisely ducked into the next stall and headed for the door with the woman right behind him. I emerged a few minutes later, unscathed, but suffering the hysterical laughter of my family.

Safely back in the car, we rode farther down the road to our next stop, the artesian center. Here we learned the difference between an alpaca, a llama, a guanaco, and a vicuna. I would love tell you what the differences are, something to do with the ears and the size, but really, they all look pretty similar. I think they would be okay with me saying that. They all seemed to get along.

We learned how the alpaca was sheared and how the fleece was dyed and then woven into rugs and other textiles. Our guide delighted in telling us that in the past, human urine was mixed in with the colors for the dyes used on the fleece. It made the colors bolder, he said. I couldn't help but take a suspicious sniff at my new sweater.

Undeniably though, the best part was when we were allowed to interact with an adorable baby guanaco only nine hours old. A guide stood with us in the pen. The baby's mother, though keeping a cautious eye on us, allowed us to carefully touch her baby, which was still moving around on wobbly legs. It was an incredible moment.

When we finished at the artesian center, Richard drove us to the Pisac Ruins. With clear skies, and at an elevation of 11,000 feet, we could see for miles. The citadel sat high on a plateau, with abrupt drop-offs into deep gorges on either side. Again, we saw the many agricultural terraces of the Incas. One fascinating thing we learned about these terraces was that even though the soil surrounding Pisac seemed thin and rocky, the crops did extremely well. The reason was because the soil was not native to the area, but had been carried in by hand by the Incas and the tribes before them all the way from the jungle, a two-day walk away. Each terrace was over 9 feet high, and it was mind boggling to see how much dirt was actually brought in.

A young, Peruvian college student offered his services to guide us through the ruins, and we accepted. Richard, our taxi driver, waited for us in the parking lot at the bottom of the ruins. Tristan and Tessa loved hiking on the cliff-hugging trails and scrambling through tunnels carved out of the rocks. The trip down took ninety minutes, and we enjoyed every minute of the warm sunshine and clear skies. During our hike, our guide played the traditional Andean flute; its somber tunes echoing off the cliffs containing Inca burial tombs high above us. It couldn't have been more perfect.

We arrived at the Ollantaytambo ruins late that afternoon. The ruins are in town, and Richard waited for us while we climbed the massive stone steps leading up the terraces. The amount of cut stones in Ollantaytambo is staggering. They line the terraces that go straight up the side of the mountain, which caused our already tired legs to groan with every upward step. One of the highlights at the top of the ruins was the unfinished Sun Temple. It was here we found the Wall of Six Monoliths consisting of six huge stones. The largest stone is over 12 feet high and over 6 feet wide. One of the stones held the faint outline of the *chakana,* or Incan cross, and on another, a puma, the symbol of the middle world. While we loved the stunning scenery at the Pisac ruins, the energy level and the stonework made Ollantaytambo our favorite that day.

At 5 p.m. the ruins closed, and we gathered our bags from Richard, who had been patiently waiting in the car. We waved as he drove away. Our train wasn't scheduled to leave until 8:35 p.m., so we had some time to kill. We hoped there was an actual train station at Ollantaytambo, but no—just a few park benches to sit on. We had eaten a large, late lunch at a riverside restaurant before we arrived in town, so we weren't hungry, but we were bored. After walking along the cobblestone streets and seeing a few of the shops, we were too tired to do much more. We found an open park bench and huddled together. As the sun went down, the temperature dropped.

We'd been smart enough to bring our sleeping bags with us, so we used them to keep warm. Everyone got out a book and a book light, and we spent the next two hours in the cold and dark reading. About forty-five minutes before the train was due, we moved to a small café by the railroad tracks and had hot tea, hot chocolate, and a brownie with ice cream. Finally, closer to 9 p.m., our backpacker train arrived.

We were very tired when our train pulled into Aguas Calientes later that night. We had tried to sleep on the train, but stumbled off still half-asleep. We couldn't wait to get to our hotel. Unfortunately, we couldn't remember the name of the hotel we were going to. That's never good. Hotel Torre Dorado had made the reservations for us, and since we hadn't actually seen the name written down, and at this point were so tired, we couldn't remember the name. It wouldn't have been that big a deal since Hotel Torre Dorado requested that someone from the hotel meet us at the train station, but there was no one there. So we were tired and had no idea what the name of our hotel was or any clue where it was located. It was a great lesson to learn—never let someone else make your reservations for you, or if you do, have them write it down and get a phone number.

Across the plaza from the train depot was an internet café that also offered phone calls. Fortunately we had the phone number to Torre Dorado, so Dan made the call. Ever helpful Danny, who covered the front desk, solved our problem immediately. He called the hotel in Aguas Calientes and instructed them to send someone to the train station to meet us. A few minutes later, the rather irritated manager from our new hotel met us at the train station and led us back to his hotel. I was embarrassed to find that it was located only a block from the train station. Even an idiot could have found it. Things weren't off to an auspicious start.

Our plan was to go to Machu Picchu at sunrise. We still needed to purchase our bus and admission tickets, but we had no idea where to buy them. The hotel owner didn't speak English, and we were too tired to understand his Spanish. I was able to communicate bus ticket, and he pointed vaguely out the window, but I was getting frustrated and couldn't understand what he was saying. This was surprising because we were becoming pretty proficient at speaking and understanding Spanish. I guess we were just too tired. Giving up, we communicated a 4:30 a.m. wake-up call and decided we'd figure it out in the morning.

We trudged up the stairs to our room and went straight to bed. We had just fallen asleep, lulled by the sound of the roaring river across the street, when loud music coming from a marching band woke us up. Seriously? It was after midnight. Who were they and where were they going? We found out later they were part of the *Tres Cruces* festival; a festival that would go on all day and all night while we were there. It was turning into a long night, so Dan and I decided we wouldn't go to Machu Picchu in the morning but would wait until the next day. It was a good decision.

19

Magical Machu Picchu

PERU

EVERYTHING WAS MUCH EASIER THE next morning. We were able to converse in Spanish with the hotel manager and learned that the office to buy our bus ticket was only 30 feet from the hotel, and the office to buy Machu Picchu tickets was just around the corner in the plaza. Once we had our tickets, we spent the day enjoying the festival. For hours, brightly costumed dancers performed in the plaza. The dancers were all ages, and the costumes were elaborately embroidered. Some of the dancers were dressed as bulls and some as devils. They danced along to traditional Peruvian music and eventually ended up at the church where they carried out a cross, and the procession danced out of town.

During the festival, we ran into our Canadian friends who we first met in Arequipa. They had just returned from Machu Picchu and told us what we could bring in and what to expect. They also told us they had been on a bus from Arequipa to Cusco, the same day we were supposed to have taken the bus but had been told it was cancelled due to the protest. They were on a cheaper bus that didn't cancel. Instead, when the bus arrived at the protest site where the road was blocked, the driver made them get off the bus and left them there. They were forced to ride on a motorcycle taxi that took them around the protesters and then dropped them off on the other side where they had to wait and pay for another bus. They said it was very scary. I was so glad that wasn't us.

The next morning we were up at 4:30 a.m., packed our bags, and headed down for a simple breakfast at 5:00 a.m. Because we were taking the train back to Cusco that day, we checked out of our hotel room. The manager showed us where we could leave our bags, in a corner, in a big pile with everyone else's bags. We weren't sure how secure that was, since we weren't given a receipt, nor could we be sure if anyone was watching the bags. We were pretty sure the manager thought we were idiots because we couldn't find the hotel on our first night, but we decided to go with the flow. Our bags joined the growing pile.

At 5:30 a.m. we lined up to get on the bus for the sunrise trip. We were so excited. We were lucky and got seats on the first set of buses, guaranteeing we would make it to the top for sunrise. The bus ride takes about twenty minutes, winding up switchbacks to the top of Machu Picchu. If you want to save yourself a few dollars, or want the challenge, you could actually walk up. Not on the road though, that would be too easy—right up the side of the mountain as Hiram Bingham the man who "discovered" Machu Picchu would have done. But I really didn't need another challenge in my life at that point, so we took the bus.

The bus dropped us off at the top. From there, we stood in a line to get in. It was still early, and the crowds hadn't arrived yet, so we didn't have long to wait. After the check-in point, we were on our own. Most people, like us, headed to the caretakers hut for the best view. It is there that many tourists take their Machu Picchu picture, the one that most people are familiar with. The rest of the crowd was in a footrace to be one of the first two hundred people to reach Huayna Picchu so they would have the chance to climb it. While it sounded like a unique opportunity, I had no desire to stress everyone out, racing across the place I really wanted to explore so I could be one of only two hundred allowed to climb up a mountain right next to it just to gain another 1,000 feet. Our Canadian friends had done this. They said that while Huayna Picchu offered a great view of Machu Picchu, the climb took awhile and took away from the time they needed to explore Machu Picchu. So we passed.

The trail to the caretakers hut was uphill. We huffed and puffed for about ten minutes before finally reaching the top. We stood on the edge and looked down. At first all we saw was white from the clouds, but as we waited, the clouds and mist slowly parted, and the sacred city began to reveal itself to us. We felt like we were back in time with Mr. Bingham, seeing the site for the first time. It really was spectacular.

While Dan waited for the sun to appear so he could capture a picture, I kept a sharp eye on Tessa. She was enthralled with the wild llamas grazing near us. I was afraid she wouldn't pay attention to where she was going and would plunge off one of the sheer sides, disappearing forever. As I kept an eye on her and the llamas, an incredible thing happened. The mountains across from Machu Picchu, to the east, are jagged, reminiscent of a picket fence. As the sun rose and the first rays of light peeked from behind the jagged peaks, the wild llamas, which had been grazing peacefully in the dim light, stopped grazing. In a slow procession, they walked to the edge of the cliff and stood there, watching, until the sun completely rose over the mountains. I had never seen an animal watch the sun rise. After the sun was over the peak, the llamas disappeared down the mountain. I watched them go in awe.

The Incas worshiped the sun. Most of the buildings in Machu Picchu face east. On the eastern side of the city, we saw several benches carved from rocks, presumably where the Incas sat to watch the sun rise. I looked around me at my fellow travelers, here at this sacred place. Half were running across the mountaintop so they could be part of the first crowd to climb the mountain next door. Another group was doing yoga but seemed oblivious to the rising sun. The hikers who had taken the Inca trail were celebrating having made it to their final destination. Many of the future visitors that day were still in bed or on their way to a souvenir market first. By the time they made it to Machu Picchu, the sun would be high in the sky. Then there was the other group, like my husband, who were trying to take the perfect photograph. Of all of us, only the llamas remembered and understood.

After the sun was up, we walked back down the steps and onto the main site. We leisurely made our way through the Temple of the Sun, the Temple of the Condor, and many other buildings. We tried to feel the energy coming off the Hitching Post of the Sun—the sacred spot where twice a year on the solstices, the sun is directly above the small, rectangular stone post protruding from a large rectangular rock. Legend has it that if you put your forehead on the stone, all the world's secrets will be revealed to you. Unfortunately, it was getting too much wear and was now roped off. Too bad because I had a lot of questions.

We had a good four hours before the crowds came in at 10 a.m. There was so much to take in. I felt sorry for the people who came on the tour buses and were allotted only two hours. That wasn't nearly enough time. If you traveled with a tour group you missed the sunrise, and you also arrived when crowds were the largest. Fortunately for us, by the time the crowds arrived, we had made it through the site for the first time and were going back to our favorite places. While there were lots of places to explore, it was also nice to sit and just take in the view.

No one is really sure why Machu Picchu was built. Very

recently, scholars proposed that instead of a city, it was actually a pilgrimage site. The Incas believed they were born of the sun and the moon in Lake Titicaca, on the Peru-Bolivia border. From there, they mingled with other humans and created the Incan race. To the Incas, the Milky Way was a celestial river, and the beautiful Urubamba River below Machu Picchu was its counterpart. Whatever the reason for its creation, it is a beautiful, peaceful place. We were so happy to have been there, not only to see such a world wonder, but also for the fact that we did it together, as a family. This was our own pilgrimage.

We stayed on Machu Picchu until well after lunchtime and caught our train back to Cusco late that afternoon. This time, we were on the Vistadome train instead of the cheaper backpacker's train. The difference? A glass ceiling overhead so we could see the mountains towering above us, a small meal and beverage service, and of all things, a fashion show. Dan and I sat in seats facing Tristan and Tessa. Between us was a small table, so we were able to play a few rounds of cards on the way back. Most of the time though we just looked out at the scenery and the snow-peaked mountains in the distance.

Our train arrived at a stop near Cusco, and we hopped into the van Peggy had waiting for us. When we returned to the hotel, our bags were in our room. Danny, still ever thoughtful, asked if we wanted to order pizza. We did, and we also wanted a Coke Zero. The pizza place didn't have Coke Zero, so Danny went to the corner market and bought some for us. Okay. How many hotels have you stayed in have that kind of service? He didn't do it because he expected something (he wouldn't take a tip). He didn't do it because it was his job. He did it because that's just who he is and who everyone is at the Hotel Torre Dorada.

Peru has a reputation for having the friendliest, most

accommodating people, but truly, I think the staff at Torre Dorada was exceptional. We really felt that they took care of us like family. When the pizza came, instead of just handing us the box, Danny brought it to our room, along with napkins, plates, and glasses and set up a table. It felt like coming home.

We stayed one more night in Cusco. There were a few places we hadn't gotten to see yet, plus we loved the city. First on the list was Qorikancha, the fabled City of Gold, the most famous temple in the Americas. It was the Incas principal astronomical observatory. When Spanish *conquistadors* first stumbled upon the city, they found the walls lined with sheets of gold and unbelievable amounts of wealth. They stole what items they could carry and came back for more. Before the *conquistadors* could return, the Incas removed the huge gold disc of the sun, snuck it out of the city, and according to legend, threw the disc into Lake Titicaca to hide it from the Spaniards. It is said the disc is still at the bottom of the lake today.

Our last Inca site was Sacsayhuaman (a fun word to pronounce, sounding like sexy woman), the site of a major Inca/Spanish battle. Of all the Inca sites we toured, including Machu Picchu, we felt Sacsayhuaman and Qorikancha still held the most energy. You could really feel the presence of the Incas at both sites. Standing in one of the rooms in Qorikancha, you swore you could see an Incan priest disappearing around a corner. At Sacsayhuaman, wandering past the stone walls built in a lightning bolt pattern, you could easily imagine the Incans and Spaniards involved in a fierce battle.

Sacsayhuaman is not too far outside Cusco, so as we toured the site from the hillside, we had a unique view of the city. It was late afternoon by the time we arrived. The air was clear, and we could see for miles. Though it was still daylight, above us in the clear sky was a sliver of crescent moon.

Before we left the site, a local woman approached me selling souvenirs. In her bag I spied a small, gold-colored llama figurine, a replica of one I had been looking for. She gave me a price, and me, loving the game of bargaining, gave her a price of half that. She said no; I walked away. My kids were outraged. They absolutely hated when I tried to bargain. The woman came back with a little lower price, and again I countered and walked away.

"Mom!" Tristan was appalled. "Just give her what she wants."

"No. It's called bargaining."

"Mom, that is so mean," said Tessa.

I couldn't make them understand how it worked, and I always ended up looking like the bad guy. They hated it. Reluctantly, and only to appease my family, I agreed on her price. From that point on, I learned to shop alone.

The next afternoon we left Torre Dorado. I had tears in my eyes. The guidebook said Peruvians weren't partial to hugs, but I couldn't resist and gave Danny and Peggy a hug goodbye. They hugged me back. We were sad to leave, but it was time for us to catch our bus and head to Puno (Lake Titicaca). Danny and Peggy walked us out to the taxi and waited by the curb until we pulled away. We couldn't have been better taken care of.

20

Mystic Waters

LAKE TITICACA, PERU

THE NEXT LEG OF OUR journey turned out to be a long one. We took the overnight bus from Cusco to Puno. The road was rougher, and it was much colder as we headed high over the Andes. Once again our sleeping bags came in handy to keep us warm.

A little information about Peru bus travel. Before this trip, we had never been on a long-distance bus. In Peru it's the main form of travel. The bus lines we took were generally nice, double-decker buses with VIP areas and onboard videos. The kids loved them, but anything that's different from what they are used to they love. (For example, they love roll-down windows on cars. They think that's so cool.)

The seats on the buses are comfortable, with the VIP seats on the bottom level being better because they are bigger and lie flatter. Plus, you don't feel the bus lean over as much when the driver is barreling down a mountain and careening around hairpin turns. The restrooms are generally clean, though hard to use when the bus is really moving. I tried to plan their use when the bus was moving slow, but I could never really count on that.

One night the bus was stopped, and I felt it would be alright to get up. It was late, and the bus was dark. Most of the people were asleep. I unbuckled my seatbelt, and the bus started forward. I decided to chance it. Normally when you are walking to the back of the bus, you can put your hands on the back of the seats to steady yourself. I did this in the dark, forgetting the seats were reclining. My hand missed the seat back, and instead, my fingers became embedded in someone's thick, curly hair, no doubt belonging to the hippie guy with the curly, red afro that was seated a few seats behind us. *Yuk!* I heard a small cry as I wrenched my hand free, a few strands of red hair still clinging to my fingers. I scurried away, hoping he hadn't seen me. After that, I didn't leave my seat.

The bus pulled into Puno around 6 a.m. and dropped us off at an actual bus station. As we stumbled sleepily inside, we were overwhelmed by people trying to sell us tours to Lake Titicaca. Before we bought a tour, we had to check the bus schedule. We needed to find the bus line that would take us from Puno to Tacna.

Though the tour operators kept shouting at us, trying to get our attention, we ignored them and kept walking. Mayra, a woman who sold Lake Titicaca tours, stayed with us. She pointed out we could tour Lake Titicaca all day, then board an overnight bus that evening to Tacna. From Tacna we could take a cab across the border to Arica, Chile. It was a workable, if not ambitious plan.

Mayra helped us get our bus tickets, then she took us upstairs to the cafeteria. We ate breakfast while she talked about the tour. The tour company provided a taxi to take us to the docks. There, we would join the others on the tour and board a small boat, not more than 20 feet long and about as fast as our dinghy. It would take us to three islands. The first two islands were the Uros floating islands, about an hour away. From there, the boat would take us to the island of Taquile, two hours away. We would eat lunch on the island and be back at the bus station by 6 p.m., in plenty of time to catch our next bus leaving after 9:00 p.m. The price was great, $10 for adults and $8 for the kids, and the timing perfect, since the boat tour was scheduled to leave at 7:30 a.m. That gave us just enough time to eat, brush our teeth, and be on our way again. We kept our backpacks with us but left our luggage with Mayra in the tourist office.

Our first stop was the Uros Islands. These manmade islands, woven from reeds, were originally built by the Uros to isolate themselves from conquering tribes such as the Incas. Several hundred people still live on the islands today, mainly very young children and the elders. Most of the teenagers and young adults have moved off to the city. The lifespan for those who stay on the island is around fifty years. While sad, it's not surprising as it didn't seem healthy living on floating, decaying reeds.

The islands are constructed from many, many layers of reeds stacked into floating blocks, eventually getting several feet thick, and then anchored in place. Every two weeks a new layer of reeds is added, and every thirty years, the natives have to redo the island, burning the old one. Everything was built from reeds: the island, the houses, the overlook tower, even a very large boat folded like origami, with reeds instead of paper, into an oversized canoe complete with the head of a swan at the bow. That was ambitious. You could ride in the boat for a small fee, and I told Dan and the kids to go without me. I would enjoy the view from the waterbed—I mean island.

In the middle of the floating island, as if there wasn't enough water around, was a fish pond. To increase their income, the Uros raise trout to sell in the market. They are definitely a resourceful group. While it was phenomenal how they built the islands, and Tristan was especially fascinated, hanging on every word the tour guide said, I found the whole place uncomfortable. The people were a little grumpy, arguing over potential customers looking at their crafts, but then again, who wouldn't be less than pleasant after walking on a giant sponge all day? I was more than happy to get back into the tour boat.

Dan and I slept the over two hours to Taquile Island. We woke up just as the boat docked. Taquile Island was nothing like the Uros islands. This island was green and fairly lush, with solid rock beneath our feet. Instead of reeds, the island was covered in grass and trees. The island wasn't always this lush. It was the Incas who brought in dirt and made the land hospitable for living and farming.

We stepped off the boat and our guide pointed up. We had five hundred steps to climb, nearly straight up, to where our lunch was being served. Five hundred steps, at an altitude of over 12,000 feet; it took awhile for the entire group to make it to the top. Still breathing heavy from the exertion, we were seated at a long table, positioned so we overlooked the brilliant blue waters of Lake Titicaca.

Our lunch was simple and delicious: soup, fresh trout, and quinoa. The views were breathtaking. Somewhere across the lake was the country of Bolivia. And somewhere under the deep sacred waters, according to Incan lore, rested the sun disk made of pure gold. Looking at the lake around me, it was a legend that was easy to believe.

While we ate, our guide filled us in on some of the Taquile culture. The Taquilenos are a very private society, heavily steeped in old customs. Tourism has evolved fairly recently on the island, and all islanders share in the profits based on community collectivism. Family and community are extremely important to them, and they still adhere to the Inca moral code: *do not steal, do not lie, do not be lazy.* The Taquilenos are hard working and are renowned worldwide for their artistic textiles. The women do the traditional weaving, while the men knit.

Our guide pointed to the hats the men wore, and he explained their significance. All the men wore hats, but which color hat they wore told something about them. Married men wore red hats, and single men wore more elaborately designed red and white hats. There was a special black hat for the tribal leader to wear. Each man served as a tribal leader for one year. The men knit the hats themselves. We saw the men's knitting circle. Knitting is apparently how they get the ladies. The better the knitter, the more interest from the ladies, because quite frankly, what woman wouldn't want a man who knows his way around a skein of yarn?

During our lunch, the local Taquile people did something they hadn't done before. In a possible attempt to bring in more tourists, they put together a dance, which they performed for us. We were warned beforehand that this was something new, and they were still working on the choreography, but it was really, I hate to say it, not good. I am not sure who sold them on this idea. Maybe there was a roving tourist consultant who stopped by the island in his fast, fancy speedboat and said, "Hey, you got to move on from this knitting thing. It's been done. Dancing is what brings in the crowds."

The performers were either shy or embarrassed to participate, we weren't exactly sure. In fact, we weren't exactly sure what they were doing. It looked like they were making it up as they went along. When it was over, we clapped, and they smiled shyly.

After lunch we climbed one hundred more stairs to the plaza. The architecture in the plaza was cut stone. Stone bricks were arranged in arches that we passed beneath to enter and exit the plaza. Tall, arched windows accented the large stone buildings in the marketplace, and outside on stone benches, we saw more single men in knitting circles. We strolled through the indoor market where many examples of their knitted and woven crafts were for sale. The prices were much higher than what we had paid for other indigenous handiwork, but the craftsmanship was superior. I bought a blue headband with a black-and-white checkerboard trim. I was thankful for it when we were in the colder parts of Chile.

We had thirty minutes to follow the paved path around the island and down to the dock. Our guide warned us to be prompt returning to the boat because they would leave on the dot without us. The boats needed to depart before the strong afternoon winds whipped the waves to an unsafe height for small watercraft. I'm not sure if anyone was ever left on the island (you can spend the night with a host family), but I didn't want to be the first to find out, so we made sure to be back on time.

We slept on the trip back to Puno. We had a few hours to kill before we boarded the bus again, so we had the van drop us off downtown. After an unusually good (for Peru) pizza, it was back to claim our luggage from the tourist company and wait for the bus. For this overnight trip, we (finally!) had the VIP seats on the lower level.

Traveling between Puno and Tacna used to be a rough trip. The bus climbs over a high mountain pass and then speeds straight down to nearly sea level. The old road was unpaved, but the guide book assured us that a new road had been built. The trip wasn't bad. The road was still a little jarring, it was cold, and the bus still swayed around the corners, but we were all so tired, we didn't care. We were snug in our VIP seats, with the seats that lay flat like a bed and a privacy partition around us. The over-the-speed-limit sign flashed all night, but we didn't care. We slept soundly. When the bus arrived in Tacna at 6 a.m., we sighed with disappointment as once again, we were dropped in the middle of nowhere.

This is what we thought would happen. The bus from

Puno would drop us off at the bus station in Tacna. We would board a *collectivo* (a small van carrying about twelve people) that would take us across the Chilean border to Arica and drop us off at a bus station. There, we would find a tourist booth and someone who spoke English who could help us find a hotel.

Here's what actually happened. The bus dropped us off in an alleyway in Tacna. This must have been common practice because there were several cab drivers waiting. Well, they weren't actually waiting, they were yelling in Spanish, jostling each other, trying to get the passengers' attention. Bleary-eyed, we grabbed our bags and were immediately swarmed with taxi offers. The problem was we didn't know where to go, and with all the confusion, it was hard to think. When in doubt in a foreign country, always head to the bus station.

A man chased our cab into the bus station parking lot. He yelled something we couldn't understand, and our cab driver yelled back and waved him away. As soon as our cab stopped, the persistent man was there, along with four other guys, trying to get our business. We'd been warned to watch our luggage at the Tacna bus station. In confusion just like this, tourists had their luggage stolen. Of course, we had been warned at every bus station to watch our luggage, and by this time our luggage had expanded. In addition to our backpacks and two small rolling suitcases, we had two more soft Peruvian backpacks to store our sleeping bags and one soft Peruvian duffel bag that held our dirty clothes and souvenirs. What was our plan for keeping our luggage from getting stolen? Tessa. She was our go-to girl. Dan, Tristan, and I unloaded the luggage, and Tessa guarded it. It may seem strange to you having a nine-year-old girl keeping guard, but it worked. Who would steal from a little girl?

Our luggage was out of the car, and the taxi drivers were in a shoving match over who was going to get our business. What did we do in situations like this? We just walked away. They all followed us into the terminal, yelling in Spanish how much they would charge to take us across the border. At least that's what we think they were yelling. We walked around the small terminal aimlessly, not sure what to do. It was so hard to think.

The guy who originally chased our car into the parking lot stayed with us, and I understood he would charge us 15 sols per person to take us across the border to Arica, Chile. This was not a simple thing. It was an hour to the border, where we would wait in line at customs and immigration, then drive another half hour or so to Arica. For US$18 total, it sounded like a great deal. Another man jumped in and offered to charge us less, but I went with my gut that said the first guy was trustworthy. We chose him.

We exchanged introductions with our driver, Gustav, and made small talk during the drive as best we could. He didn't speak English, but we were pretty fluent in Peruvian Spanish by now. Our first stop was checking out of Peru. We left our luggage in the cab and walked through the customs and immigration checkpoint. If we were the suspicious type, this would have been the perfect opportunity for Gustav to ditch us and drive off with our luggage. Instead, after he parked his car, Gustav guided us to the front of the line and quickly through. A short cab ride down the road, we checked into Chile without a problem and then were back in the taxi on our way to Arica.

We had little information on lodging in Arica, so we asked Gustav to drop us off at the bus station, again thinking we could get some hotel information. This bus station turned out to be more of a strip of ticket counters for the bus lines. The station and parking lot were empty except for a few men milling about. We looked around in concern while we unloaded our bags, but Gustav took care of us.

During the ride into Arica, Gustav had asked us if we

needed Chilean pesos. We said yes. It turned out this wasn't just a bus station, it was a place we could exchange money. Thank you, Gustav! We followed him to where a Chilean man was standing at the edge of the parking lot. This was the "money man."

We had a vague idea of the exchange rate, but we really weren't prepared for the transaction. The rate at the time was 567 Chilean pesos to 1 US dollar. We gave him our money, and he gave us back several 1,000-peso Chilean bills and some coins.

In Spanish, I asked Gustav if this was the correct exchange rate, and he said it was. I then asked the Chilean man, "*Cuanto cuesta taxi*" or "How much is a taxi?" Sometimes, actually a lot of the time, I'd get mixed up and ask, "*Cuanto quesa*" or "How much cheese?" I knew it must have hurt the locals' ears when I spoke Spanish, but this time I got it right. We couldn't understand the money-man's answer at first because now the amounts were in *mil* or thousands, so he took some money, folded it up, gave it to Dan, and said, "Taxi." That cleared it up. A taxi should run us 1,500 pesos. We thanked him for his help and then consulted the Lonely Planet guide for a place to stay in Arica.

So Many Colors, So Many Stars
CHILE

D AN HAILED A TAXI, AND the driver took us to the Hotel
Sotomayor, which was conveniently located about
a block from the plaza. The hotel was a bit old, but the
room, with one double and two twin beds, was clean, and
the manager, without asking, gave us a family discount.
Breakfast was included. The bellhops carried our bags to
our room and refused a tip. Our room was on the second
floor. There was an elevator, but it was only big enough for
two people and one bag of luggage. It was like riding in a
phone booth. Tristan refused to go near it.

The hotel staff couldn't do enough for us. They even
stopped using their work computer to let me use it to look
up hotels at our next destination and then let me use their
phone. For US$50 a night, right next to the plaza in a
resort town, Hotel Sotomayor was a great deal, and even
better, there was a restaurant nearby that sold delicious,
cheap *empanadas*.

Arica is not a big city, the population is about 185,000,
but it's a very popular beach-resort town, complete with
casinos. From the beginning, we knew we weren't in
Peru anymore. For starters, we were having trouble with
the language. We prided ourselves on becoming fairly
competent with the Spanish spoken in Peru, but Chilean

Spanish was much harder for us to understand. The pace there was much faster than in Peru. The people seemed very preoccupied and in a rush. It felt hectic, so we didn't stay in the city long. We had two areas of Chile we wanted to see before our trip ended: San Pedro de Atacama, located in the high Atacama Desert; and La Serena, located on the coast. The next evening we were back on the overnight bus to San Pedro de Atacama, the place we would all fall in love with.

May 9, 2009 San Pedro de Atacama, Chile
(from the blog of Alegria)

Chileans love their rules and their checkpoints. It was late. I was sleeping on the bus when Dan woke me up. He couldn't understand what the bus steward was saying. The steward was trying to explain to Dan something about passports, then control, then *dos horas*. Half asleep, this meant nothing to me. Luckily Tristan translated that the bus steward needed our passports for passport control and would bring them back in two hours. Oh. Okay.

Later we were again woken up. The bus had stopped, and we were told to get off for another checkpoint. Well, some of us were. You never wake Tessa up. Never. The result was like throwing a cat in bathwater. While Tristan and I joined the freezing passengers on the side of the road, Dan tried to coax Tessa into getting off the bus. Finally the bus driver, sensing the futility in this said, "*Nina* stay, okay." Tessa stayed. Dan joined us outside.

We waited while the bus was searched inside and then searched underneath with a mirror. A tall, unfriendly guard searched through my backpack, though I'm not sure what he was looking for. Then he looked through Tristan's backpack. We read somewhere that they were looking for Peruvians or Bolivians trying to sneak into their country illegally. I know Bolivians and Peruvians are small people, but there was no way I was smuggling one in my backpack.

When we were finally allowed back on the bus, we found Tessa busy gathering up all our belongings. She thought we had left the bus and forgotten our luggage. She was doing her best to retrieve all the bags, struggling under their weight. Remember what I said earlier about her guarding the bags? She took her job very seriously.

The rest of the night passed uneventfully. I woke up early in the morning and was treated to a beautiful sight. The sun was just coming up, unfolding a plush blanket of pink and purple for the setting full moon. It was breathtaking. The desert sky was so clear, the colors just popped, something I'd never seen before. It was magical, a phrase we couldn't stop using during our time in the Atacama Desert.

As I watched the moon slowly fade, I was overcome with sheer happiness and gratitude; so happy that I was here and so grateful to share this time with my husband and children. Before our trip, a friend had given me a magnet that said, "Wherever you go, go with all your heart." All my heart was there that morning. [*End blog*]

The road eventually gave way to a dusty, desert town, reminiscent of a scene from an old western. The bus stopped next to a small adobe building. As we gathered our bags and stepped off the bus, the usual crowd of tour and hotel solicitors were there wishing us a "Welcome to San Pedro de Atacama." We had arrived.

We weren't interested in talking to anyone; instead we strolled down the street. The town was a surprise to us. Cars were a rare sight. People moved around by either walking or bicycling. I'm sure we looked strange, wandering through town with our luggage, but we didn't have hotel reservations. I had called a few hotels, but they were expensive and fully booked because it was Mother's Day weekend. Most people wouldn't show up in a remote desert town without a place to stay, but we weren't most people. During one of my phone calls, a helpful, English-speaking hotel clerk gave me some good advice. He said we should walk into a hotel in San Pedro de Atacama without a reservation and ask for a discount. So that was what we did.

We walked past the many quaint, brown adobe buildings housing restaurants, shops, tourist agencies, and hotels until we found a place we really liked: the Lodge Andino Terrantai. I think we startled the manager by showing up without reservations, but she did have one room, a large family-style room, available. She showed me the price, and I asked for a discount. She looked at me in surprise, not sure what to do, then reduced the price. Nice. The hotel was unique, with its river-stone walls both outside the hotel and inside the hotel room itself. Each night, on the patio near the pool, a large fire was lit, and though it was very cold at night, we would sit by the fire and relive our day.

There were many tour operators leading adventures into the desert, but we decided to go with two offerings from the hotel. Max, our guide, described the scenery late that afternoon as our family joined a couple from Belarus on the *Valle de la Luna* (Valley of the Moon) tour. Max pointed out the fantastic moon-like landscape of the Atacama Desert. The desert is rich in minerals, particularly salt, which leaves a glistening white covering, resembling snow or the surface of the moon, across the landscape. Because the Atacama Desert is the driest desert in the world, everything stays preserved. It was a remote, desolate place, but also incredibly beautiful and peaceful.

The desert air was so clean and clear, we could see for miles. San Pedro De Atacama sits at an elevation of nearly 8,000 feet. Max drove us even higher to a mountain plateau and set up wine, drinks, and snacks. We gazed into the distance and watched the setting sun paint the surrounding mountains and volcanoes various shades of red and purple.

May 11, 2009 San Pedro de Atacama, Chile
(from the blog of Alegria)

This was what we came for—the stars at San Pedro de Atacama. We signed up at the SPACE agency in town, and that night we were driven by bus to the Atacama Lodge. The French astronomer Alain Maury and his wife, Alejandra, established the lodge in 2003 and lead observations every night. We had been warned to dress warmly, which for us meant wearing just about everything we had.

We were so excited we could hardly stand it. Our sailing trip had given us several opportunities to see magnificent night skies, but this was different. This was the Southern Hemisphere, and we would be seeing stars we had never seen before. Imagine that for a moment. Think of how old you are, how many times you've seen the same stars in the sky, and then think that there's a totally different night sky with stars you may never see in your lifetime. Crazy isn't it?

After a short ten-minute ride, the bus stopped outside a very dimly lit house. Stepping off the bus was like stepping into another universe. The stars were so close, so bright, that out of reflex we ducked our heads. We were awestruck, amazed, rooted to the spot, even a bit dizzy. The Milky Way, at best seen to most Americans as a small, cloudy group of stars, blazed across the sky here—a thick band of white, from one end of the horizon to the other. We couldn't take our eyes off it.

Alejandra was there to greet us and kept everyone moving along into a candlelit room where Alain gave us a history of the lodge. He is French and came to Chile because, as he said, "There are more stars in the southern sky." He married Alejandra, and from their passion came the Atacama Lodge.

After a brief explanation of what we would be seeing in the sky, our group headed outside. Alain used a laser pointer and a good bit of humor to point out the different stars, planets, and constellations. He encouraged us to get a closer look through the several large telescopes scattered around the yard.

Each telescope was aimed at a different part of the night sky. These weren't your average telescopes. Alain had the largest group of telescopes in any public observatory in South America, and they were big—between 20 and 60 centimeters in diameter. The telescopes were so powerful, making the stars so clear, we almost couldn't believe what we were seeing.

One telescope, pointed at Saturn, clearly showed the rings and all the vibrant colors. In fact, Saturn was so clear it seemed fake. Tessa and Tristan were blown away by what they saw. They (we) were so excited, going from telescope to telescope, asking each other, "Did you see that?" "Did you see that?"

We drooled over distant galaxies, star clusters, and blue, red, yellow, turquoise, and green stars. I never knew stars came in so many colors. Alain's enthusiasm never let up as he and Alejandra patiently answered questions and aligned the telescopes to show us different parts of the sky. Without a doubt, the Milky Way was my favorite. Nearly every ancient civilization has some history with the galaxy, with some civilizations believing we were born or created through the Milky Way. The Incas and Mayans, in particular, viewed it as a link from the upper world to the lower world.

Looking at the Milky Way, it's not just the stars you can see that are important; the lack of stars, or blackness, is equally revered. The Incas saw animals, such as a llama, a snake, and a toad, swimming in this celestial river. In the middle of Alain's presentation, Tristan whispered to me, "Mom. I can see the llama in the Milky Way." We easily could.

At 8,000 feet and with no cloud cover, the desert gets extremely cold at night. Even with all our layers, we were cold. When Alain felt everyone had gotten a good view, we went back inside the lodge. While Alejandra served the best hot chocolate, making sure Tessa got hers first, Alain told us more about the night sky. Some things he told us were obvious, but made you think. For example, there are no "shooting stars." These are dust particles or debris burning up in our atmosphere. When you look at the night sky, you are always seeing the past. And a big surprise to me, all stars are suns with the possibility of having their own planets, a combination that Alain is interested in finding. We could have listened to him talk for hours, but it was time for our tour to end and the next one to start. Back at our hotel, we ended our day reliving our experience around a blazing fire. [*End blog*]

May 12, 2009 San Pedro de Atacama, Chile
(*from the blog of* Alegria)

One of the things we enjoyed most about this trip was setting our own pace. We were supposed to stay in San Pedro only two nights, but we so enjoyed the town, we exchanged our bus tickets (no charge) to leave a couple nights later. It was hard to leave San Pedro. We loved the food. The days were warm, the nights cold, and the desert exotic.

On our second tour with the hotel, we again joined with the couple from Belarus. Max drove us to a very small nearby town, and we toured a charming adobe church, visited a local dwelling, and got as close as we could to the pink flamingos with black tail feathers, feeding in the salt flats. A pack of llamas crossed the horizon in the distance. The landscape was beautiful but harsh and uninviting, and it amazed us that people and animals would choose to live there.

Back at the hotel later that night, we sat around the campfire and talked to the Belarusian couple. We actually had a lot in common. The husband worked in the financial arena, and they had two children close to Tristan's and Tessa's ages. They were surprised we had brought our kids on the trip and impressed with how well they traveled. Their children were back in Belarus, staying with family. They would have loved to have brought them along, but the kids had school. They wondered how our government allowed us to homeschool. The evening turned into an interesting conversation on children, countries, and politics, until eventually the cold desert air forced us to retire for the night.

Surprisingly we didn't see any other tourist families here. San Pedro definitely attracted a younger twenty-something, adventure crowd, or an older, newly-retired crowd. The people we met, especially the twenty-something group, were very happy to see our kids exploring the world. They all wished their parents had done that for them.

The next afternoon we left San Pedro and began our seventeen-hour bus trip, our longest yet, to La Serena. [*End blog*]

May 15, 2009 La Serena, Chile
(*from the blog of* Alegria)

We awoke to the worst weather we have seen on our entire trip, overcast and foggy. La Serena is on the Chilean coast, and this is their normal weather. We took a taxi from the bus station to our hotel. The Hotel Costa Real was more expensive than what we usually paid, but it was close to the Plaza de Armas where most of the tourist information bureaus were located.

Our taxi stopped in front of the hotel, and the bellhops came out to help with our luggage. We didn't have a reservation and didn't know if they would have anything available. I went inside to see about a room. My plan was to talk to them before our ragtag, just-off-an-overnight-bus group, with our less than chic backpacks, descended upon the lobby. This, after all, was not a hostel, but a businessman's hotel. We needed to have a sense of decorum.

I gave a friendly smile to the woman at the front desk. "I'd like to see about a room."

She looked at my uncombed hair, my backpack, and my several layers of clothing, including the Peruvian sweater I had been wearing for nearly a month now. Then she looked over my shoulder, alarmed when she saw Dan and the kids enter the lobby.

"Do you have a reservation?" she asked haltingly in English.

"No."

Again, the look of alarm on her face. "Just a minute please." She called for backup. The manager came to the counter, equally alarmed. Again, I asked about a room. She asked if we had a reservation. Again, I said no. Again, she looked distressed.

"Do you have a room available?" I asked a little more assertively. I mean really, reservation or not, you either had a room or you didn't. End of story. Finally she came up with a room option. A room with a king-sized bed, a sleeper sofa, and they would bring in a rollaway bed. She gave me the room price, which included a breakfast buffet. The price was very reasonable, considering the location and the fact this was listed as a top hotel, but I had to ask, "Can you give me a discount?"

The manager looked at me as if I had just asked if we could sleep naked in the lobby. After a moment she said she could take US$10 off the price. Sold!

Our room was incredible. Located on the second floor, it overlooked the small, outdoor swimming pool. The bathroom was large and beautifully tiled, but it was the sight of the stereo system and 48-inch, flat-screen TV that sent me scrambling for the phone to book another night.

After showers, and dragging ourselves away from the TV, we walked toward the plaza for lunch and to find a tourist office. La Serena is Chile's second oldest city. Of course, it has the beautiful, tree-lined, well-enjoyed plaza, but we were also in a major business and shopping district. Everyone was well dressed, and I felt out of place.

The Chileans, for the most part, totally ignored us as if we didn't exist. It was surprising to us. When you dealt with them one-on-one, they were mostly friendly and helpful, but out on the streets, the atmosphere was different. We spent the day wandering the city, taking in the sights, enjoying the cool air, and checking out the grocery store. That may not sound exciting to you, but you can really learn a lot about a country by checking out its grocery stores. It's one of our favorite things to do.

The next day we found El Qui Valley Tours, where a very friendly, English-speaking tour guide sold us a tour to the Humboldt Penguin Reserve. The van to the penguin reserve would arrive at eight the next morning, so even though we would have enjoyed watching TV all night long, we were in bed early. [*End blog*]

22

Penguins!

CHILE

OUR DRIVER ARRIVED RIGHT ON time, and after picking up a few more tourists, we were on our way. La Serena is overcast and foggy at least 90 percent of the time, but about an hour outside of town, the sky cleared, and we were again treated to a desert landscape. We traveled over an hour north to catch a ferry that would take us out to Isla Damas and Isla Choros where we hoped we would see penguins and dolphins. Many times due to bad weather and high seas, the trip was cancelled, but the call from the coast was that everything was good.

At Caleta de Choros we met our ferry, a small wooden boat with plank seats and a large outboard motor. It was a chilly ride. I kept my ears warm with the headband I had purchased on the island of Taquile. The sky was overcast. It was damp, but luckily no rain. It was hard to believe we were headed into the Pacific Ocean to see penguins. I mean, really; I grew up in a small farm town in Illinois, and here I was, in Chile, about to see penguins in the wild. It was surreal.

Our first stop was Isla Damas, a bleak, desolate island that we were allowed to explore for about thirty minutes, which was just long enough. The island had a very small, rather pretty white-sand beach, but the rest of the island was rocky, had a few birds, mostly vultures, and a lighthouse.

Back in the boat, we motored to Isla Choros. Landing on the island was prohibited, so we conducted all our sightseeing from the boat. Isla Choros is even bleaker than Isla Damas. Gunmetal gray rocks shoot straight from the surprisingly clear, turquoise water. The water was so clear, the white-sand bottom so beckoning, that I wanted to jump right in. It looked like Caribbean water, and I couldn't resist pulling off my gloves and dipping my fingers in. Not surprisingly it was extremely cold, which explains why the penguins and the sea lions liked it.

The boat driver did an excellent job of getting us close to the shore. Close enough to see the wildlife, but just far enough to avoid crashing on the jagged rocks. Marcel, our guide, pointed out the various birds, such as the cormorants, but we were all holding our breath to see if we would spot the main attraction. We didn't have to wait long. There, high above us on a ledge, trying to blend into the charcoal-colored rocks, stood two of the most adorable penguins. Penguins! Just standing there. Not in a zoo—in real life. In my real life.

Humboldt penguins are medium sized, about 26 to 28 inches high, and weigh about thirteen pounds. They are endangered, with less than 10,000 in the world now. The first two we saw, I guess were a couple. They were so adorable. We watched them for a long time, getting all the photos we wanted. The penguins tired of us well before we tired of them, and it was cute to watch them make their way up the rocks, hopping, scrambling, head down, flippers out. Our boat driver and our guide enjoyed the penguins as much as we did.

When the birds disappeared, the boat was maneuvered to another spot where we spotted a few more penguins off in the distance, but none as close as that first pair. That was alright though. We had gotten what we came for.

There was one more major surprise waiting for us. Off in the distance, we could see dolphins and sea lions playing in the water. I began my usual yelling and calling to get their attention, and my kids did the usual, "Mom, stop! You're embarrassing us!" I didn't care.

Years ago in Florida, we went on a dolphin-encounter. When we spotted dolphins in the distance, our guide said, "Dolphins love children. Have the kids make as much noise as possible." We all yelled, especially the kids, and sure enough, the dolphins came right over. Now whenever I spot a dolphin, I yell, clap, make a lot of noise to let them know I'm happy to see them. They always come to the boat. So here, on this boat in the Pacific, Tristan and Tessa were the only kids, so they needed my help. "Here dolphins! Dolphins, dolphins!" I yelled and guess what? They came, bringing the puzzled sea lions with them.

Within moments we were treated to an incredible show. Dolphins jumped out of the water next to the boat. The more we yelled, the higher they jumped. I think they were as excited as we were. The sea lions were a bit on the shy side, not sure what all the yelling was about, but eventually they too were caught up in the moment. One curious sea lion came very close to the boat, while the sea lions farther away entertained us with dives beneath the water. The dolphins were huge, the biggest we'd encountered. They leapt from the water, as close to the boat as they dared. We knew they wanted to see us as much as we wanted to see them.

Our show lasted over forty minutes, and our guides were gracious and wouldn't move the boat until the dolphin and sea lion show was over. At lunch later that day, to prove a point to Tristan and Tessa, I asked Marcel if it was true that calling to the dolphins helped. He said yes, dolphins are very good at reading the energy of humans. The more excited the people are, the more excited the dolphins become. But, he added, this day was special. In his fifteen years of leading these tours, he had never seen them put on a show like that. He was honestly and sincerely amazed.

I gave Tessa and Tristan a look that said, "Told you so" and basked in my ability to speak dolphin.

We were down to our last week of traveling and wanted to see as much as possible of the Chilean countryside, so we rented a car and headed to the Elqui Valley, northwest of Santiago. The drive out of La Serena was fairly easy; it was like driving in the US, only on better roads. The skies cleared and the countryside changed from coastal, to rugged mountains, and finally to green valleys with numerous vineyards. Out there, horseback riding was the preferred method of traveling, and we passed several cowboys on their well-attended horses.

On the way to Elqui Valley, we stopped for lunch at the Solar Kitchen, a restaurant that cooked all its food using solar ovens. They had several ovens set up outside the restaurant and two big mirrored disks that heated water. The food was good, and the kids got an education in solar energy.

Later that afternoon, we arrived at our cabin. The Elqui Valley is known for its mystical properties, and the area is filled with new age centers and spiritualists. The energy in the valley, especially at night when we were stargazing, was intense. At times it made us dizzy. We lingered there a few days, luxuriating in the good energy and basking in the limitless stars in the valley before heading back to La Serena and catching a bus to Santiago.

We'd had such good luck with the bus systems, I guess we were due. On the way to Santiago, our bus broke down. We noticed the first sign of trouble when the bus slowed and pulled onto the shoulder of the highway. The driver made an announcement and then disappeared with an empty bottle. We surmised that the bus must have overheated, and the driver was looking for water. When he came back with the bottle still empty, we knew that wasn't good. The driver made another announcement, and the other passengers immediately jumped up and quickly exited the bus.

Dan and I looked at each other. What just happened? Where did everyone go?

Tristan looked out the window and said, "They're getting their stuff and getting on another bus."

Sure enough, our fellow passengers were getting on a bus that had pulled in behind us. Is that what we were supposed to do? Our bus driver, finally noticing that we hadn't moved, tried to explain what we needed to do. In Spanglish, and lots of hand motions, he conveyed to us to quickly get our luggage and get on the other bus.

By the time we got our bags organized and boarded the other bus, no one was happy to see us. I scanned the bus for empty seats and was greeted with less-than-friendly faces. Dan helped Tristan and Tessa find a seat. Once they were settled, I looked for a place for me. There was an open seat by the bathroom, but I knew better than to take that one. On the bus we had just vacated, the toilet was filled almost to the top, threatening to slosh urine and feces onto the next unsuspecting user. If you had to use it, you prayed the driver would not make a sudden stop. I figured the bathroom on this bus was probably in the same shape.

My other choice was the seat next to the guy who gave me the feeling he would be less than thrilled if I sat next to him. I picked him. I sat down and turned to say thanks for allowing me to have that seat, but before I could say anything, he threw his coat over his face, making it pretty obvious he wasn't interested in chit-chatting with me. How welcoming! This was going to be an interesting ride. I couldn't see where Dan was sitting, but I could see Tristan and Tessa, and their seatmates seemed much friendlier, so at least they were fine.

The ride got even more interesting when later on, just outside the city of Santiago, some passengers exited the bus in the middle of a major highway. We hit rush-hour traffic, and I guess they thought this would be a good opportunity to disembark—on a major, four-lane highway, in bumper-to-bumper traffic. When the bus stopped, a passenger and the bus steward rushed off, opened the luggage department under the bus, found the luggage, and the passenger dodged between moving cars and made his way to the side of the road. This happened several times. When the traffic cleared so the bus could move, the driver moved. We often saw the passengers and the bus steward jogging next to the bus, trying to get luggage while the vehicle moved on. For the life of me, I couldn't understand why they would risk their lives like that, but it was entertaining to watch.

The bus passed through some seedy back streets near the outskirts of Santiago, and I grew anxious that we would be dropped in the middle of nowhere like we had been in Peru. Instead, the bus pulled into a bus station. I breathed a sigh of relief. It was nighttime now, and we were happy we were able to easily find a taxi. Within a few minutes of getting in the cab, we were hurtling through downtown, racing through stoplights in major intersections, until we were delivered in a panicked state to our hotel. I needed a drink bad.

The guidebook said our hotel was good, but we had mixed emotions. On the positive side, our hotel room was located on the top floor of a five-story building, and we had good views of the mountains and volcanoes surrounding the city. On the negative side, the elevators only went to the third floor, so we had to hike up a narrow, rickety staircase to the fifth floor, giving us the impression that the entire floor was put on as an afterthought. In fact, the hallway we had to walk through to our room was actually an enclosed overhang off the building. I shuddered every time I walked on it.

Breakfast the next morning was a small buffet of fruit, bread, cereal, and some eggs. While it wasn't outstanding, Tristan and Tessa were happy to have something beside the biscuit-and-jelly meals in Peru, especially since we had a full day of walking ahead of us.

The city of Santiago is situated in a valley, surrounded by mountains—jagged, snow-peaked mountains—and volcanoes, wherever you look. The surrounding extreme elevation causes this city of nearly six million people to sit in a "bowl" of generally poor air quality. Fortunately when we were there, the air was fairly clear. The residents of Santiago were friendlier than we had encountered in La Serena and Arica, and that made us feel better. They seemed to be enjoying life more, and why not? The city was beautiful, they appeared to have money, and there was plenty to spend it on.

We enjoyed strolling through the city. The streets were extremely clean, and the city was very pedestrian friendly. The weather was warm, and people were enjoying coffee or eating lunch at small tables set up outside the cafes and restaurants. Trees were an integral part of the landscape; nowhere in the downtown area did we feel overrun with concrete. The mix of old architecture and cathedrals existed easily with the modern buildings. We felt very comfortable and safe walking everywhere.

On our last day, we did the full city tour, on foot, including the presidential palace, cathedrals, and the Cerro San Cristobal cable car. Back at our hotel that night, the friendly hotel clerk ordered us a Domino's pizza, and we spent the rest of the evening packing. While we enjoyed our trip through Peru and Chile very much, it was time to go home. Early the next morning we boarded our flight to Aruba.

May 25, 2009 Aruba
(from the blog of Alegria)

The flight back to Aruba was uneventful. *Alegria* was waiting patiently for us, bobbing gently in her slip. We were so happy to see her. The Renaissance Marina had taken great care of her. Being back on the boat was easy, getting used to the heat was not. For the next few days, we moved slowly, still wrapped in the blanket of memories of soaring condors, mysterious valleys, the colors of a Chilean desert at twilight, and the beauty of the Peruvian people.

To say we had a life changing experience would be a huge understatement. I am still amazed we were able to go on such a big excursion, planning it along the way, living out of backpacks, and putting the whole thing together on a moment's notice. I'm extremely proud of how Tristan and Tessa never complained about anything, including lugging a heavy backpack around. They were always very organized, a side of them I'm not sure I saw before, and there wasn't anything they weren't excited about doing. I'm also proud of us as a family, acting on a gut feeling and trusting in the goodness of people to help us along the way. While we are a little sad to get back, I think we all feel there are many more of these trips ahead of us. [*End blog*]

The summer in Aruba passed slowly. Our friends from North Carolina and my niece and nephew came for a visit. Family members back in the US were still having health issues, so in September we remained in very hot Aruba and were not on our way to Colombia as planned in case we needed to fly to the States on short notice. In order to have access to Wi-Fi, and most importantly the pool, we stayed in the marina. We finally broke down and used the air conditioner we'd bought in the USVI, but now we felt we were warehousing ourselves. It could have been worse. It was just as hot, if not hotter in Colombia.

I loved Aruba and the people, but I hated just sitting there. We needed a plan. After much discussion, Dan and I decided that instead of flying to Illinois at Christmas and losing good sailing weather, we would fly back now. I could get schoolbooks for next year, we could see our families, and we could spend some time touring the US. When we came back, we would head to Colombia. It was the perfect plan.

23

The Train, the RV, and the Bear

USA

THE SEPTEMBER WEATHER IN CHICAGO was fantastic. It had been awhile since we had experienced an early fall in the Midwest. After spending a week with our families, we made plans to head out west to see the Grand Canyon. Tristan and Tessa had seen so much of other countries; it was time to see the US.

Our first idea was to rent a tent and camp, but Dan found a great deal on RV rentals. A one-way, 31-foot RV rental was only $9.95 per day. We had to pick it up in San Francisco and deliver it to Nashville Tennessee, but that wasn't a problem. Dan booked us on Amtrak, and we took the California Zephyr, a fifty-three hour train ride from Chicago, through the Rocky Mountains, past the Sierra Nevada mountain range, to San Francisco.

September 14, 2009 The Amtrak California Zephyr, Chicago
(*from the blog of* Alegria)

> At 1:30 p.m. we found the line forming to board our train. It was a very mixed group of passengers. There was, of course, the long-haired, bearded, poncho wearing, Jesus look-alike, who I'm sure is mandatory on every Greyhound

bus and train in America. He contrasted nicely with the Amish (I think that's what they were), with their old-fashioned trousers and vests, hats, and beards. I thought Amish shunned the modern world, but this family must have needed to travel far. The final destination of our train was San Francisco. Dan and I couldn't see the Amish in San Francisco, and figured they would be exiting somewhere around Nebraska, although we never confirmed this.

Senior citizens formed a majority of the riders. We didn't see any children, but there were several twenty-somethings and a few international travelers. There seemed to be an unusually high number of musicians, or people carrying guitars or other instruments. They didn't seem to be together, but maybe train travel brings out the musician in all of us.

We had coach seats. Since there were no reserved seats in coach, I wanted to board as soon as possible to make sure we had seats together. Dan wanted to board as late as possible to make sure we had seats not near the poncho guy or the musicians. I thought it might be fun to sit next to the older Latino gentleman with the guitar. The fact that the guitar was not in a case signaled to me he was ready to play, and ready to play often. Unfortunately it signaled the same thing to Dan, who didn't have quite the same romantic notion of a Spanish serenade. We didn't have a choice though. The agent assigned us a car and seat by our destination. Our seat assignment put us in the second-to-last car, in front of a senior-citizen group headed to the casinos in Reno, Nevada.

To say we were overwhelmed by our train's seats would be an understatement. They were wide and extremely comfortable. Even when the seat in front of us was fully reclined, we had plenty of room. A huge window allowed an uninterrupted view of the ever-changing landscape. It was a far cry from cramped, airline seating and better than the Peru buses because we didn't have to worry about the engineer driving off a cliff. We departed on time and so smoothly, we only knew we were moving by the changing scenery outside our window.

The high rises and lofts of Chicago were gradually replaced by smaller urban neighborhoods and towns with brightly painted, old-fashioned depots. The train glided past large, green lawns, main streets, and parks with children, through people's backyards, and behind businesses. It seemed as if every small town was having some type of festival, with small crowds gathered near tents in the middle of town and children on miniature carnival rides. It was a glimpse into Midwestern, end-of-summer days. Some people ignored the train completely, while others waved enthusiastically. After years of waving to people on passing trains, I was excited to be the one waving back.

The train rolled on gathering speed, and gradually the chic towns were replaced farther west by working class, down-on-their-luck towns, until these too were replaced by endless rows of corn and soybeans. It was then that Debbie, our car attendant, introduced herself and encouraged us to get out of our seat and explore the observation car, the snack car, and move around the train in general. We took her advice and headed to the observation car. Dan got us drinks from the snack bar, and we relaxed and watched the world go by.

As we were enjoying ourselves, two women came into the car and sat next to a couple they had met earlier on the train. Some of the people on board had started their journey on the east coast. One of the women, in a thick southern accent, said she'd gotten on in Charlotte. Then she thought again and said maybe it was Charlottesville. Anyway, she was sure it was someplace in Virginia. She and her friend traveled a lot. "I always travel," she drawled, "even when I'm hung over."

They were funny, and we enjoyed listening to them talk. Even the Amish weren't immune to their charms. I was a bit surprised later to find one of the Amish men enjoying a root beer and the ladies' company. You can take the man out of the city, but you can't take the city out of the man.

The senior-citizen group was fun too. You could tell they were together because they wore matching shirts. They told us that twice a year they all got together and headed to the casino in Reno and gambled. I loved their energy.

The next morning we passed through Denver, Colorado and the Rocky Mountains. We had been told to be sure to have seats in the observation car during this leg of the trip. Dan, Tessa, and I sat at a table. Tristan sat next to an elderly gentleman, a veteran train traveler, who gave Tristan a bit of history about the route. The view was impressive. Switchbacks snaked their way up the mountains, peaks in the distance still clung to a bit of snow from last winter, and if you looked closely, you saw mule deer grazing near the tracks. We passed ski resorts and then for a long time followed the Colorado River.

The river was in heavy use with rafters and fly fishermen, surprising for this late in the summer. The colors were vibrant; the glistening river lined with red rocks gave way to green grasses and bushes just hinting at turning brown. There was so much to see, and I soaked it all in. Even after Dan went back to our car to take a nap, I stayed and wrote in my journal, played games with Tristan and Tessa, talked to other passengers, and gazed out the window. The only time I left the observation car was to eat in the dining car; another experience I absolutely loved.

The wildlife we saw from the train was amazing. In Colorado we saw a big antelope with large antlers, sitting near the tracks. I woke up early one morning to see a herd of wild mustangs, three adults and a foal, running on the plains outside my window in Nevada. We saw deer everywhere. I couldn't have been happier.

Our time on the train flew by. We even arrived early into Emeryville, California. Reluctantly, we got off the train and boarded the bus provided by Amtrak, which took us into San Francisco. The bus driver was so nice, he took us right to our hotel. It was time for our next adventure. Dan and I had both been to San Francisco several times before on business, but this was the kids' first time, so we spent one night in the city and did as much sight-seeing as we could. The next day we took a taxi to pick up the RV. [*End blog*]

I can't say enough good things about our time on the train. We loved it! The most surprising thing to me was how well everyone got along, even people from such different backgrounds. Everyone, including the Amtrak workers, was relaxed, friendly, and really tried to get to know the other passengers. It was very reminiscent of the sailing community.

We weren't sure what to expect, but we were pleasantly surprised. The RV was in great shape, almost like new, and it was big. Dan only had a short time to get used to driving it before he had to test his skills in a packed, shopping center parking lot, but he did great. We provisioned at a dollar store and a grocery store, then took the freeway out of town. We stopped for the night at a campground in Mariposa and left early the next morning for Yosemite.

We all fell in love with Yosemite National Park from the moment we drove in. We didn't know what to look at first: the towering pine trees, the granite-faced mountains, the flower-filled meadows, or the signs warning of bears. The park is extremely popular, and most people make reservations to camp at least a year in advance. Unfortunately we didn't know that, so we didn't have reservations. The park's website and a sign at the entrance said the campground was full, but we hoped, somehow, we would be able to stay the night.

The park ranger at the visitor's center confirmed the

campground had no vacancy. He told us to check at Curry Village, but he didn't sound optimistic. A Curry Village ranger put our names on a waiting list for campsites that would be assigned later that afternoon. If the campers with reservations hadn't shown up by then, the sites would go to the people on the waiting list. At 3 p.m. on the dot, the ranger assigned the remaining campsites. Our name was called (yes!) for a site at the Upper Pines campground. The campsite was quiet, shaded and, as the name suggested, beneath towering pine trees. Life was good.

After we had secured the RV, which by this time the kids had nicknamed "Awesome," we caught the free shuttle bus for a tour of the other areas in Yosemite. The big question on our minds as we went through the park was about bears. Would we see them? Everywhere in Yosemite, you were reminded to be careful with your food. It was mandatory each night to lock your food in the bear-proof lockers at your campsite. No food could be left in your car because bears could break in and did all the time. We watched a shocking video showing a bear taking his paw and actually bending down the metal window frame to get potato chips inside a car. If a bear wanted to, he could rip through Awesome's sides like a can opener. It was a frightening thought.

We roasted marshmallows over our campfire that night and made s'mores. Every noise we heard conjured up bears in our minds. When we went to bed, far off in the distance, we heard the sound of the bear patrol. A park ranger told us they patrolled the park nightly for bears. If they saw one, they would blow whistles and make banging sounds to scare it back into the mountains. It was important to keep the bears away because once they had a taste of human food, they wouldn't stop invading the campground. As a result, the bears would have to be totally removed from the park, or even sadder, they could accidentally get hit by cars and be killed or injured as they roamed in high-traffic areas. After hearing that, we no longer wanted to see a bear.

It was such beautiful weather that evening. We slept with the windows open. Later that night I was awakened by a noise. It was a loud crunching noise. I sat up in bed trying to figure out what it was and where it was coming from. After a moment I realized the sound was coming from outside our bedroom window. Groggily, I pulled back the curtain and looked out. I gasped. There sitting at the picnic table, as calm as could be, was a big bear munching on potato chips! I hit Dan repeatedly to wake him up.

"Bbbbear!" I could barely get the words out, I was so excited.

Dan shot upright, barely awake. "What? Where?"

I pointed out the window. "He's at the picnic table eating potato chips. Get the flashlight!"

I kept my eye on the bear, while Dan fumbled for the high-powered flashlight he kept next to the bed in anticipation of an event like this. I was worried about the people in the campsite next to us. While we were safe in our RV, even if the bear could have ripped open the door had he wanted to, our neighbors were in a tiny, flimsy tent, also known to the bear as a "Hot Pocket." I needed to warn them.

Dan lit up the intruder with an intense beam from our flashlight, while I screamed "Bear!" to alert our neighbors.

The bright light from the flashlight caused the bear to freeze. One paw was frozen halfway to his mouth, while the other paw plastered the bag of potato chips to his chest. The bear's jaw dropped open in surprise.

Except, it turned out it wasn't a bear. It turned out to be the camper next door, the one I was trying to warn, noisily wolfing down a late-night snack.

When the light hit him, the crunching stopped and our terrified neighbor froze. He had heard me yell, "Bear!" so when Dan shone the flashlight, he must have thought the bear was right behind him. I think we nearly scared him to death! At the very least, I am sure he soiled himself.

Dan managed to shout out, "Sorry!" before we collapsed into uncontrollable laughter. We were laughing so hard, Tessa and Tristan ran into our room to see what was going on. The crunching stopped, and we think our neighbor crawled into his tent to change his pants. Our window was still open, and I'm sure he heard us laughing late into the night. We never did see a real bear in the park.

We spent the next two days in Yosemite, and we were lucky to have a campsite each night. We spent our days listening to lectures about the park, hiking, and biking. The kids finished their Junior Ranger program at the park. They had to attend one ranger-led discussion, answer questions in a booklet about Yosemite, and then answer test questions asked by the park ranger. They passed, and the ranger swore them in, gave them badges, and announced to the group in the visitor's center that Tristan and Tessa were new Junior Rangers. People applauded. As a reward, we treated them to ice cream.

Later that night, we took our chairs to the "boardwalk," a wooden walkway crossing the open meadow in the valley. We had attended a ranger talk earlier about the tarantulas in the park, so now we were worried about them as much as the bears. We kept our feet off the ground as we sat in our chairs. For a long time, we watched the stars in the night sky framed by tall pine trees and sheer-rock faces. We would be sad to leave the next day, but we had a lot of miles to cover to our next national park, the Grand Canyon.

September 22, 2009 The Grand Canyon, Arizona
(*from the blog of* Alegria)

Around noon when the sun was directly overhead, we had our first look at the canyon. We thought it was beautiful, not spectacular. We tried the view from different overlooks, but we had the same reaction. I think it was just us though. I think we were jaded by seeing Colca Canyon in Peru first. Also, it felt like we had just driven off a major highway, parked the car, and looked down, almost anticlimactically. I don't know what I was expecting, but I didn't expect it to be almost a drive-up view. We gazed at the canyon for what we hoped was an acceptable amount of time, then disappointed, we wandered off to find something else to see.

A ranger walk was starting, so we tagged along, hoping to get a better feel for the canyon. During the walk the ranger told us to be aware of the elk in the park. It was mating season, and they were unpredictable. There were signs all over the park warning visitors to stay 45 feet away from the elk. Fine. I was really interested in seeing a bear. An elk? Not so much.

As the sun set, we decided to give the view one more try. What a difference lighting makes. We sat at the Lookout and watched the sun's dying light cast purple and red shadows on the rocks, highlighting a few deep canyons we hadn't seen before. The sunset gave the canyon a three-dimensional look not seen in harsh daylight. We were impressed.

Our campground didn't have lights, and our campsite was a fair walk from the shuttle-bus stop and hidden in a thicket; without sunlight or a flashlight, we would never find it. Reluctantly, we headed to the bus stop. Tessa sat across from me in the bus shelter. Suddenly she pointed behind me and yelled, "Elk!" I turned around and sure enough, coming towards us, was a huge male elk. It was my first wild elk sighting, and I was speechless. The male elk came from the parking lot below and headed for the grass near the lodge and bus shelter, passing within 15 feet of us (a blatant disregard of the recommended 45-foot safe zone). He was huge. I imagined an elk would be very much like a big deer, but there was no comparison. He walked calmly by us, head up and proud, eyeballing us the whole time. He wasn't worried about us, but wanted us to know we needed to be worried about him. We got the message and remained in the shelter until our bus arrived and took us back to our campground.

It was warm enough in the early evening that we were able to eat our dinner outside at the picnic table. Dan built a fire and the kids roasted marshmallows. Afterwards Tristan and Tessa went inside to work on their homework and Dan followed. I stayed outside a little longer, watching the stars and calling friends. It was nice to be able to talk to someone without losing the phone signal like we did on *Alegria* every time the boat moved. Soon it was too cold for me, and the dark campground was emitting scary, rustling noises, so I decided to go inside. As I walked around the front of the RV, I heard a tree branch snap. I froze, sure an elk was lurking in the darkness. When I thought the coast was clear, I dashed inside.

Inside the RV, it was quiet—too quiet. The door was locked, and all the shades were drawn. It was weird being enclosed and not knowing what was happening outside. The kids and I felt uneasy, and we weren't sure why. Tessa glanced toward the closed shades and whispered, "I saw a light or something go by the window."

I looked at her. Tristan looked at me. Our imaginations ran wild. I thought of the scary movies I had watched of people camping in the woods. Dark nights, no lights, no one around, suddenly...bang! Bang! There was a loud rapping on the door. The kids and I nearly jumped out of our skin.

"Dan," I almost screamed, "Someone's at the door!"

Dan, who'd been in the bedroom working on his computer, looked at us like we were crazy as he answered the door. The would-be axe murderer was actually a park ranger. First, she informed us that we couldn't run our generator because it was quiet hour. (Yes, we noticed the quiet!) Second, we (I) had left our fire outside unattended, and all the signs clearly stated that we were at the peak of fire season. Don't leave fires unattended. As she said this, her hand reached for the gun on her hip and she said to

Dan, "Just give me a reason."

Sorry. She didn't say that. She did tell him to turn off the generator and put out the fire though. Still, it was scary.

You know, people ask me all the time: Don't you get scared out on the ocean? You're in a strange country, maybe the only boat in a dark cove, aren't you afraid of pirates? I can honestly say, I was more afraid in the US, locked inside an RV. On the boat, we are as much outside as inside, even at night. If something or someone comes up to the boat, we'll likely hear it. In an RV, once you go inside, everything is closed up—the doors, the curtains. You lose your sense of what is going on outside. Even when we slept with the RV windows open, we locked ourselves away from the outside. That made me more afraid. [*End blog*]

24

Unless You Speak German

W E STOPPED FOR A FEW days in Sedona, Arizona to hike and meet up with friends. Fred and Kathy, our sailing friends normally on *Makai.* were taking a break from their boat and just happened to be in the same area as we were. It was a nice reunion. The last time we'd seen them was nearly a year before in Grenada. They picked our brains on Peru and gave us advice on places to see when we passed through Utah. When we parted, we had no idea when we would see them again. They would go back to *Makai* and sail east, and we would be sailing west. There is so much to be said about the friendships you make while cruising. I think those are friendships you keep for life.

September 27, 2009 Monument Valley, Utah
(from the blog of Alegria)

The changing landscape never ceased to impress us as we crossed through Arizona and Utah on our way to Colorado. The sky was clear and we could see for miles, our sight blocked occasionally by the giant, red-rock formations of Monument Valley. This was a long stretch of road, devoid of trees and towns. We stopped for the night at Goulding's Trading Post campground, hoping to get into a campsite. It was late, and it was the only campground around for miles. When I called for reservations earlier, the attendant had told me she had one site left and asked me the size of our RV. When I replied 31 feet, she said we were too big for the site, but we could camp across the street for $10 less without water, sewer, or electricity. That seemed a high price for us to park in a parking lot, but it sounded like we had no choice.

When we pulled into the campground a few hours later, I went to the office and again asked if there was anything available, hoping our luck had changed. The attendant asked me what size we were, and this time I replied *30* feet. She said she had one spot left and it would be very tight, but we were welcome to try. Loving a challenge, as well as electricity, we decided to give it a shot.

Dan drove Awesome carefully down the very narrow road cutting between the campsites. The sites were so small, the RVs were nearly on top of one another. We found our spot, and it would be tight. On one side was a Danish couple in a smaller RV, backed in at an angle. On the other side, parallel parked and taking up two spots, was an RV occupied by a German couple. They were traveling with another German couple, who had also parallel parked. A fence lined the back of our site, and across the road, other RVs and an oversized pickup truck crowded right to the edge of the pavement. There was little room for Dan to back in, but that was what he had to do.

Tristan took his usual spot at the back of Awesome, right on the fence line, and I guided Dan from the front and side. As soon as Dan started to back up, everyone came out to give advice. The Danish guy was saying something in Dutch and pointing a finger toward the road. Two German men were at Dan's window, giving him directions in German; one of them pointing one way, and the other pointing the opposite way. Getting no response from Dan, the Dutch man changed tactics and started talking to me, then so did the Germans. All I could say was "Yes. I see." Which, of course, I didn't.

At one point, Tristan was by the fence motioning Dan to keep moving back, while I also signaled for Dan to back up. At the same time, however, a German man was in Dan's window signaling him to turn his wheels the opposite way Tristan and I were saying, the other German guy was signaling Dan to stop, and the Dutch guy was telling him what, I have no idea. Dan was a deer in headlights. He kept turning the wheels, first one way then the other, but was too confused to actually step on the gas. I stepped up to the window, parting the crowd "Dan. What's the problem?"

"Everyone is telling me different ways to go. I don't know who to listen to."

"Well, unless you speak German or Dutch, you need to listen to the person speaking English." That seemed fairly obvious didn't it?

We finally cleared everyone away, and Dan backed the RV perfectly into the spot. Well, not perfectly the first time. It took several times of going in and out, but finally Awesome was in with the back bumper an inch off the fence and the front tire just barely off the road. We did it. Triumphantly, we swaggered up to the office to pay our fee.

On the way back, we stopped to talk to one of our German neighbors. He didn't speak a word of English, so he fetched his wife. She told us they were traveling in a big group of RVs touring the Western US and loving it. They had parked their RVs parallel because the site was too small for their 20-foot RV (score one for team BeDell and our parking prowess). The woman was very nice and told us she and her traveling companions loved the US. After spending so much time enjoying other countries, it was nice to see people from other countries enjoying ours.

Even though we were packed in like sardines, we liked the campground, which was encircled by high canyon walls. That night it was pitch-black, there were thousands of stars, and we were serenaded to sleep by the far off yip-yips of coyotes. The next morning Dan and I got up early and walked around the grounds. We were treated to a beautiful gold and red sunrise. Hanging high above, between the canyon walls, was a cloud shaped in the form of an angel lying on its side. We watched as the sun came up, eventually washing the gold to white, and our angel gradually blended into the sky. [*End blog*]

We kept heading east, stopping at the Four Corners, the spot in the US where the four states of Colorado, Utah, Arizona, and New Mexico come together. Yes we took the classic picture of us standing in each state. Then we moved onward, stopping at Mesa Verde National Park and Telluride, both in Colorado. We were trying to stop at as many National Parks as we could so Tristan and Tessa could earn their Junior Ranger badges. It was impressive to see how much they were learning.

September 30, 2009 Rocky Mountain National Park, Colorado
(from the blog of Alegria)

We really weren't expecting snow on this trip. I mean, late September and snow?

Driving from Mesa Verde to Rocky Mountain National Park was tough on our RV. The roads were steep and Awesome was really straining at times. Then we had the wind. The forecast called for gusts of up to 75 miles per hour (*what?!*) and we reached our KOA campground in Estes Park just in time. Even though we were protected by trees and other campers, the wind still rocked the RV hard. The next morning storm clouds were gathering over the distant peaks.

Our plan was to enter the park and drive across Trail Ridge Road. Trail Ridge Road is 8 miles across and 11,000 feet high, connecting the east side of the park to the west side. Its highest point is 12,183 feet. With the winds and the coming storm, we knew this was not a job for Awesome, so Dan rented a very small car. We loaded up with drinks, cameras, snacks, and as we found out later, not nearly enough warm clothes, and headed into the gathering storm.

The roads inside the park are very well marked. It was easy to find our way. First stop was the ranger station to pick up the Junior Ranger books and watch a movie about the park and the building of Trail Ridge Road back in 1920. Later, as we drove through the park, we stopped at a turnout to watch a large herd of elk lounging in a beautiful meadow below a snow-kissed peak.

From there, the road climbed quickly, and as it did, the sky grew darker and the wind stronger. Suddenly the snow came, gently at first, then harder and harder. Dan pulled the car onto an overlook, and we all got out. The wind whipped the snow harshly into our faces, making it very cold and very hard to walk. We loved it though. We laughed, jumped up and down to keep warm, and the kids tried to catch snowflakes on their tongues. When we couldn't bear the cold any longer, we raced as best we could against the howling wind back to the car, laughing all the way.

The higher we went, the faster the snow accumulated. We reached the highest spot, 12,000 feet, and we could barely see the road. I told Dan we needed to turn around. Not only could we not see, but there was a real danger of us getting to the end of Trail Ridge Road (we were almost there) and the park rangers closing it, not allowing us go back the way we came. If that happened, we would have to drive four or five hours all the way around the outside of the park to get back to Awesome and the campground. Since it was nearly 4 p.m. already, that wouldn't be fun...or safe.

But where to turn around? It was impossible to see if anything was in front of us or coming from behind us. On my side of the road was the mountain wall; the other side was a sheer drop-off. Thankfully the car was small and didn't need much room. Dan took a chance, and after executing a very cumbersome five-point turn, had us heading back down the mountain. As we hit the lower altitudes, the snow turned into rain. Later we found out that at 4 p.m. that day, Trial Ridge Road was officially closed for the winter. [*End blog*]

We spent the rest of our time at the lower altitudes, stopping at the Royal Gorge before leaving the state. New Mexico was new to all of us. Our favorite moments were basking in the hot springs of Ojo Caliente outside of Taos, learning the legend of the mysterious staircase in the Loretto Chapel in Santa Fe, and being camped close to the grounds for the hot-air balloon rally in Albuquerque.

The strong winds seemed to follow us south from Colorado. It made for intense skies over New Mexico. One night we found a small campground just off the road, outside of Santa Fe. It wasn't very scenic, but with the wind and the fierce-looking sky, we chose to stop. Dan paid for our campsite, and the attendant warned him to be careful walking around the grounds. The night before, a mother bear and her two cubs had crossed the road not too far from there. Later that evening, over the howling wind, we swore we heard the sound of a baby bear cub. We were too scared to open the door and look. Instead we hid the potato chips.

After New Mexico, we settled in for the long drive to Tennessee. Tristan and Tessa earned their last Junior Ranger badges at what became one of our favorite parks, the Smoky Mountains National Park in Tennessee. While I loved the taller, rockier mountains in the west, the rushing waterfalls and the mist-covered, lush, green mountains in the Smoky Mountains National Park will always hold a special place in my heart.

We spent our last night in a campsite close to the Grand

Ole Opry, in Nashville. The next morning we dropped Awesome off at the delivery point, rented a car, and drove seven hours back to Illinois.

We really enjoyed our camping adventure and loved the RV. The campgrounds were nice, and most had Wi-Fi, making it easy to keep up with homeschooling. During that time, we used a lot of free homeschooling resources off the internet, so that really helped.

We never really got the hang of making the RV "heel proof." On a monohull sailboat, before you take off, you have to make sure everything is put away so it doesn't slide around during your sail. On a catamaran, like *Alegria*, you don't have to be as vigilant because it rides fairly level. Well, the RV was no catamaran. No matter how careful we were, cabinets would open, pans would fly out, and drinks would roll down the aisle.

One time the coffee maker flew out of a top cabinet and hurled right into a screaming Tristan. The cans of soft drinks and bottles of water never remained in one place. The joke became that if you wanted a soda, just wait until Dan stepped on the brakes; you could catch one as it rolled by. But all in all, we loved Awesome and would definitely rent an RV again.

A Change of Plans

ARUBA

W E RETURNED TO *ALEGRIA* SHORTLY after Halloween, which allowed the kids to trick or treat in Illinois. After celebrating the past two Halloweens in the Dominican Republic and Venezuela, Tristan and Tessa deserved a US Halloween. They scored more candy than they could ever possibly eat. I dutifully carried it on the airplane (I didn't want it to melt in the checked bags) and promptly forgot about it and left it on the plane. I wasn't the most popular person after that.

It was November—time to head to Colombia. I again provisioned, this was my third time, I believe, and we had a great weather window. We were excited until Dan changed the oil and found a leak in one of the saildrives. This was bad news. We couldn't leave without repairing it. The crew of *Alegria* was at a low point.

There are very few things that require the boat being hauled out of the water to fix, but this was one of them. Unfortunately for catamaran owners, Aruba is not where you want to be hauled out. The boatyard didn't have a travel lift wide enough for *Alegria*, so we had to rent a crane. It was expensive and dangerous. Having our home picked up out of the water by a giant crane and swung across the boatyard was not something we wanted to witness, but we had no choice. Thankfully, it went smoothly and *Alegria* wasn't dropped onto the pavement.

Once the boat was out of the water and Dan could perform a thorough inspection, he realized parts of *both* saildrives had electrolysis damage. This would be a major and time-consuming repair. Add the need for new boat batteries, and we realized another trip to the US was necessary. It was the cheapest (but still very costly) and fastest way to get everything we needed. In the back of my mind was a constant worry, would we ever get out of Aruba?

Dan was set to buy an airplane ticket to Florida when we got the news. In three days, the crane operator would be taking off for the holidays. If we couldn't get the repair completed by then, we would have to wait until after the first of the year before *Alegria* could be put back into the water. There was no way the repairs would be done by then. We needed a new plan. Christmas in Cartagena, Colombia, turned into Christmas in the US. Colombia seemed very far away.

It took some time for Dan to find the parts he needed. December stretched into late January before he flew back to Aruba by himself. There was no way I was going to live on the boat in the boatyard any longer than I had to, so the kids and I stayed with my parents in Illinois. My parents were in their late eighties, and my Mom had cancer, so it was nice to for us to be able to spend some good, quality time together. I also was able to spend more time with my sisters and brother. Tristan and Tessa worked diligently on their homeschooling. We took advantage of the free museum days in Chicago, and by the time we left Illinois, they were ahead in their schoolwork.

A wonderful added bonus to my time in Illinois was that I was able to reconnect with my old high-school friends. What started as a small dinner, turned into a late night gabfest with many of my long lost girl friends, including Jackie, Penny, Stacie, Angela, and Lori. Since I had missed the last class reunions, I hadn't seen many of them for years. It was great to reconnect, but also great to remember who I was, or more specifically, who I had been. As we talked about the crazy things we'd done in high school, it took me by surprise. More and more, the stories of the instigator of the fun times led back to me. It really came as a shock to me. Was I really that fun and crazy with my friends back in high school? I was. What happened to that girl?

Before the boat trip, I had gotten so serious with trying to be the best in the corporate world. The constant competition meant that I had to live in the right neighborhood, ensure my kids went to the right schools, make sure I was as good a mom as the stay-at-home moms, and make sure I made the money, and lots of it, because in my old world, money defined you. I had been constantly stressed and tired. While I'd known that this couldn't be how life was supposed to be, I'd felt too trapped to change it. I had forgotten that life wasn't meant to be so serious. Life was meant to be fun. In order to find out who I was meant to be going forward, I'd needed this trip backwards to find out who I was, and to no longer let society define me. That trip down memory lane with my girlfriends was an unexpected gift.

Back in Aruba, the boat repairs moved along slowly. The best mechanic Dan could find was the one who worked on the tourist submarine. The mechanic could only work in his spare time, so he and Dan spent many late nights working on our installation. When it was nearly complete, I made arrangements for the kids and me to fly back to Aruba. We finally returned to *Alegria* in late March, but still in boatyard hell.

April 16, 2010 Boatyard Hell, Aruba
(from the blog of Alegria)

It is awful living on the hard in Aruba, or for you non sailors, living in the boatyard. Really, it's not the place to live on board. The wind is constant, and our boat is forever buried in dust. No matter how diligent I am, I can't keep it clean. But we pray for the wind because when it dies, the mosquitoes are vicious. And if the mosquitoes don't drive us mad, the constant inundation of flies absolutely will. There are no restroom or shower facilities at the boatyard. We could shower on the boat, but bathrooms? Well, we had to improvise.

Before Dan came back to Aruba in January, we went to Walmart and found a Porta-Potty (portable toilet). Well, not actually a Porta-Potty, that was too big and heavy for Dan to bring back on the plane. Instead, we purchased the Fold-To-Go, a unique product which is like a small lawn chair with a toilet seat. A replaceable bag attaches to the seat for the waste.

Who thought of this? Was someone sitting in a lawn chair at their kid's soccer game, realizing they had to go to the bathroom, but where? Idea! "What if I could just go where I sit?" Ding! Ding! The Fold-To-Go was born!

The waste bags were expensive, and of course, sold separately. Knowing we would go broke buying enough bags for our stay, we opted to use garbage bags. Such is my life. Emptying the bags is our worst nightmare. I am responsible for removing the bag, but the carrying-to-the-dumpster job falls to whoever has irritated me the most that day. Our boat motto is "Stay on Mom's good side!" [*End blog*]

The repair was finally finished. We had touched up the bottom paint, and we were ready to go back in the water, but we still had to wait until the crane was available. While we waited, we had a decision to make. Were we going to sail to Colombia or was our trip coming to an end?

When we started the trip, we had only planned to be out for two years. We were starting on our fourth year. Sailing to Colombia just wasn't feeling good anymore, but I didn't want to keep sailing in the same areas we had in the past. Obviously, financially, we couldn't stay out forever. Maybe it was time to go home?

April 30, 2010, Aruba
(from the blog of Alegria)

Alegria was finally fixed. The crane was coming the next day to put her back into the water, and we needed to decide what we were going to do after that. One of the best parts of the last several years, besides being together, was sailing to new places. That came to a standstill once we arrived in Aruba. Flying to Peru and Chile had worked out great, but we didn't like being stuck in Aruba (or anywhere), waiting until a weather window opened up to allow us to sail on to Colombia. In fact, that was the hardest part of this trip and the biggest source of problems between Dan and me—the waiting for good weather. We had tried three times to sail to Colombia, and every time something prevented us from going. Maybe that was a sign.

With an hour to play with before finalizing our next day's commitment to put *Alegria* back into the water, I looked at Dan and asked, "Want to go somewhere?"

The boatyard, while not great for living on the boat, was perfect for *storing* the boat. After getting out the kids' world atlas, talking with them, and deciding where each person's interest lay, we made plans. A week later, we had our tickets purchased to Ecuador, flying back through Colombia.

It was a tough call at first between South America and Central America, but the airfares were much better to

South America. Then it was a tough call between Argentina and Ecuador, but eventually the fact that it would be much colder in Argentina gave Ecuador and Colombia the win.

Our current plan is to keep the boat on the hard until our return from Ecuador in July, then head back east instead of west—unless plans change. [*End blog*]

It really wasn't until later, when we were back in the US permanently, that we realized what an affect this had on the kids, especially Tessa. Someone asked her what was the best thing about the boat trip. She replied, "When you wanted to go somewhere, you just went." We sure did.

26

Lost in the Amazon

ECUADOR

May 5, 2010 Quito, Ecuador
(from the blog of Alegria)

Our flight from Aruba into Quito, Ecuador arrived at close to midnight. It was raining. Our hostel, the Chicago Hostel, seemed dark, and we were getting a touch of altitude sickness. I was extremely thirsty, but the hostel was out of bottled water, so I had to settle for an orange soda. We were not off to a good start. *(We decided that this trip, we would stay in hostels instead of hotels. We had a good experience with the one in Peru, and hostels would be cheaper and help us connect more with our fellow travelers.)*

The next morning everything was better. Our rooms and the rooftop terrace have great views of the mountains, or rather volcanoes, surrounding the city. The altitude here is 9,400 feet, yet the active volcanoes in the distance still tower above us.

Quito, the capital, is divided into Old Town and New Town, and we walked to Old Town first. We toured the massive cathedrals and churches. Most of them were free. La Campania de Jesus was well worth the price of admission. The interior of the church is covered in 23-carat gold. It is beautiful if not excessive. The rest of the day we visited the presidential palace, the parks, and plazas. By the end of the day, the extensive walking and the altitude got the better of us. [*End blog*]

Ecuador is a small country, about the size of Nevada, but there is so much to do. Quito is situated right on the equator, but its altitude keeps it a spring-like high of 60 degrees. It's very diverse ecologically. The country is almost split down the middle by the Avenue of the Volcanoes. To the west, you have cloud forests, then the coast. To the east, you have cloud forests, then the Amazon jungle.

Ecuador is a volcano lover's dream. It boasts fifty-nine volcanoes on its mainland, fourteen of them over 15,000 feet tall, and these can all be seen in a five- to six-hour car ride. Most of the volcanoes are active. Cotopaxi is one of the highest active volcanoes on earth, and Chimborazo is not only the tallest peak in Ecuador, but is also the spot on earth closest to the sun. There was so much there for us to explore, it was hard to decide what to do first. We put it to a vote and unanimously decided on the Amazon.

May 8, 2010 Quito, Ecuador
(*from the blog of* Alegria)

Pablo at Dracaena Tours put our tour together. He gave us several options: three nights in the jungle; four nights in the jungle; or even eight nights, where you traveled by canoe and camped on the river bank each night. Dan's interest was piqued until Pablo said we would bathe in the river and dig our own toilets in the jungle. Hearing that, Dan decided the four-night trip was better. The biggest issue was getting to the Amazon and back. It was a ten- to twelve-hour bus ride and the Ecuadorian buses were not nearly as nice as the ones in Peru. Pablo gave us the option of taking a private taxi to the jungle, then flying back to

Quito. It would cost more, but along the way we could stop at Papallacta, the hot springs high in the Andes. That sounded good to us. We would leave the next morning, on Mother's Day, and be in the Amazon on Monday. [*End blog*]

Mother's Day was off to a great start. At 8 a.m. sharp, Pablo and our driver Ricardo arrived outside our hostel. Since Ricardo spoke even less English than we did Spanish, Pablo came along to get us settled. The language barrier would make for an interesting seven-hour trip.

Before we left, Pablo again reiterated we could stop wherever we wanted. As we hopped into the dual-cab pickup, the weather in Quito was a comfortable 60 degrees with sunny skies. Over the course of the trip, the weather would change dramatically.

The ride started out smooth. Not too far outside of Quito, we headed straight up. That was a surprise. We were already over 9,000 feet, and I had expected we would be heading down to the Amazon, not up. The higher we climbed, the more the clouds and patches of rain moved in and the temperature dropped. Ricardo anticipated this and handed us a blanket. Tristan looked up the route in the guidebook, and it showed us going up to 13,451 feet. It would definitely get much colder.

There wasn't much to see at this altitude because the clouds covered everything. Occasionally we saw a small house or a cow, but mainly the view was rocky soil with little growth. Two hours later, and at a little lower altitude of 11,000 feet, we arrived at the town of Papallacta, home of Termas de Papallacta, the best hot springs in Ecuador.

It was still early, so the springs were not crowded, but the weather was cold and rainy. There were multiple pools in large medium and small sizes, secluded behind lush trees or bushes with red and orange flowers. It was a beautiful garden, with the baths tiled in blue and stone paths leading from one pool to another.

We hurried to the closest one. People were staring at us, but they smiled and we smiled back. On a clear-weather day, the sunlight would have been intense, allowing us to see snow-capped Antisana, a volcano that erupted in 2002, but today the clouds blocked our view. But still, sitting in the hot springs at 11,000 feet with my family, the rain gently falling, the clouds incredibly close, an active volcano standing guard; it was a great Mother's Day.

A little over an hour later, we were back in the car, continuing our journey. We had just driven out of Papallacta when Ricardo's cell phone rang. He pulled to the side to take the call. The conversation was in Spanish, but we were able to understand that he was telling someone we were just leaving the hot springs and had about five or six hours to go. Later he received a second call and began to drive faster.

The scenery along the road to Lago Agrio was stunning. It seemed that every time we rounded a hairpin turn, we spotted yet another waterfall. Tessa amused Tristan by quoting from the Spanish phrasebook, trying to find the funniest phrases. First the Spanish, then the translation— then they'd both dissolve into giggles.

Tessa: "*El pasajero se comporta de forma sospechosa.* The passenger was behaving suspiciously." Tristan and Tessa would then crack up.

Tessa: "*Necesito una bolsa parael el mareo.* I need a sickness bag."

More laughter. She was doing a good job with the Spanish, but I cautioned her: "Stop it! You know, Ricardo can understand what you are saying!" This made them laugh hysterically. My admonishment only fueled the fire.

Tessa: "*Huelo algo extrano.* I smell something strange."

Side splitting laughter that time. Even I was laughing. Ricardo was chuckling too. This went on for another half hour before things turned dark.

Ricardo's phone rang again. Dan and I were starting to

put the picture together. It was Mother's Day, and he was supposed to be somewhere else, not driving us to Lago Agrio. Every time the phone rang, Ricardo drove faster. This wouldn't have been a problem, but, as I mentioned, the roads were very winding.

"Mom, I think I'm going to throw up," said Tristan.

"No. No you're not." I handed him a wet wipe to put behind his neck. It didn't help. Again he said he was going to be sick. "Take your finger and start tapping on the middle of your forehead."

Okay—I know this sounds strange, but sometimes it works. Tristan started tapping, but he wasn't doing it with much enthusiasm. I leaned over Tessa, who was in between us, and started tapping on Tristan's forehead. I wasn't sure how long I could keep it up. When Ricardo made sharp turns, my finger landed in my son's eye.

"Ow!" Tristan said, adding that he felt better. Was that true or was he afraid of going blind?

By now it was lunchtime, and those of us who weren't carsick were starving. We kept thinking Ricardo would stop for lunch soon, but he showed no indication.

Tessa yelled, "I'm going to throw up!" and clamped her hands over her mouth.

"No! Tap your forehead!"

The scenery was rushing by. Ricardo was nearly on two wheels around the sharp curves and I—like a crazy woman—was tapping on my daughter's forehead.

"It's not working," she cried.

"Pinch your earlobe instead." At this point I was just making stuff up, but what would you have done? There was no place to pull over, and I didn't even know the proper phrase.

I tapped Ricardo on the shoulder. "*Mas despacio, por favor.*" He understood and slowed down. Meanwhile I kept tapping Tessa's head and pinching her earlobe. My Mother's Day bliss was fast heading for the toilet. Ricardo finally pulled off onto a side road, and I had Tessa walk around, hoping it would settle her stomach. Over the next twenty minutes we had to stop the car twice more. Finally I got smart and had Tessa sit by the door where, for the rest of the trip, she hung her head out the window like a dog. She felt better. Problem solved. Now it was my turn to sit in the middle and become sick.

We passed through a small town with a roadside restaurant. I said to Ricardo *"Necesito almuerzo* (lunch)."

He shook his head and replied in English, "No. Not good here. Lago Agrio eat." The restaurant looked fine to us, and we'd eaten in all kinds of places, but it was clear he had no intentions of stopping. He said it wasn't much farther, about 95 kilometers. He did stop at a gas station when I asked him to, and we were able to get some Gatorade. It seemed to help everybody.

Throughout this drama, we were passing by an ever-changing panorama. We spotted so many waterfalls springing from the sides of lush, green mountains, that I stopped taking pictures. Gradually the road became straighter and the terrain more open. Even the rain gave way to sunny skies.

But soon the beauty of the landscape was marred by a very large, rust-colored pipe running parallel to the road. An oil pipeline. It brought oil from the Amazon to the Northern Provinces in Ecuador. The Amazon, home to some of the most unique and endangered flora and fauna in the world, was also home, unfortunately, to oil.

As the landscape flattened, the temperature rose. There were fewer trees and more grass, also small communities and more traffic. Large oil-company trucks dominated the road. It was close to five that afternoon when we pulled into the unglamorous, oil town of Lago Agrio. Ricardo dropped us off at our hotel. Although it wasn't great, it was the best available on the strip and was where we would be picked up in the morning for the remainder of our journey to the Cuyabeno Reserve in the Amazon. Most importantly, it had air conditioning. The heat was absolutely stifling.

The next morning we joined Ricardo in his pickup truck for the two-hour ride to the river, where we expected to spend three hours on a canoe trip to the Cuyabeno Reserve. It would be a long day, but hopefully fun.

Again, the drive was a very long two hours. The paved road soon gave way to a bumpy gravel road, with people standing along the side, usually a family with a baby, hoping to catch a ride. Ricardo picked some of them up in the middle of nowhere and dropped them off farther down the road, a place equally in the middle of nowhere. We passed an oil facility with armed guards, but other than that, there were just miles of tree-lined road. Finally, Ricardo pulled off the main road and came to a stop by the riverbank. This was as far as we could go by car.

While waiting for the canoe, we ate the lunch Ricardo provided: chicken with salsa and rice. For dessert there was *maracuya*, a yellow, egg-shaped type of passion fruit. The outer coating was thick, and we had to rip it open to get to the seeds covered in pulp. You eat both the seeds and the pulp. The taste was refreshing, not too sweet and not too tart.

The canoe arrived just after we finished eating. The workers loaded our luggage in the front and covered it with a tarp. They also loaded eggs, crates, and a few large heavy barrels. The long canoe was made of wood and had a fast motor. The plank seats were wide enough for two people. Dan and I sat in front of the kids, the two guides behind them, and the driver in back.

Before departing, the guides handed each of us a thick, rubber poncho. As we started down the river, the sky was cloudy. A short while later, the clouds opened up and for the next hour, we endured a torrential rain so strong it was like being in a car wash. There was nothing to do but huddle under our ponchos and hope the driver knew where he was going as we raced along in the whiteout. When the rain finally ended, the blue skies returned.

It was a busy day on the water. We passed barges carrying trucks, barges loaded with supplies, and smaller canoes like our own, carrying families. Many people were bathing in the water or doing laundry. When Dan was growing up in Illinois, he'd spent many days boating and fishing with his grandfather, who lived on a river, so he was really enjoying this part of the trip. This was a new world for our kids, however, seeing how communities lived and worked near a major waterway.

Our driver steered us off the main river and onto the Cuyabeno River. About thirty minutes later, we again branched off and soon arrived at the lodge. Okay, it wasn't really a lodge. There was one open-air building and some cabins. The big building was right beside the river. Hammocks hung from its ceiling, and there were a few long dining tables. Behind this were the cabins, cute wooden buildings with thatched roofs, more like huts. Paula, a petite, friendly young woman, not much taller than the kids, met us as we got out of the canoe. She showed us around and told us to take any cabin we wanted.

The cabins were identical. We picked a weathered one in the second row. It was built about 3 feet off the ground, had a small front porch with a hammock, and was divided into two sleeping areas. Each section had three twin beds and a bathroom with a sink and shower. The thatched eaves came down low on the sides to prevent rain from coming into the large open windows. In the bathroom, another long open window ran almost the length of the room, which meant no privacy but an excellent view into the jungle close behind the huts. A large, black cistern out back collected rainwater for our showers. The kids took the right side and we took the left. It was nice to have them next door so we could have some privacy. We dumped our bags onto one of the beds and headed off to find our guide, Paula.

Dinner was served at 6:00. We quickly understood we wouldn't go hungry here. First course was soup, then the main course of a meat and vegetable, followed by fruit for dessert. Paula ate dinner with us and filled us in on our itinerary. After dinner we would go out into the rainforest for an hour or so walk in the jungle...in the dark. Were we ready for that?

The night was pitch-black. We followed Paula into the supply building to get our rain ponchos and rubber boots. A giant cockroach scurried across the floor. Unfazed, Paula cautioned us to store our boots upside down at night so nothing crawled in, and to always be sure to check them before we put them on. After seeing the size of that cockroach, there was no way we would forget. A young man approached, and Paula introduced him as Claudio. He was of an ethnic group indigenous to the rainforest, a Quichua Indian, and spoke only Quichuan and Spanish—no English. He would be our guide for the night hike.

Tentatively, we put on our boots and ponchos, made sure our flashlights worked, and headed into the jungle just as it started to rain. To say we were a bit nervous was an understatement. It was raining, it was dark, there were all kinds of sounds we'd never heard before, and every so often there was a sound like something big crashing through the trees. The sound was getting closer. The vegetation was thick, and there was no discernible path. We gripped our flashlights tightly and stuck close to Paula as our guide, Claudio, channeled Sacajawea and led us deeper into the jungle. Sometimes he would motion us to stay where we were, and he would head off into the dark, leaving us alone with Paula. I'd panic after a bit, thinking he wasn't coming back, but then he would reappear and lead us to an extremely large spider or a multi-legged bug he had found. Sometimes he and Paula left together, leaving us huddled closely, flashlights pointed shakily at every sound. It was so dark and we were so disoriented; we had no clue what was going on.

Sacajawherearewe? I was sure we were lost. I was so sure we would be spending the night in the jungle that I seriously started taking inventory of what I had on me. Did I have food in my pockets? Could we start a fire? Would anyone ever find us? I was certainly not going to sit on the ground. Could I sleep standing up? Would those giant fruit bats flying overhead lay eggs in my hair and drive me crazy?

For our final bit of jungle fun, Paula had us stand in one place, turn off our flashlights, and listen to the sounds of the jungle. It was spooky. The Amazon is very noisy at night: buzzing, screeching, chirping, croaking—plus that crashing noise, which still seemed to be getting closer. After less than a minute in the dark, I felt a sharp bite on my leg. It hurt. I whispered to Dan that something had crawled up inside my pants and bit me. A few seconds later he was bitten too. So was Tristan. I snapped my flashlight back on and told Paula we must be standing on top of an anthill. What were the odds?

Claudio led us out of the jungle and into the clearing at the back of the cabins. It seemed to us, we had trekked to the middle of nowhere, but in reality we had not ventured far from the lodge. A flock of huge fruit bats zigzagged past us and disappeared into the rafters above one of the huts. Thankfully it wasn't ours. Minute by minute I was becoming less and less enamored of the jungle.

We followed our guides down a long wooden walkway that connected the jungle path with the cabins. The walkway kept us from the mud that results from the Amazon's frequent rain. Our rubber boots had slick bottoms and made us feel like we were skating down the walkway. Twice that first night, I nearly fell.

Paula and Claudio were leading the way, Tristan and Tessa followed them, and Dan and I brought up the rear.

Suddenly Tristan jumped and screamed, "Ow!" He lost his balance, his poncho and flashlight headed skyward, and his butt hit hard on the wooden boards.

I rushed to help him. "Are you ok? What happened?"

"Something bit me! It really hurt!"

Paulo and Claudio looked at us with concern. Dan and I checked Tristan over for bugs but couldn't find anything. "You need to be careful," I cautioned. "This walkway is slick."

We hadn't walked 10 feet when it happened again. The scream, "Ow!" then the feet flying up in the air, the poncho and flashlight heading to the sky, and the hard landing on the walkway. It was as if someone had tasered him. Dan and I picked him up. Tessa was wide eyed. Claudio and Paula were less concerned this time.

"What is going on?!" I was losing patience.

Tristan shouted, "I keep getting bit!"

Again we checked him over and found nothing. "There's nothing on you. You have to stop jumping. You are really going to hurt yourself."

We were on our way to the river where we would wash off our boots. We still had to traverse about fifty feet of slick boards and had moved forward only another few feet when the same thing happened again. Paula and Claudio didn't even stop this time. Tristan was nearly in tears. I was getting less and less sympathetic.

"Something keeps biting me!" *(Later we found out it was ants.)*

"I understand, but there's nothing we can do about it now. We'll get your clothes off in a minute, but for now you need to stay off the boards and walk in the grass so you don't get hurt!"

But he refused to leave the walkway. On we went. Next time I was ready. When Tristan cried, "Ow!" I shoved him onto the grass. I know, not exactly a "Mom of the Year" move, but I had no choice. In the process of pushing him off, I stepped on a rotted end of a board and nearly fell myself. I was starting to think the jungle was cursed.

Tristan recovered once we rinsed our boots in the river. Dan and I breathed a sigh of relief, and we headed back to our cabin, thinking the worst was over. One lit taper candle leaned precariously on the steps outside our hut and another was inside next to our bed. How cute, we thought, until we realized this would be our light for the evening. The bathroom light was electric and went out at 10 p.m. Each sleeping area was lit by a single candle, open flame, placed ominously close to what I'm sure was a highly flammable mosquito net.

Tessa walked into our room and announced, "There are ants in my bed."

Great. Dan and I swept them out, put down her mosquito net, and assured her all was fine. I believe the words we used were, "The ants won't bother you."

We all went back into Dan's and my room where we had left our backpacks and bags. Dan opened the snack bag and jumped back. Ants swarmed out. Not a few ants—a seemingly never-ending mass of ants. They poured down the sides of the bag, onto the bed, and from there who knows where. We had brought a few individual packets of lemonade with us. I think the sugar was what attracted them. Whatever it was, they were having a party.

My backpack was half unzipped, and ants were happily making their way to and fro. Slowly I leaned closer to get a better look. A cockroach, as big as my palm, was about to disappear into its depths. The horror of it made me act on pure instinct. I screamed, reached my hand in, scooped out the vermin, and gave it a fling. Dan asked, "Where did it go?" A few seconds later he was yelling and trying to get something out of his hair. Found it!

The four of us stood, frozen, in the center of our hut. What were we going to do? We couldn't stay there with biting ants and cockroaches, but there was no way to leave. Another canoe would come the next day to bring more guests, and my thought was we needed to be on it. Dan and I noted the candle on the table, our only source of light besides our flashlights. We had only 3 inches of light left.

We huddled together, a horrified American family deep in the Amazon, wondering what to do. Finally our survival instincts kicked in. Dan said we must be doing something wrong. There was no way people would live like this nor would tourists stay here. We took a deep breath and rallied. The BeDell family was better than this. We swept the ants, which were leaving on their own anyway, from our bed and the bags and tucked the mosquito net tight under the mattress. Then we took Tessa and Tristan into their rooms and got them settled. Tristan used the bathroom and calmly informed us that there was a mouse in there cowering in the corner. Really? What else? We left it alone. The mouse was apparently as scared as we were.

We hustled Tristan and Tessa into their beds, mindful of their fast dwindling candle. I didn't know which was worse, leaving the lit candle inches from their mosquito netting or blowing out the candle and leaving our kids alone in the dark. I chose the gradual approach and told them to let the candle burn itself out. I was so proud of the kids. They didn't complain or say they wanted to leave. They sucked it up and made the best of it and trusted us when we told them they would be safe under the mosquito nets.

There was no way I was sleeping alone, so Dan and I shared the twin bed. Once in bed with the mosquito netting tucked in tightly and the candle extinguished, we heard all kinds of rustling sounds in the rafters. I shuddered, thinking about the bats. The kids called Dan in a few times. I am proud to say he responded every time. Tessa thought she had a few lingering ants, so he made a thorough search of her bed. Tristan wanted Dan to find out what was casting a giant shadow on his netting. I heard a loud smack and then Dan assuring Tristan it was nothing, but when he came back to bed, he told me there had been a huge spider on Tristan's mosquito net. He'd killed it. Morning could not come soon enough.

27

The Jungle

ECUADOR

DAYLIGHT, AND THE BUGS SEEMED to have miraculously disappeared. Since we had survived the night, we figured we might as well stay. We were up and into the smaller paddle canoe before seven. Paula and Claudio paddled quietly, steering us down winding stretches of river. We were looking for monkeys. We couldn't see them, but we could hear them jumping in the trees. An hour later we returned to the lodge for breakfast. I was thinking we might have a relaxing afternoon. Maybe I would do a little reading. Paula informed us we would be going hiking in the forest for about five hours. Was she serious?

She was. Claudio joined us on the hike. There was so much to see and hear in the jungle. As we became more acclimated, we could tell where we were by the sounds. Bird sounds meant we were close to the river. If the jungle was quieter, we were more inland. Paula and Claudio were both great about taking time to point out things of interest. The *chicle* tree was a favorite. Claudio cut a small gash in the tree, and we all tasted the sweet white sap. It tasted a little like marshmallows. The sap is used as a medicine for upset stomachs and in making chewing gum, like Chiclets. It was a nice treat in the middle of our hike.

The hike was long but fascinating. The jungle contains so

many important medicinal plants, as well as giant spiders and ferocious ants. Our main concern was mosquitoes, but they turned out to be a nonissue. It was ants we had to watch out for. Claudio took a stick and picked up a very large black ant from the ground. It was a bullet ant, over an inch long. Its bite is intensely painful, the pain lasting 3 to 5 hours and so bad you want to end it by taking a bullet. I hoped I wouldn't find that in my backpack.

Ants aside, we loved exploring the jungle. Tristan and Tessa had a great time, swinging on the vines and putting bird-of-paradise flowers on their noses to look like toucans. Claudio cut open a coconut, and Paula explained that the rainforest tribes eat the small, white worm inside. Did any of us want to try one? To my surprise, Tristan stepped up and chomped down on the fat, white worm. Not to be outdone by my son, I tried one too. Not bad. The body was soft, but when you bit the head there was a gruesome pop. Not surprisingly, no one else volunteered.

The Cuyabeno Reserve is very close to Yasuni National Park, which scientists have recently documented as the place with the greatest variety of plant and animal groups in the world—from amphibians to trees to insects. And here we were, like something out of a National Geographic special. As I walked along I repeated to myself, "We are actually in the Amazon. We brought our kids to the Amazon."

After lunch Claudio and Paula paddled away from the main part of the river toward a new area of exploration. The smaller canoe allowed us to slip into narrower branches. We were disappointed that we still did not see monkeys, but we did spot a rare sight—an owl high in the trees.

We returned to the lodge and found the other guests had arrived: three single women, two from the US and one from Pakistan. We gave them some tips on how to prepare their cabins against the bugs. After dinner we decided to enjoy the hammocks and play games with the kids instead of doing the night hike. When we heard screams from the jungle, we knew we hadn't missed anything. I nearly screamed myself when I almost sat on a huge lime-green frog that blended into the hammock I was about to plop down in.

Because there was no electricity in the main dining area, we played games that night by candlelight. It was a little spooky because earlier two tarantulas had been in the eaves above where we were sitting. I was afraid one of them would drop on my head. As the other guests entered their cabins after their jungle walk, we heard what would become the familiar nightly scream as someone found a tarantula, a huge frog, or the world's biggest cockroach in their room. The screams were a nightly entertainment.

During our remaining time, we were constantly out exploring. Before breakfast was a trip by paddle canoe. After breakfast we went on a long hike or a trip in the motorized canoe, which was steered by Alex onto the main river in a search for caimans or monkeys. Claudio was skilled at using a repertoire of animal sounds to locate wildlife. The animals often answered his calls. By the end of our stay, we had spotted seven species of monkeys, but unfortunately, no caimans.

While the monkeys were a highlight, I think the kids were most excited about seeing the sloth hanging on the side of a tree. Apparently that was a rare sight for Paula and Claudio too. I couldn't keep track of all the birds we saw, including white-billed toucans, parrots, and macaws. Electric-blue butterflies danced around our canoe. And though we fished for piranhas, we didn't see any—a disappointment, but one we could live with because there was something a great deal more important to us. We wanted most of all to see pink river dolphins.

The Amazon dolphins, also known as pink river dolphins, live in fresh or brackish water, have a very small dorsal fin, and sport a big hump on their forehead. Their snout is much longer and skinnier than a saltwater dolphin's.

Paula warned us that dolphins are elusive and shy, and we would need to sit quietly. Even then we might not spot any. Alex stopped the boat, and Claudio tried calling them by making a sound we assumed must be the sound of a river dolphin. Nothing happened. It looked like this was going to be a bust. Everyone on the boat was disappointed, though we all felt Claudio was trying his best. Well, most of us felt that way. One American woman was particularly obnoxious and vocal. "This is just great! We didn't see caimans, we didn't see piranhas, and now we're not going to see dolphins? This is the worst trip!"

We were slightly disappointed that we hadn't seen those things either, but this wasn't Disney World. Wildlife wasn't summoned up on command. Besides, we were more than happy with the things we did see.

That said, this being quiet around dolphins didn't feel right to us. We may not be indigenous guides, but we knew dolphins. We spoke dolphin. The kids and I started yelling, "Dolphins, dolphins!" We whistled and clapped—and sure enough, within a few minutes two river dolphins surfaced. Claudio and Paula were shocked. Soon, we were all yelling and whistling—and more light pink and light gray dolphins surfaced to check us out. I think it's universal; dolphins love to see people, especially kids.

Late one afternoon we visited Claudio's Quichuan village. A few men were playing an intense game of volleyball. We were surprised to learn that though the village people are mostly under 5 feet tall, volleyball is a favorite sport. Every day after lunch, Claudio, Paula, and Alex played volleyball at our lodge. Most days, Tessa played too. The Quichuan village, though poor, also had a nice volleyball court. Who would have guessed?

When we arrived at Claudio's village, he immediately joined in the game. Tessa went off to play on the playground with the local children while Paula showed us around.

The village was small and quiet. The very small local

school served kids through what we call middle school. For further education, the students had to go to Lago Agrio. This option was out of the question for most families, so the teenagers either moved to the city to look for work or the girls became pregnant. In Ecuador school is mandatory and free for ages six to fourteen, but in every city, we saw children selling gum or candy on the streets. Most Ecuadorians are very poor, and everyone in the family has to work, including the children.

The people of Claudio's village made and sold crafts as a way to earn money. The village had also set up a turtle sanctuary. Some of the younger children took us to see it. The villagers gather the eggs, raise the turtles in a protective pen inside the village, and when the turtles are large enough, they are released back into the river. During our visit, Paula said they had thousands of turtle eggs in one of the two pens.

Before we headed back to the lodge, Paula wanted to show us one more thing. We headed in the direction of a small plantation, and by the time we reached it, the daylight was gone. That didn't deter Paula. By flashlight she walked us around the small fields and past coffee trees, coco trees, pineapples, and rice fields. We were familiar with most of these plants, having seen them growing throughout the Caribbean, but they were new to the other guests. We approached the house, and Paula trooped us inside to meet the family—and their pet monkey.

The wooden-plank house was built on stilts, presumably because of flooding and to keep out animals. The floor plan was open, there were no bedrooms. The five small children shared a bed in one corner, and I'm not sure where the parents slept. Maybe the parents slept in the bed and the kids slept on the floor, I had no idea. The house was clean and neat and everything had its place. Paula pointed out the monkey hiding in the rafters. The owners found him when he was a baby.

The house was dark, lit only by candlelight. I didn't see any signs of electricity. I was so intent on getting a picture of the monkey, that I didn't pay attention to where I was going. I tromped across the floor in my giant rubber boots, insanely thinking I could take a picture of a monkey hiding in a dark rafter, in a house lit by candles. In my haste, I kicked over this big, smoking, metal can-like thing that I presume was burning something to get rid of mosquitoes. When I tripped over it, the can spun around on the floor, smoldering and leaking flammable liquid. I apologized and apologized, but the family just laughed and righted the thing.

I couldn't believe what I had done. I could have set the house on fire, which in turn would have set the Amazon on fire. Imagine sitting in your living room, minding your own business, when some tourists stop by, bumble through your living room, and accidentally set your house and business on fire. Unbelievable!

Thank goodness there was no harm done. The mother even engaged me in conversation, through Paula, and asked me about Tristan and Tessa. She was curious about their ages, and I told her how old they were and asked her about her children. That was nice, two women, from very different parts of the world, sharing stories about their children (and one of them nearly killing them all in a blaze of stupidity.) The world just got a little smaller.

It was late, and Paula herded us back into the canoe. There wasn't a light anywhere. I had no idea how Alex, our driver, could see where he was going. What if our boat hit a log or ran up on a sandbar? Could another boat even see us? We didn't need to worry. Alex had lived and worked on this river all of his life, and he delivered us safely back to camp. It was our last night in the Amazon.

Reluctantly, the next morning we packed our bags,

making sure they were free of any bugs. We wished the mouse in the bathroom good luck. From what we had seen of the jungle, he would need it. We boarded the canoe and headed back to civilization. This time the sun was shining, and it was hot. On the way, we stopped at a house so our cook, who was going on vacation, could buy a live chicken. How odd. You could buy a live chicken virtually anywhere in Ecuador. Why did he have to drag one back from the Amazon? We would soon find out this chicken was meant for a higher purpose than stew.

When we reached the end of the canoe ride, Alex pulled the boat over to a small dock, and we climbed out and hiked up the steep riverbank to the road. We were putting our backpacks into the van when we saw a strange sight. An indigenous man, dressed in a bright pink tunic, wearing beads and red and yellow feathers around his neck, and donning a flower headdress was walking toward us, carrying a long machete. Well, that's something you don't see every day. From the way he carried himself, and how Paula and the rest of the crew acted around him, we knew he was a man of importance. I wanted to take a photo, but when he saw my camera, he put up his hand, and Paula moved to block him from my view. Our driver informed me that pictures were not allowed.

Our entire group watched fascinated as our colorful new friend took the live chicken from our cook. He had the chicken in one hand and the machete in the other. Was I about to witness a chicken sacrifice? Forgetting no photos were allowed, I got my camera ready, sure I was about to capture a shamanic moment. The man turned quickly and glared at me. Jeez! Did this guy have eyes in the back of his head or what? I was inside the van, and his back had been toward me, but the look he gave me told me he knew exactly what I was thinking, and I'd better not do it. At that moment I felt pretty sure he put some kind of curse on me. (Case in point, I broke my arm a few days later.

Coincidence or shaman?)

I put my camera down. All of us in the van were curious as to what was going on, but the crew did a good job of blocking our view. One thing was certain; things were not going to end well for the chicken.

Curious as to who this guy was, I asked our driver, "Is he a shaman?"

Our driver answered, "Secoya."

I didn't know what that meant. I asked again, "Shaman?"

"No. Secoya."

I waited a few minutes, not sure I had heard correctly. "Is he a shaman?"

He patiently repeated, "Secoya."

Okay. Are you ready for my comeback? "Is that Spanish for shaman?"

Our driver was a model of patience. He explained that the man was the leader of the Secoya tribe. The Secoyas live in the Amazon, close to where we currently were. They were involved in a lawsuit with a US oil company. The Secoyas claimed that the oil company had dumped oil and poisoned their land. The tribe's population, now around five hundred, had been decimated by a huge increase in cancer rates and aborted pregnancies that they blamed on the dumped oil. The lawsuit had been going on for several years, and it was now looking like the oil company was going to win.

The driver's voice sounded sad. He never did tell me why the man was killing a chicken.

We were tired and not very talkative on the drive back. Everyone else took a bus, but we flew from Lago Agrio back to Quito. Flying within Ecuador was cheap, and we were again given a discount for Tessa. We flew on TAM Airlines in a new and spacious plane. I looked out the plane's window, and my jaw literally dropped. We were flying directly over a volcano. I yelled for Dan, Tessa, and Tristan to take a look. I could see the center, which was a deep rich rusty brown color encircled by snow and ice. I was so excited. "It's a volcano! We're flying over a volcano!"

The sight thrilled me. It was one more reason to add to my list of why I was enthralled with Ecuador.

May 14, 2010 Quito, Ecuador
(from my journal)

After our Amazon adventure, we headed back to the Chicago Hostel in Quito, which would remain our base in Ecuador. We had to get acclimated again to the elevation, which meant a day of taking it easy. We took the trolley into New Town to find a pharmacy. Dan was covered with some kind of Amazon funk, giving him a weird rash on his body. Tristan had the same thing on his arm. Someone told me to put toothpaste on it. The fluoride in the toothpaste acts as an antifungal agent. I put some on Tristan's arm, and his rash was gone the next day. Dan wanted no part of that, hence our visit to the *farmacia*.

"I don't have any idea how to say the word 'rash' in Spanish," I told Dan as we stood at the pharmacy counter. "I can't find it in the phrasebook." The pharmacist politely stared at us, unsure of what to do. "Just show her the rash."

"Are you crazy? I'm not going to show it to her," he replied. Instead, he tried the talk-loud-and-slow approach that involved lots of hand gestures. "I have a rash. You know," he mimicked itching something on the back of his hand. This was not where his rash was, so how he expected her to know what he meant was beyond me. "A rash."

Nothing. She was a deer in headlights.

"Can't you just show her?"

"I'm not going to do that," he replied.

A few more minutes of Dan scratching and making itching motions, and I lost my patience. I was hungry and I wanted to eat, not play charades with the pharmacist. "For goodness' sake, just show her!" The rash was on his butt.

"I am not showing my butt to a pharmacist!"

"She's a professional. She's seen it all before. Just drop your pants and let's go. I'm starving."

Dan looked around. The pharmacy was wide open to the busy street. Reluctantly he pulled the waistband down and hitched his hip up onto the counter, giving the confused pharmacist an idea of what he was talking about. She took a look and disappeared into the back room, where I'm sure I heard her say *"Ay Dios mío"* as she made the sign of the cross then came back with a cream. Problem solved, temporarily. Dan used the cream for a few days and then finally used toothpaste, which healed the rash completely. [*End entry*]

28

Want to Climb Up a Volcano?

ECUADOR

THE TOWNS OF MINDO AND Banos are two of the most popular ecotourism/adventure towns in Ecuador. Mindo lies to the north, so we decided it could wait and went south to Banos—an adventure-lovers paradise on the side of Tungurahua, a very active volcano. The town's official name is Banos de Agua Santa and was named after the Virgin Mary, who is believed to have appeared in the nearby waterfall. The cathedral in town houses a sculpture of the Virgen de Agua Santa and many Ecuadorians come here in pilgrimage, as well as for adventure.

We took a bus to Banos. This bus wasn't nearly as nice as those in Peru, but it was clean and the seats reclined a bit. We thought we were on the express bus, but shortly after the bus left the station, we stopped alongside the road to pick up more passengers. Boarding along with them were vendors.

There was a guy selling ice cream, a woman selling drinks, and another woman selling plantain chips. They boarded the bus and walked down the aisle selling their goods. This was a surprise, but our mouths really dropped open when a guy boarded, selling meat on a stick. He had these shish-ka-bob sticks, about 10 inches long, and the sticks were overflowing with chicken, sausages, and vegetables. The food wasn't wrapped or covered. The man was holding the bottom of the sticks in his hands, walking through the crowded bus. The shish-ka-bobs smelled great. They weren't very sanitary, but people bought them. The vendors stayed on the bus until it stopped again a few miles down the road. The woman selling plantain chips stood next to my seat, staring at me. I felt so guilty for not buying chips from her that I reached into my own bag and gave her a package of my cookies. She took them without a smile and continued to stare at me. That was awkward.

So much for our "express" ticket—our driver stopped everywhere to pick up passengers, even when all the seats were full. Where did these extra passengers sit? On the armrests of our seats. No kidding. For nearly thirty minutes, Dan had to share his armrest with an elderly man who was almost in his lap.

After we left the town of Ambato, the last major city before Banos, the trip was all downhill. Literally. We dropped from Ambato's elevation of 8,400 feet, down to around 6,000 feet. The bus driver seemed reluctant to touch the brakes the entire way down, unless it was for someone wanting a ride, then we came to a sudden stop, tires squealing, and we were forced to peel our faces off the seat backs in front of us. As we careened around hairpin curves, we'd catch a glimpse of Tungurahua. Over 15,000 feet high, the volcano is magnificent.

The first time I saw Tungurahua, I gasped. It has such a powerful presence. In Peru, standing in a low valley like Colca Canyon with the Andes towering above you, jagged peaks touching the sky, you felt safe. The mountains seemed like friendly ancestors watching over you. Not the Tungurahua. Nothing about Tungurahua seemed friendly. Tungurahua was to be respected, admired, and treated with deference. In Peru the towering peaks stand shoulder to shoulder. In Ecuador the mountains seem to move back in homage to the volcanoes. The volcanoes in Ecuador are top dog, and Tungurahua is one of the rock stars.

The bus dropped us at the station in Banos, and under a light rain, we scurried to find our hostel, Plantas y Blanco. It quickly became one of our favorite hostels. We had two private rooms, each with private baths and twin beds. One of the rooms had a great view of the church, Basilica de Nuestra Senora del Rosario de Agua Santa, which was beautifully lit at night. There was a restaurant that served breakfast on the hostel's roof. The rest of the time, the enormous kitchen was open for anyone to use.

Half of the rooftop was enclosed in glass so we could sit inside, enjoy the internet, look out through the wall of windows at the sacred waterfall, or sit outside and enjoy the fresh air. It was a great gathering place, and we spent many nights talking to other travelers or playing the many games the hostel provided. Though our plans were to stay only two days, after seeing the town and the views, we knew we would be there much longer.

Banos is a town for the adventurer. Everything was so cheap, about a quarter of the cost of the same things in the US, that we did as many activities as we could. One day we all went white-water rafting. Another day the kids and I went horseback riding up Tungurahua, where Tessa and I drank water bubbling up from a stream directly from the volcano. Yes, I know in Ecuador you aren't supposed to drink the water, but no one said anything about not drinking volcano water. It tasted a lot like baking soda.

The highlight and lowlight of our stay in Banos was the day we went canyoning. Canyoning, a sport new to us, involved rappelling down a series of waterfalls, the last one being over 120 feet tall. We donned wetsuits and helmets, and with only a few minutes of instructions on how to hold the rope, how to brake, and how to descend, we were rappelling down the face of a waterfall. The first descent was 30 feet. Tessa bravely went first. We couldn't see her descend to the bottom because once she went below the top of the falls, she was out of our sight. One of the guides went down next to her the first time. They did the same with Tristan his first time too. Dan and I were on our own. Once we got close to the bottom of the first waterfall, we released the brake and jumped into the cold pool.

The next waterfall was about the same height. I went first this time. The guide warned us to go slow. I should have listened. Everything was great until about half-way down. I was descending too fast, and I hit the wall hard. I made a big mistake, the mistake they told us not make—I extended my left arm to brace myself against the impact. When my hand hit the wall, I heard a snap, then felt a sharp pain. Having broken several bones in my lifetime, I knew my left arm was broken.

I hung there for a moment, trying to see how bad it was. One of the guides rappelled down to help. Dan called down from the top of the falls, asking if I was alright. I told him what happened. My arm and thumb really hurt, but I couldn't just hang there. I had to continue down. I slowly fed the rope through the brake with my right hand, lowering myself as gently as I could to the bottom. Once there, I examined my arm. Though there was some swelling and what looked like a raised lump on my arm at a spot just before my wrist, it was my thumb that hurt the worst. While I waited for the others to descend, I soaked my arm in the cold, rushing water. It helped a little. The worst part was that I still had the biggest waterfall, 120 feet, to get down. That was tough, but I made it. My arm was actually feeling a little better, until I jarred it sliding down the small waterfalls at the end.

The guides were very sorry about my injury. They blamed themselves, but I knew it was my own fault; I was going too fast. Banos must see its fair share of adventure accidents because there is a medical clinic in town, which we visited the next day. It was our first exposure to international medicine.

The clinic was located a short walk from our hostel. We arrived as soon as it opened. I only had to wait a few minutes before I saw the doctor. He was Ecuadorian, quiet, very formal looking, and didn't speak English. His wife, the doctor in the next office, was Russian and was a study in contrasts. She was tall, stout, had extremely pale skin, large eyeglasses, wild blond hair, and spoke some English with a shout. She was an obstetrician and had a patient, so she couldn't help me. I had to use Tristan's Spanish skills and the Spanish phrase book to communicate with her husband.

I could tell it was bad by the way he kept grimacing and sucking in his breath between clenched teeth as he examined my arm. He pushed down on what I thought was the lump on my arm (I think it was actually broken bone), and when I jumped in pain, he sucked in his breath again. He shook his head in despair before leaving the room and returning with his wife. She shouted at me, in her limited English, that I needed an x-ray. Unfortunately they didn't have an x-ray machine there. I needed to go to the much bigger town of Ambato, an hour bus ride away. The odyssey continued.

The doctor in Banos wrote down the address of the radiologist (we assumed that's what he was). When the bus dropped us off at the bus parking lot in Ambato, we flagged down a taxi and gave him the address. He found it easily. We walked in the front door of the plain, brick building, up the stairs and into a dimly lit waiting room. There were at least ten people ahead of us, so we resigned ourselves to a long wait, but a nurse came out immediately. She spoke little English, but it didn't matter because the Banos doctor had written everything down on the paper I gave her. Within minutes, a young man x-rayed my arm. I was happy to be seen quickly, but I also felt a little guilty as it seemed I was being taken care of in front of the other waiting patients. Afterwards I joined Dan and the kids in the waiting room. Less than ten minutes later, I was called into the office where the doctor had my x-rays displayed. Tristan came with me to translate. The x-ray showed my arm was clearly broken.

"*Como* (How)?" the doctor asked.

Using basic Spanish and a lot of hand motions I explained what happened. He got the idea.

"*De donde eres*?" he asked.

I knew that one without Tristan's help, and I knew how to answer in Spanish. "*Yo soy de los Estados Unidos. Notre Carolina.*"

He looked surprised and told me he spent some time in North Carolina, he and his family, when he was studying at a hospital there. After chatting as much as we could, he wrote down a prescription for a painkiller, gave me my x-rays, and after paying my bill of US$18, I was on my way back to Banos.

When I returned to the clinic and showed the doctor the x-rays, he again sucked in his breath. He called in his wife. What I and Tristan understood, trying to decipher her over-the-top gestures, while at the same time visibly flinching from what I am sure she felt was a mastery of the English language, was that her husband couldn't set the break, and he needed to call in a specialist from Ambato. He left the room, came back a few minutes later, and said, "*Especialista. Aqui. Dos horas.*"

"Two hours," his wife shouted from the other room. Sure enough, two hours later the specialist from Ambato arrived.

I was thinking it wouldn't be so bad to have a cast on my arm; the new casts were small and lightweight. But apparently that was in the US, or maybe the break was too bad for a lightweight cast. Whatever the reason, my cast was made from very heavy plaster, and it was an ordeal to get my arm set. Everyone got involved: the specialist, the doctor, and even a man who I presumed to be the janitor. Apparently it took a village to put on a cast in Ecuador.

The cast was thick and heavy. I was afraid it was going to be hot. Tristan helped me with the words to ask how many weeks I would have to wear it, *cuántas semanas?* The doctor's reply? *Cinco semanas*, five weeks—only a few days less than the remaining time on our trip. Not good.

A bright spot during this was that even though I couldn't understand all of what the doctor was saying, Tristan was able to translate perfectly. He definitely earned an A in Spanish.

The next day we went to the market. I was looking for fresh tomatoes and other vegetables so I could cook chili for dinner in the hostel's kitchen. There were so many vendors selling much the same fruits and vegetables, I wasn't sure who to give my business to. When I saw a nun buying produce from a woman on the far edge of the market, I felt that was probably a good recommendation. Tessa and I went to the woman's stand and picked out some vegetables. When she saw my broken arm, she pointed to her own deformed arm, then put her hand on my cast and gave me a sympathetic smile. After that, she was the only person I would buy from.

We had already spent more time in Banos than we had planned, and there was still so much of Ecuador to see. We boarded another so-called "express" bus for the eight-hour trip to Cuenca, in southern Ecuador. The trip involved going up over the Andes, then dropping back down to Cuenca's elevation of 8,000 feet. Again, at every stop, vendors boarded the bus, hawking their wares. Tristan couldn't resist a bag of fried plantains, and Dan watched in disbelief as I ate a huge ear of corn on the cob slathered in butter. When in Rome, Dan; when in Rome.

Later that night in Cuenca, we were stunned to learn that Tungurahua had erupted shortly after we left. The town of Banos was fine. The lava and pyroclastic flows cascaded down the northern and western sides of the volcano, away from the town, but a large, ash cloud drifted to the coastal city of Guayaquil, shutting down the international airport. We were grateful we weren't there when it exploded, but we knew we had to return and see it before our trip was over. In the meantime, we would enjoy Cuenca.

Cuenca is the third largest city in Ecuador and home to a surprising number of US expats. The cab driver who picked us up at the bus station was doing his best to tell us the perils of Cuenca. Dan was sitting in the front, and the kids and I were in the back, but the driver chose me to direct his tirade of the dangers of the city. He said the city was *peligroso* (dangerous), and then he said something about *anillo* (ring) and made the motion of someone cutting off a finger to get your ring. Next he said something about *arete* (earring) and made the motion of someone yanking on your ear. Then more animation and a motion of a knife.

Tessa was worried. "Mom, what is he saying?"

"Nothing honey. He's just telling us to be cautious." Goodness! He obviously didn't work for the tourist bureau.

Fortunately we didn't have any problems. In fact, we really liked the city. When we weren't enthralled with the cathedrals, including the majestic, blue-domed Cathedral of the Immaculate Conception, we were enchanted by the huge assortment of roses the street vendors were selling. Ecuador is a major supplier of roses to the US, and many of the farms are in the Cuenca area. The roses were simply stunning, and at a price of 10 and 15 cents apiece, I had to have a few.

Cuenca was interesting to visit, and there was certainly much more we could have seen, but we have never been fans of big cities. We used it as a short stop on the way farther south to the small village of Vilcabamba, also known as the "Valley of Longevity."

Vilcabamba gained international attention awhile back when it was first reported that the inhabitants lived to well over one hundred years old. While that has since been disputed, there is some truth that the healthy climate, mineral-rich water, and relaxed lifestyle enable a long, happy life. The main reasons we chose to visit were for the area's beauty and to check out an interesting hostel, Izhcayluma, we'd found advertised in a brochure. The hostel seemed more like an upscale spa than a backpacker's hotel.

Izhcayluma is located just outside the town of Vilcabamba and is very unique. The hostel features a beautiful pool and a delicious, well-priced restaurant onsite. We could be as active as we wanted, from watching the nightly movie, playing pool, getting a massage in the tranquil spa, swimming, or just hanging out and meeting the rest of the guests. Tristan, Tessa, and I spent many hours horseback riding through the lush, green hills, exploring the fruit and coffee plantations surrounding the town. Every afternoon a brief rainstorm rolled in and treated us to a vibrant rainbow, sometimes two, over the towering mountains surrounding our snug valley. As had happened so often on our trip, our expected two-night stay turned into four.

Dan and I left the kids at the hostel one day and went to explore the sleepy town of Vilcabamba. The town was easy to navigate. It consisted of a plaza bordered on one side by an old church and on the other sides by small shops, a few restaurants, and several small stores selling drinks and limited groceries. The pace was very slow, and the streets were unpaved, adding to the charm.

It was warm, so Dan and I decided we would get a drink and sit down on the shaded sidewalk. I walked into the *tienda* and took two Pilseners, the local beer, from the cooler. The owner asked if I needed a *vaso* and pointed to two cold glasses in the cooler. I said yes. He set the glasses on the counter and brought out a small round table with two chairs for Dan and me and set them on the sidewalk. He then poured our beers into the ice-cold glasses. We spent the next hour just sitting and talking, watching the world go very slowly by.

A downside to such easy living, for Ecuadorians, is that it has attracted the attention of foreign investors, which at the time of our visit were mainly Americans. Americans love Ecuador because of the climate, the healthy living, and the fact that Ecuador uses the US dollar. Plus, the Ecuadorians are friendly, and the cost of living is low. The American retirement dollar goes far in Ecuador. The problem is that, instead of building homes consistent with the smaller Ecuadorian homes, the expats have built mansions. Though they loved the safety of the country and the friendliness of the people, they realized that their extravagant homes flaunted their wealth, so they now live in gated communities, walling out the lifestyle they fell in love with, and driving up the prices for the locals. It is sad.

After a brief return to Banos to see Tungurahua, which was still belching out smoke and some ash, we continued our journey and settled into a hostel near another active volcano, Cotopaxi. The Secret Garden hostel was in the middle of nowhere and was totally self-contained. The price of our room included all our meals and drinks. We thought we were spending the night in a cabin, but somehow the reservations were mixed up, and all they had available were the tents located on the property.

The tents were on a raised platform. All the sides of the platform were open, but the top was covered. At first I was a little upset. Camping? At 11,000 feet? I have a broken arm, people! It was cold and I didn't want to be sleeping outside in a foreign country. I asked the owner if it was safe, indicating my children. He assured me it was fine.

A couple of times a year, the wolves came down from the mountain, but that was about it. I noticed the goat tied out in front of one of the tent platforms. No, I'm sure that won't attract wolves to our tent.

We didn't have a choice, and it was only for one night; we would have a cabin the next evening. Tessa and I shared a tent, and we were toasty warm. The mattress was comfortable, and one of the workers brought us a hot-water bottle to warm up our bed. At first I scoffed at it. How could a hot-water bottle warm up a bed? It did. Amazingly well. Before we fell asleep that night, Tessa and I snuggled together and watched the moonlight reflecting off the glacier on top of Cotopaxi. It was stunning. The sun rising over Cotopaxi the next morning was nearly as incredible. I have to admit it; the tent was really the best place to sleep. I thought of all the luxurious resorts and hotels I had stayed at over the years. None of them could hold a candle to this experience.

The Secret Garden hostel was popular and quickly took on an international feel. There were guests from all over the world. There was so much to do. Dan, I, and the kids joined a few others on a climb up to the glacier on Cotopaxi. This was a last-minute thing. We were relaxing around the fire when the owner asked, "There's a group hiking up Cotopaxi. Want to go?"

Uh, hike up a volcano? To a glacier? Heck yes! Without hesitation, and without even knowing what that would entail, we dressed in our warmest clothes, which in this case meant wearing all our clothes at once, and joined our much younger group.

Our climb was broken into two parts: one to the refuge and the other to the glacier. The refuge was a small building that sold food and hot drinks and was used as a staging area for climbers who would be going all the way to the peak. Our hike started at the parking lot, and we climbed slowly, straight up. The altitude of 15,750 feet, combined with the thick, loose ash and gravel we were trudging through, made the climb difficult. We all used different styles to conquer the mountain. Tristan and Wendy, a young woman from Ireland, took the straight-on approach and would stop every so often to catch their breath. Tessa went slow and steady; she never stopped and never looked up. Instead of walking straight up, I used the serpentine method—five steps angled up to the right, and then five steps angled up to the left, stopping often to catch my breath. Dan went with a combination of all three. It took us about forty-five minutes of constant movement just to reach the refuge.

When we arrived, we had the option of staying and enjoying a hot drink and snacks or going on up another four hundred feet or so to the glacier. The kids really wanted to see the glacier. Dan was having a little trouble acclimating to the altitude, so he opted to stay. I sent the kids off with the rest of the group and decided to stay with Dan. But as I thought about it, the chance to see a centuries-old glacier was irresistible to me too, so broken arm or not, I was going. I raced out of the refuge and after the group.

As we started up the slick side of Cotopaxi, it began to snow. The farther along we went, the harder the snow came down. I looked at my ragtag family, totally unprepared for a hike to 16,000 feet. I was wearing the thin jacket I had bought in Chile the previous year. Tessa was layering two long-sleeved shirts under my very thin yoga jacket. Tristan was wearing his new sweatshirt purchased in Cuenca. We all wore jeans and cheap tennis shoes. Luckily we had the gloves and hats that we purchased at the park entrance, or our hands would have froze.

I contrasted that to what we would have bought in the US had we planned on climbing up a volcano. At the very least, we would have bought top-quality hiking shoes, hiking pants, heavy coats, warm gloves, and maybe a hiking stick. But here we were, wearing the only things we had, on a spur-of-the-moment trip, and having the time of our lives.

The climb to the glacier was much steeper than our earlier climb. It was so steep that you could feel the pull of gravity behind you, but because the terrain was more frozen mud than thick ash, it seemed an easier hike. Tessa and Tristan were farther ahead, walking with the younger group. I didn't worry about them because I knew they would be looked after.

When I finally made it to the glacier, I was shocked by how thick the ice was. It towered well over my head. The whiteness of the glacier set off the deep red of the mud and rocks on the steep slope. A vein of light-blue ice was clearly visible inside the ice. I had read somewhere that the blue ice was the oldest ice, and this was what I wanted to see. Excitedly I showed it to Tristan and Tessa, who seemed equally impressed. Happily, we collapsed onto the snow, gave each other big hugs, and reveled in the fact that we were sitting at 16,000 feet, on a glacier, on the side of an active volcano.

As a child growing up in a small farm town in Illinois, I dreamed of going to exotic places. My favorite shows were the nature shows. I would watch them over and over, fascinated by the beauty of the world. I envied the hosts when I saw them sweating in the Amazon, exploring the mysteries of Machu Picchu, or being obscured by a glacier so thick, it was over their heads. I never thought that would be me, but now, I had done all those things. And most importantly, we had done them as a family. I thought back to my former co-workers who thought I was crazy for throwing everything away that I had worked so hard for. "Only go for six months and try it out. That way you can always come back." Really? How could I go back to being confined to an office? How could I go back to a world where overachieving and then desperately clinging to the status quo were valued over saying yes to adventure? How could I go back to restrictions when I had been living a life without borders?

29

Did He Just Hiss At Me?

ECUADOR

B Y NOW THE SNOW WAS falling harder and a heavy fog had rolled in, limiting our visibility to less than 10 feet in front of us. Our guide said we needed to go, so we reluctantly started down. I was thankful for the fog as I'm not sure I wanted to see how far up we were. With my broken arm, the descent was a challenge, so I was unable to help Tristan and Tessa. Our new friends were there and immediately offered to assist. Adam from England led the way. JC, who was Canadian, walked with Tessa. Wendy paired up with Tristan again, and they equally helped each other, while Courtney, a California nurse, helped steady me down the steep slope. We met up with Dan at the refuge and feasted on hot chocolate and delicious banana bread, fresh from the oven.

The following morning we were off on another adventure, a three-hour horseback ride to an extinct volcano. We could see for miles across the high Andean plain, and for miles there was nothing but newly turned dirt or green rolling hills. Farther in the distance stood the ring of volcanoes. During our ride we cut across fertile farmland. The soil was rich from the volcanic ash, making it easy to grow crops, but the rolling terrain made the work difficult. In one small field, women, dressed in traditional clothing of colorful skirts and bolo hats, were working the field by hand. On a nearby steep section of land, a large modern tractor carved the black earth. It was a study in contrasts.

Later that afternoon Dan took a nap, and I lay in the hammock on the porch of the Secret Garden, listening to someone strumming the guitar and gazing out at the eight volcanoes in the distance. Tristan found me and asked if I wanted to play Monopoly with him, Wendy, and Courtney. I answered no, I was enjoying myself looking at the view and enjoying the music.

"You know who that is playing the guitar don't you?" he asked.

I shook my head no.

"It's Tessa."

Sure enough it was. One of the guys at the hostel had shown her how to play the guitar, and now she was entertaining. My children never ceased to amaze me.

The next day we headed back to Quito, tired and a little sad to leave our new friends. When we reached the Chicago Hostel, it was pouring down rain. The day was gray, like our mood. It was hard to leave the fresh country air and the lush open vistas to return to the gray of the city. A little dejected, we ate a quick dinner and went straight to bed.

The nice thing about always returning to the same hostel in Quito was that I developed a ritual. In the mornings I would enjoy a quiet walk down the road outside our hostel, gathering things for breakfast. I'd stop at the shop across the street for eight eggs and juice. The woman behind the counter would patiently work with me on my Spanish. I'd then walk two more blocks and buy fresh-baked buns. Farther down, I'd buy ham and butter from the woman anxious to improve her English, and we would talk about our children and what life in America was like.

Waving goodbye to her, I'd cross the street. On the corner was a small shop selling fruit where I purchased bananas and 50-cent pineapples. The shy, young woman dressed in the traditional attire of a long, embroidered skirt, peasant blouse, and hair in a long braid would give me a tired, sad smile as she swept the floor and tried to rein in a rambunctious toddler who alternated between watching the TV blaring cartoons and running out the door. Her sadness was palpable.

Taking my groceries to the communal kitchen, I would whip up a quick breakfast, and the kids and Dan would carry it up to the tables on the rooftop. We would talk about ideas for the day while enjoying the panoramic views of the city.

We still had two areas of Ecuador we wanted to see before we left. We rode the bus two hours north of Quito, to Otavalo, home of the renowned indigenous market. The towering volcanoes of Imbabura, Cotacachi, and Mojando dominate the horizon. The indigenous people of Otavalo have a very spiritual relationship with the land. Imbabura is considered the sacred protector of the region and its people. There is definitely a special, peaceful feeling about Otavalo. There, the land felt more like a protector, more so than anywhere else we had been in Ecuador.

We shopped in the market, and I bought some rugs, a blanket, and a few other souvenirs. The prices were great (after bargaining, of course), and the quality was very good. We spent two nights in the Rose Cottage Hostel on the outskirts of town, which strangely had a tennis court and was next door to a primary school. Again, as I've said over and over, the scenery was spectacular. The next day Tessa and Tristan played tennis. The neighboring kids playing in the yard nearby watched them the whole time. Our room had a window on the same side as the tennis courts. Later, I was talking to Tristan and Tessa in our room, and I was shocked to look out the window and see the faces of several young Ecuadorian boys. I was even more shocked when I heard them calling, in English, "Tessa. Tessa. We love you, Tessa!" I looked at Tessa. She just shrugged her shoulders and smiled.

When we returned to Quito from Otavalo, we took a cab from the bus station back to the hostel. Along the way we passed a Kentucky Fried Chicken. We were hungry and tired and thought something familiar would be nice, so we had the driver let us off.

Ecuador is a country filled with fresh food, deliciously prepared with exotic fruits and spices, and very inexpensive. We were eating at a KFC that was expensive and virtually indistinguishable from a KFC in the US. When we finished eating, we swore never again.

Something interesting happened as we tried to catch a cab outside of the restaurant. A cab stopped for us. Out of the corner of my eye, I saw a group of young boys approach Dan. They had large poster boards in their hands. It looked like they were holding large greeting cards. Tessa and Tristan were already in the cab, and I started to get in when I heard Dan call for help.

The boys were surrounding him and trying to press the cardboard up against him. I had seen this before on an episode of 60 Minutes that showed how street kids in Brazil pickpocketed tourists. The kids would rush up to the foreigners with the pretense of selling them one of these poster boards. When the tourist was surrounded and distracted, one of the young hoodlums would take their wallet. That's what they were trying to do to Dan. He was doing his best to hold his backpack and mine up over his head, out of their way, while also trying to hold onto his wallet. He couldn't walk forward because they were pushing him backwards.

"Carla," he tried to get my attention.

"Dan. They are trying to get your wallet."

"I know. I know. But I can't move."

I wasn't sure what to do. I didn't want to leave Tristan and Tessa by themselves in the taxi—the driver could just drive off with them, but I could see Dan needed help. The street kids were becoming more aggressive. A few people walked by, but you could tell they were doing their best to avoid getting involved. I would have to help out, though I wasn't sure what I could do. I told Tessa and Tristan to wait in the taxi. I told the taxi driver to wait. From the taxi I yelled to Dan, "Dan, you need to get in the cab."

"I'm trying, but I can't move!"

I yelled at the street kids, "Get out of here."

One of the kids sneered at me and yelled something back that I was sure was unflattering. This kid, about ten years old, was cursing at me. Are you kidding me?

"I said get out of here," I yelled again.

The kid held his ground, said something in Spanish, and then made a hissing-like sound at me. *Oh no he didn't!* I was tired. I had just eaten a large, very unhealthy meal, which was undeniably working right now to harden my arteries and shorten my lifespan, and, at the very least, had put me in a bad mood. I was carrying around what felt like a twenty-five pound cast on my arm, and now a street punk thought he was going to rip us off and give me an attitude? It was so not happening.

I clumsily extracted myself from the cab. Tristan and Tessa tried to stop me. "Mom. Mom," they cautioned.

I looked at them and replied, "Mom will be right back.

The street urchin took a step toward me and hissed. I hissed back. He took another step toward me and hissed again. I hissed louder. (I know, exceptionally immature behavior on my part.) He made the move to do it again, and I became a crazy woman. I hissed even louder and started waving my cast around. Tessa, Tristan, and the taxi driver were all looking at me as if I had lost my mind.

And I had. But it worked. The urchins backed off and moved on down the street, shouting insults at us as they went. Dan and I got into the cab and calmly told the driver where we needed to go. The driver didn't even think about overcharging us.

A few days later we arrived in the cloud forest of Mindo. The town is known for bird watching and zip lining. I would have loved to have gone bird watching, but when I heard it entailed getting up at 4 a.m. and squatting down in a wooded area for hours, I realized I could live with my disappointment. I especially didn't like the fact that because of my cast, I had to miss the over two-mile-long, zip-line tour that Dan and the kids got to experience. I stayed at the hotel and checked out the hammock, while my family happily zipped through the tree tops.

I wasn't totally left out of the fun though. Tristan, Tessa, and I took a two-hour tour of the cloud forest on horseback. We rode through rushing streams, mist-shrouded valleys, and tall, dense forests. The climate and geographical diversity in as small a country as Ecuador was simply amazing, and we hadn't even gone near the coast.

Mindo was our last adventure in Ecuador. In a few days we would be in Colombia. The country we had spent over two years trying to get to by boat.

Our journey to Colombia started off badly and didn't end much better. On the way to the Quito airport, Tessa was complaining that her stomach hurt. We were running late, so I didn't give it much thought. As we started to walk into the airport, Tessa stopped and threw up all over the sidewalk—twice. Dan and I were unsure of what to do. Our flight left in two hours. I felt Tessa's forehead and she didn't feel feverish. Hopefully it was just from that nasty-looking hotdog she ate the night before. The one I fixed for her.

A young woman approached us and said there was a doctor's office inside the airport if we needed it. I thought Tessa would be alright. I took her into the bathroom, got a wet towel for the back of her neck, and then went to find her a Sprite. By the time the plane took off, she was feeling better.

After all the drama we had endured trying to get to Colombia, first by boat, and now by plane, we discovered Colombia was definitely not worth it. It probably wasn't Colombia's fault, but we just didn't like it. Part of the reason, was that it was hotter than Hades. We'd left a spring-time 60 degrees in Ecuador, flown to the country next door, and had disembarked into Cartagena's 100-degree temperatures with 90 percent humidity. We just couldn't adjust.

All the cruisers we spoke to loved Cartagena. They went on and on about what a lovely city it was. The city was pretty, but not as pretty as others we had been to. The fort was nice, but the fort in Old San Juan, Puerto Rico was better. We stayed in Bocagrande, which was a mistake because it was very much a tourist area. Walking anywhere was enough to try our patience because we had to run the gauntlet of street vendors. In the length of one block, we would dodge six guys selling sunglasses, four people selling some God-awful artwork, and another few selling t-shirts. Over and over again, we politely said no, but it became unbearable.

Dan chose our hotel because it was close to the beach. We only had a short walk, but the beach was dirty, littered with cigarette butts, and the water looked murky. We were very disappointed.

In the old part of Cartagena, we found some great restaurants, so we did enjoy some good, authentic Colombian food. The Museo de Oro, or Gold Museum, was a treat. It had beautiful artifacts, told us a lot about the indigenous tribes of Colombia, was free, and most importantly, it was air conditioned. In Cartagena anything with air conditioning was a treat.

One day during a walk in the steaming heat, we spotted an air-conditioned grocery store. We walked in, anxious to cool off. We strolled around for awhile, pretending to be interested in the merchandise until we all felt refreshed. Then we walked out an exit on the opposite side of where we entered. The difference was shocking.

Gone was the clean sidewalk next to the lovely colonial building. We were spit out in the middle of a dirty side street. Immediately, women of questionable repute and clothing sidled up to Dan. When they began touting their skills, I covered Tessa's ears. Tessa and Tristan looked at me in disbelief. Where were we? It was like we had come out the door and crossed into another dimension. We had fallen through a black hole in the universe.

We couldn't find our way back to the store, so we walked as fast as we could to the nearest taxi stand, grabbed a cab, and headed back to the safety of our hotel. We spent the rest of the day holed up in our room. We were so happy a week later to be back in beautiful Aruba.

After visiting Colombia, I really felt that the Universe was looking out for us by thwarting our plans to sail there. The harbor we would have anchored in was dirty, so we wouldn't have been able to swim. The heat was oppressive. Because there were no available marinas, we couldn't have left the boat and traveled anywhere. We (I) would have been absolutely miserable. Dan and I learned a valuable lesson; if a plan doesn't work, don't force it.

PART 3

30

Woman, Calm Down!

CURACAO TO VENEZUELA

THE REST OF THE SUMMER flew by. *Alegria* was back in the water, and we started our journey back east toward Grenada. From there, our plan was to head north to St. Martin, where we would put *Alegria* up for sale. We arrived in Curacao in September. You'll remember that we were not huge fans of Curacao, with all the drama in 2009 taking place in the boatyard. This year, the commotion would play out in the anchorage. Spanish Water was where everyone anchored. It was crowded and the holding was bad. Every time a storm hit, which was often that September, several boats would drag, luckily not ours. One night we were playing board games when an intense storm blew in. Suddenly there was a loud bang from the front of the boat. I looked at Dan and asked, "What was that?"

He knew instantly. "Someone hit our boat." We ran to the front of *Alegria* where, sure enough, *Seven Seas*, a very heavy, 50-foot monohull sailboat, was t-boned on our port hull. The boat had been anchored next to us for at least a week, but obviously not anchored well. Her bow faced to the left, and she was pivoting on our port hull, about a third of the way from her stern. The wind was forcing her hard against us, and *Alegria's* anchor held the weight of both boats. If our anchor popped, we would be on the rocks before we could even react.

Dan was at the bow, trying to shove *Seven Seas* off. He wasn't getting any leverage because he had to squat down, nearly under the bow seat, to avoid their stern-mounted solar panels. The sharp, steel edges of the panels just barely cleared the seat and Dan's head. If he stood up too soon, he would be crushed, or worse, decapitated. Luckily Tessa shouted a warning to me before I was sliced by the panels.

I pushed hard on *Seven Seas*, but the wind was too strong and the boat too heavy. Tessa and Tristan hung back, assessing the situation. Dan yelled to Tristan to start our engines. With the engines running, if our anchor didn't hold, hopefully our engines would keep us off the shore behind us.

The man on *Seven Seas* was yelling at his wife to start their engine too. This was dangerous because his prop (propeller) was over the bridle that attached to our anchor. If he snapped our bridle, that would put more stress on our anchor, and if he got our bridle wrapped around his prop, it would disable his ability to steer his boat off of *Alegria*. His wife, Lisa, whom I had just met the day before, couldn't get the engine started.

"Don't start the engine. You'll snag our bridle," I yelled to him. "You need to get your dinghy and use it to push your boat off."

He looked at me and hollered, "Woman! Calm down!"

What? Are you kidding me? You slam into my boat, and you tell me to calm down?

"Don't call me woman!" I was furious. "You can't start your engine. Our bridle will get tangled in your prop. Get your dinghy!"

He didn't like my advice.

"Woman! I said to calm down!"

"Don't tell me to calm down! Get your dinghy!"

He started in again with the "woman," but I cut him off.

"I swear to God, if I you call me woman one more time, I will come across this boat and—"

"John," interrupted Lisa with a near-hysterical cry. "Her name is Carla!"

Tristan stared at me wide-eyed. Dan was still trapped under *Seven Seas'* solar panels. I looked behind me and spotted Tessa.

"Tessa! Run inside and get on the VHF. Tell them a boat has dragged into us, and we need help!" Without hesitation, she took off while I continued to push. Lisa had the idea that maybe we could just hang on until the storm subsided, but if anything, conditions were getting worse.

A few minutes later, the cavalry, alerted by Tessa's call, arrived. Four dinghies, whose owners I had never seen before, zoomed in to help. With more power and a back up should something go wrong, Tristan and I dropped *Alegria's* bridle to get it out of the way, hoping to retrieve it later. All the pressure from our chain, anchor, and the weight of both our boats was now solely on our anchor windlass. Lisa cranked *Seven Seas'* engine again, and it slowly caught. She put the engine in gear, and with a push from the dinghies, *Seven Seas* slowly inched off *Alegria* without doing any more damage and motored off into the crowd of other boats. Dan let out a sigh of relief and unfolded himself from his cramped position. It was too dark to tell how much damage had been done. We stumbled back inside, exhausted.

The next morning we congratulated each other on what a great job we'd all done and had a good laugh over the "Woman!" episode. During breakfast we listened to the morning cruiser's net as boaters thanked other boaters for helping them out the prior evening when their boats also got into trouble during the storm. (This was really just a nicety because all cruisers consider it their duty to watch out for each other.) We hoped to hear someone from *Seven Seas* call out thanks too, but they remained quiet, so Dan got on the VHF and thanked everyone.

Seven Seas was anchored next to us again. The net ended, and Tristan and Tessa jumped into the water to look for the bridle. To our delight, they found it, still attached to the anchor chain. Later we were well into schoolwork, when there was a call from the back of the boat. It was Lisa and her husband, John (Lisa formally introduced him), our unwanted visitors from last night. John was apologetic, especially about the whole "woman" thing. He explained he was a retired fire fighter and that was how they were trained to react. (Well, if that was true, they needed to rethink that training because every woman knows you never yell, "Calm down woman!" to an irate female.) I accepted his apology. They told us they would pay for any damages to our boat. We showed them where their solar panels had gouged into the metal on our stays (part of our rigging). We had no way of getting them replaced in Curacao, so we weren't going to pursue it. We were simply thankful our Spade anchor had held the weight of both boats. It would have been a disaster otherwise.

Before Lisa and John left, they complimented us on Tristan and Tessa. They were very impressed with how calm the kids had been and how well they'd handled themselves during the ordeal. Several people told me later that they'd heard Tessa on the radio, and she'd done a great job. They said she hadn't gotten on the VHF and just yelled that we needed help. She'd followed procedure, starting out with "Break. Break. This is Tessa on *Alegria*." She had calmly stated the problem and said we needed help. When someone had asked where we were, there were three zoned anchorages within the same harbor, she'd even known which zone. I was very proud of her.

Hurricane season was coming to a close. I was anxious to get out of Curacao. Many cruisers were making plans to leave, and the harbor would be empty except for the most diehard Curacao fans. Most would sail north to Puerto Rico or the Virgin Islands, a three-to-four-day sail. I longed to go with them, but our captain was adamant about heading back up the chain. I just wanted to be moving. I was tired of watching my neighbor on the trimaran come on deck every morning in his dingy, gray underwear. But I guess that was better than the tiny Speedos the European men loved to wear. During our stay in the anchorage, Dan's name had gotten around as the computer whisperer, so there had been a string of dinghies showing up at our boat. Once, when a British guy brought his computer to be fixed, he came on board wearing Speedos and a t-shirt. I could tell by the look on Tessa's face that she thought he wasn't wearing pants and was about to point it out when I shushed her.

Before we left Curacao, we found another boat sailing to Venezuela and on to Grenada. Because of the potential for problems with pirates, we, like most cruisers in this area, preferred to buddy boat. We didn't know too much about our new travel companions except that they were an older American couple. They seemed alright, but a bit paranoid. Our first passage together, to Bonaire, went well.

You can generally count on good weather in Bonaire, but we had a bit of a Halloween scare when Tropical Storm Tomas blew through. It's very unusual for a hurricane-potential storm to come through that late in the season and this far south and west. There is no anchoring in Bonaire, instead boats must use moorings. The moorings aren't storm secure, so during a tropical storm, the government mandates that all boats must leave their mooring and go into the marina. So we celebrated Halloween in a marina slip. We had a good time. Tristan and Tessa had candy, I made Jack-O-Lantern burgers, they read the Halloween stories they'd written, and we stayed up late, listening to the storm howl around us while we watched scary movies.

Tristan was up in the middle of the night, helping another boater retie the lines on the sailboat next to them. The high winds and swell coming into the marina were putting stress on the lines, causing the vacant boat to bounce around, coming perilously close to another boat. Tristan has a knack for knowing the best line configurations and soon had the boat locked down. The next afternoon, the woman he helped took him out for ice cream.

Tessa spent time with Judith and her dog, Dottie. Judith, an older, beautiful Austrian woman, who reminded me of Zsa Zsa Gabor, owned the 50-foot Bavaria yacht in the slip next to us. It was her and her late Argentine husband's dream to sail across the Atlantic, but before their dream was realized, he'd died of cancer. To honor him, she learned to sail, bought a sailboat, and sailed solo from Europe to the Caribbean. Her boat was immaculate, and she had a closet full of the most beautiful clothes, not the normal t-shirt and shorts the rest of the cruisers wore. She was refined, elegant, fearless, and full of life. I was in awe of her.

Judith made a big impression on Tessa. Tessa had too much stuff, wouldn't get rid of anything, and her room was always in chaos. After one afternoon with Judith, she cleaned her room, filling up three garbage bags with papers, toys, and clothes. Judith told Tessa that if she hadn't used or worn an item in a year, she needed to get rid of it, so that was what she did. Her room stayed fairly neat the remainder of our trip.

November 3, 2010 Bonaire
(*from my journal*)

The best grocery store is on the outskirts of town, about 2 miles from the anchorage. The store has a bakery, so while we dreaded the long walk in the heat, we looked forward to *pastechis*, a Dutch island's version of the *empanada*.

We bought too much, as usual, and our backpacks and bags bulged dangerously on the long trek back. There are no sidewalks, so we walked on the busy road, being careful to stay well clear of the mud puddles when the cars drove past. Momentarily I longed for the days back in the US when I drove the short distance to the air-conditioned store in my air-conditioned car. Grocery shopping was mindless then.

The heat, the weight of the bags, and the dodging of cars could have made for a miserable experience. Instead, Tessa started singing, "It's All Been Done," by the Barenaked Ladies, and soon we all joined in.

As I trudged along, ahead of everyone else, I thought back to our old life before the trip. I remembered the time, way before we had kids, when Dan and I bought our first sailboat, a small 25-foot Catalina. Out on the lake one afternoon, my friend Karen had asked me, "Do you feel rich?"

It was a strange question coming from her, and it always stuck in my head. Dan and I had worked hard in the corporate world and measured our success in dollars, possessions, and the amount of hours we worked. Even though money-wise, we were very successful, we hadn't felt rich. We'd felt tired and stressed, but never rich.

Maybe it was the heat, or maybe it was the fumes from the passing cars, but I could hear Karen's voice again asking me, "Do you feel rich?"

The words made me catch my breath. At that moment, for the first time ever in my life, in the least pleasant conditions, the answer was absolutely yes. I realized being rich wasn't about how much money I had in the bank; instead it was about doing what I wanted to do, when I wanted to do it, with the people I loved. Right now, and for the last four years, there was no place I'd rather be than walking down this road, under a blazing sun, singing a song with my family.

I stopped, took a deep breath, smiled, and waited for

them to catch up. [*End entry*]

Traveling with another boat is a lesson in diplomacy and patience. To be a buddy boat, you don't need to be best friends or even hang out with each other in the anchorage, you simply need to have the same travel plans and stick to them. Our buddy boat, both the boat and crew of which I shall refer to as simply *Jewel*, planned to sail the same direction as us, and they had a catamaran, but that was as far as the similarities went.

We have always lived our life with the glass-is-half-full philosophy. Theirs was the glass is not only half empty—it's dirty, dangerous, and will cut you to shreds given the chance. After several conversations with our new "buddies," we were already growing tired of them, and we still had a long way to go.

Another difference, that later proved to be critical, was one of their engines didn't work. If they couldn't sail, their boat speed would be much slower than ours. Our engines were great, but our mainsail had a small tear, so we had to motor. Both boats would most likely have to motor anyway if we were heading into the wind, but the engine issue would be a game changer. In Bonaire things started to deteriorate until the final disillusionment in Venezuela.

We were scheduled to leave Bonaire late Friday evening, around midnight, to arrive in daylight at the outer edges of Los Roques, the Venezuelan out islands. It was important to arrive with plenty of light, because we needed to navigate through the coral. That day we picked up our laundry and enjoyed a street festival in town. Instead of making water, we thought we would take the boat down to the marina, get some fuel, and fill up our water tanks that afternoon.

At 1 p.m. *Jewel* was in a fluster and wanted to leave. They were afraid the passage was going to take longer than what we had planned and wanted to leave earlier. We told them we had made the trip before and knew how long it took. Leaving this early, we'd probably arrive in the dark. They were adamant we leave by 3 p.m. at the latest. They reminded us they could only travel on one engine, so that would slow us down, but we had already factored that in the time. Instead of sticking to our guns, we said fine. We spent the next two hours running around crazily, trying to check out of the country, and getting everything ready to leave. We didn't have time to get more fuel or water, but Dan thought our fuel should be fine.

We left Bonaire, motorsailed using our jib, and made really good time, in fact, too good of time. We arrived in the dark, just as we feared. We circled around for a few hours until daylight. Later we anchored just outside of the town of Gran Roque. We weren't planning on checking into the country, and had agreed to keep a low profile. Except that it was my birthday, and I wanted to go into town and visit our friend Pedro, of Pedro's Pizzeria. While we got ready, *Jewel* visited the 60-foot Venezuelan-flagged catamaran anchored nearby to get a weather update. They stopped back at our boat just as we were heading into town.

The weather report was fine, but the captain of the mega catamaran, who was American, warned *Jewel* of the dangers of going into town and of traveling through the islands. Our now-terrified buddies relayed stories of pirates, robberies, and beatings, which they tried to repeat in front of the kids. We stopped them and told them we'd heard all these stories before, and most of the incidents pertained to boats traveling to the mainland or Los Testigos, none had been here. They wouldn't listen. They were shocked by what they perceived as our lack of interest, especially since we had kids on board. They thought of all people, we should be more concerned.

We let that one slide and decided to go into town anyway. Since it was my birthday, I put on my new white dress that, I have to admit, was a little low cut.

Dan took one look at me and said, "You can't wear that."

"Why not?"

"We're trying to keep a low profile," he said.

"But it's my birthday, and I want to wear it," I replied. Tessa really wanted me to wear it too.

"You'll get the attention of every Latin man in town," Dan said.

"Dad!" Tessa protested. "Maybe Mom wants a Latin man for her birthday!"

Well, yes she does. Thank you, Tessa!

The next day we left early for another long motorsail to the island of Blanquilla. We hit some storms, and we changed course to go around them, but this didn't sit well with *Jewel*. They chastised us for not sticking closer to them, for protection against pirates I guess, so we slowed down. It took us six extra hours to finish the passage.

As we pulled into the harbor, Dan worried that we were running low on fuel. We didn't have a fuel gauge; Dan calculated how much fuel we had based on past experience of engine hours. He was always spot-on with his estimates, and now he was worried that the extra hours of motoring, because of slowing up for *Jewel*, were burning up a lot of our fuel. Thankfully, there was only one more long leg to go, and we would be done with each other.

Blanquilla is a deserted island, except for a small Coast Guard station. A few French boats were already anchored, and not too long after we settled in, *Big Bird*, a boat we recognized from Curacao, arrived. *Jewel* made a beeline over to *Big Bird* under the guise of getting a weather report. We decided it might be best if we found out the weather report on our own, so we visited *Big Bird* after *Jewel* left. The couple on board was leaving the next day to head north to Puerto Rico. They were also worried about pirates and weren't going to chance passing Los Testigos. We got the weather and left. Shortly afterwards, we saw *Jewel* dinghy back to *Big Bird*. Dan said, "You watch. *Jewel* is going to leave with *Big Bird* to Puerto Rico tomorrow."

"No way," I said. "They're going to Grenada with us. We're buddy boats. You can't leave your buddy boat."

But apparently you could. Before lunch, our soon to be ex-buddy stopped by and informed us that they were leaving the next day with their new friends on *Big Bird* and sailing to Puerto Rico. Our ex-buddy explained that because of their engine, it was better for them to sail. We could come too, he offered.

Dan was furious. "We can't sail. Our sail is damaged. You know that."

Dan added that because we held up for them, we had used a lot of fuel and wouldn't have enough to motor to Puerto Rico. Dan reminded *Jewel* of what they had said about sticking with your buddy boat when we had gotten too far ahead of them the night before.

Jewel's reply? "Think about it. If something did happen, how could we really help you?"

So we were supposed to help them if they had a problem, but apparently they had no intention of helping us. Nice. I was so frustrated. Dan wanted to continue the discussion, but I just wanted the guy off *Alegria*.

Jewel skulked back to his boat, leaving Dan and me shocked and without a plan. We had three options: follow them to Puerto Rico; head back to Curacao, fix the sail, and then redo the passage again; or continue on to Grenada by ourselves. Before he left, *Jewel* said, "You know, there's no shame in going back to Curacao." Apparently there was no shame in abandoning your buddy boat either.

"We could follow them to Puerto Rico," I offered.

"We can't sail, and we don't have enough fuel to motor that far," said Dan. "We could go back to Curacao." This downwind sail would allow the use of our jib and the consumption of less fuel.

Going backwards was never my favorite thing to do.

Going backwards for almost 300 miles was out of the question. I shook my head no.

The other option was to continue to Grenada as originally planned. The distance to Grenada was half of what it would be to return to Curacao, but now we would have to pass Los Testigos by ourselves, not what we wanted to do since lone boats were the ones being targeted. All I knew was that none of the options felt good. Tristan and Tessa, who had witnessed the entire conversation, looked at us nervously. "Let's go up front and talk in private," I said to Dan.

Dan and I sat down on the bow of the boat. Neither of us said anything for a long while. We just sat and watched the waves crash onto the beach. What were we going to do? More waves crashed on the shore. A few pelicans lazily circled above us. The day was moving on peacefully, oblivious to our situation.

There were no answers to be found. None of our options *felt* right. We both knew it at the same time, though I said it out loud, "I don't feel we are supposed to do anything. I don't feel we are supposed to make a decision right now."

As crazy as that seemed, that was exactly what we were supposed to do; just go on with our day and see what would unfold. So that's what we did. I made lunch for the kids, we did a little schoolwork, and basically we just waited. For what, we had no idea.

We didn't have long to wait. Later that afternoon, a dinghy pulled up. Richard was an American and owner of *Mystic Rhythms,* a catamaran anchored across the harbor. The woman with him, Daria, was his first mate. We had seen them talking to *Jewel* earlier. In another example of how small the cruising world truly is, Richard had helped *Jewel* with his mast when they'd both been in the South Pacific a few years earlier. Blanquilla was the first time they had seen each other since then.

Richard asked us where we were going, and we told

them our dilemma. He said he and Daria planned to sail to Puerto La Cruz, on the Venezuelan mainland, in a few days for boat repairs. He was aware of the dangers of the Venezuelan coast, but he had talked to the captains of a few French-flagged boats who had just come from there, and they assured him it was fine. The French cruisers said they could get all their boat work completed in Puerto La Cruz and cheap. Dan shot me a look. Go to Puerto La Cruz? Actually go to the mainland? We hadn't considered that. We could get cheap fuel and have our sail repaired inexpensively. With sails and fuel, our options would open back up on how we could travel. We needed to go to the mainland. As soon as Richard and Daria left, our plans went into overdrive.

Puerto La Cruz was about 100 miles away, nearly straight south of us. According to the outdated Venezuelan cruising guide we had, it was home to several marinas. The pictures of the Bahia Redonda Marina looked enticing. The marina included a beautiful, palm-tree-ringed pool and a restaurant. There was a boatyard and sail-repair shop next door. It seemed too good to be true. Yes, we'd have to pass by Isla Borracha, the island just outside of Puerto La Cruz where an American cruiser had recently been killed, but the marina itself was supposedly safe. We trusted what Richard said. We decided the ability to get our sail fixed quickly was worth the risk. We left at sunup the next morning.

The Dreaded Mainland

VENEZUELA

W E ARRIVED IN PUERTO LA Cruz mid-afternoon. I hailed the Bahia Redonda Marina on the radio over and over again but didn't get a response. Just when we were about to give up, an American voice came on the VHF and told us how to navigate into the harbor. Someone would be at the dock to help us.

With the help of one marina employee and a few other cruisers, who left before we could properly thank them, *Alegria* was soon secured to the dock. It was a Sunday, not a great day to arrive because everything, including the marina, was closed. Jose, the dockhand, set us up with electricity, but we couldn't get internet or check into the marina until the next day.

After getting the boat settled, we took a quick walk around the complex. The pictures from the guidebook hadn't lied. The large pool was clean and well landscaped. There was a small store onsite as well as a restaurant, both of which were closed. The marina was fairly large, but there were many empty slips. Of those that were filled, we saw only two US-flagged boats, one British boat, and the rest were Dutch, French, and Venezuelan.

We stumbled upon several women playing Mexican Train dominoes in the closed restaurant near the pool: an

American named Diane; Margaret, who was Dutch; and two French women, one of them named Ann. They were very helpful and gave us a little information about the place. Diane said she would be happy to help me with anything I needed. As we were leaving, I noticed a guy sitting by himself in the corner, using his iPad. As I was talking to Diane, he was trying to catch my eye. It seemed like he wanted to say something to us but then decided against it. I chalked him off as strange and promptly forgot about him, until the next morning.

Our priorities the next day were as follows: check into the country, check into the marina, find the sailmaker to repair the sail, and get fuel. On our way to the marina office, we walked through the restaurant. The same strange guy from the day before sat at a corner table, working on his iPad. I was feeling so good about being in Venezuela and in a nice marina that I overlooked his strangeness, smiled at him, and said hello as we walked past. He stopped us. I asked him how he liked the marina. He glanced around as if to be sure no one was listening, leaned in, and whispered a warning, "Get out."

What? I stepped back. He leaned forward and continued, "This is a hell hole. There's nothing here."

In an unsure voice, I replied, "But... We need to get our sail fixed... We need fuel."

"You can't get fuel here. They won't sell fuel to Americans. I'm Canadian. I have been trapped here for over two weeks trying to get out."

I was so dumbfounded that I couldn't reply. In a few sentences, he had stripped away my blue-sky feeling with storm clouds of negativity. I was totally caught off guard and instead of deflecting it with my usual shrug of "your fear not mine," his fear clung to me like a cheap pair of nylon underwear in the summer. Dan gave me a nudge to get moving. When I tried to talk to him about it, he told me the guy was crazy. We would find out everything once we checked in.

Just as when we checked in to Venezuela two years before, we needed to use an agent. Diane told us to use Ana, a very attractive Venezuelan woman who worked at the French Consulate conveniently located next to the marina restaurant. Ana spoke perfect English, took our paperwork, and explained the process. The check in would take several days, maybe even a week, because the paperwork was sent to Caracas. We needed to pay the fees in bolivars, which was easy because this was the French Consulate and Ana could make the exchange. Their rate wasn't great, 5 to 1, but Ana told us we may be able to get a better rate later in the week from the guy at the French travel agency, located around the back of the marina.

While she copied our paperwork, Ana asked us what brought us to Puerto La Cruz. Dan told her we needed to get our sail repaired. He said our guidebook mentioned a well-respected sailmaker here who did repairs. She looked at us in surprise. "No. Not anymore. Business was slow, so he moved last year."

What? Oh, this wasn't good. My stress level was moving to panic mode. Dan saw the look on my face and whispered for me to be calm. Okay, fine. Breathe. Who needs a sail? We can get fuel and motor our way out of here. We passed the fuel dock on the way in. It had easy access. We would be fine. Dan asked Ana about fuel.

"No, you can't get fuel. They can't sell fuel to Americans here." Damn! The crazy Canadian was right. No fuel! No sail! My children will spend the rest of their lives in a Venezuelan marina, possibly working at the French travel agency. Is there no end to this hell?

I was about to pass out. I started hyperventilating. On our way to the marina office, I kept asking Dan, "What are we going to do? What are we going to do?" Usually I am the calm one, but this time Dan was calm. "Relax," he said. "We'll figure something out."

Figure something out? *Figure something out?* You don't just "figure out" how to get out of a pirate-surrounded foreign country with no fuel and a ripped sail. Oh my God! What have we done?

Dan was totally shocked by my reaction. What was wrong with me, he wanted to know. He was right. This wasn't me. I needed to get a grip. That crazy Canadian had really messed with my head.

Maria checked us into the marina. She confirmed that the sail-repair man had left long ago, but she knew a guy who used to work for him. She would try to find him. (Yeah!) She also confirmed that we couldn't get fuel at the fuel dock. I was truly about to cry, when she gave us hope, "We can't sell you fuel, but we can get you fuel."

Uh...come again?

"The taxi driver brings back fuel from town. In jugs."

Alegria holds around 130 gallons of diesel. We had two 5-gallon fuel jugs. I asked her if we could get more jugs.

"Of course! From the cleaning lady. She has big jugs. From the cleaning supplies."

This just got stranger and stranger. We found out later from other cruisers that this was how it was done. In Cumana, an anti-Chavez state to the east, marinas would sell Americans fuel at the dock. Puerto La Cruz was a pro-Chavez state, so the taxi drivers took jugs into the gas stations, filled them up, and delivered them to the boats. Of course, there was a premium attached to this. At the fuel dock, it cost 15 cents a gallon. For the taxi driver to bring fuel to the boat, plus the cost of the jugs, it worked out to 45 cents a gallon. Contrast that to the last time we bought fuel in Aruba at over $4 per gallon. Things were looking up.

We left Maria's office and again passed the crazy Canadian. We stopped to talk. I was interested in his story. He said he'd bought the old trawler docked in the slip next to us from a Venezuelan who had kept it at the marina.

Now he had to get the boat back to Canada with the help of a captain. He had been waiting nearly two weeks for the captain to arrive. In the meantime, he was trying to do some of the boat work himself, but he wasn't sure what to do. He didn't know how to get things done in Venezuela and was very frustrated. He had never traveled in a Latin American country before, so he was unfamiliar with how everyone networked. He was out of his element, and I felt bad for him.

After we left him, we ran into Diane and asked her about sail repairs. She said there was a guy that did some sail work, and we should check with Anne at the mini-mart. Of course. Look for a sail-repair man at the mini-market. That made as much sense as anything. We later learned that Mini-Market Anne had her finger on the pulse of the marina. You needed something or someone, check with Anne.

We met Anne, and sure enough, she knew Lorenzo, the guy who used to work on sails. She would find him for us. As we left the store, we met an English couple, long-term residents in the marina. They introduced us to one of the Venezuelan dive-shop owners. He knew Lorenzo too, and he immediately grabbed his cell phone and began making calls. (Love the Latin network!) Everyone was working to help us. Everything would be alright. Once again, in a very short amount of time, we had been taken in by a small international community with such genuineness and warmth.

Things got better every day. The favored taxi driver of the Brits, Carlos, showed up the next morning to get our fuel order. Diane introduced Tristan and Tessa to a ten-year-old boy named Dillon. His mom, Nancy, ran the dive shop at the marina. She is French-Canadian, so Dillon spoke French, Spanish, and English fluently. He helped with the translation a few days later when Lorenzo came to our boat and left with our mainsail. Everybody was getting in on the act, and we really appreciated it.

We settled into a nice routine as we waited for our sail to be repaired. Dan played Mexican Train dominoes. Dillon played Nintendo DS with Tristan and Tessa, either on our boat or in his marina apartment. When she wasn't with Dillon and Tristan, Tessa played with two French girls close to her age. Neither spoke the other's language, but they had the best time. Some days, Mini-Market Anne's Venezuelan granddaughter would join in.

Tessa helped Diane take care of the many cats in the marina, a job that required waking up at 6 a.m., but she loved it. Dan made friends with Jacques, a French-Canadian boat captain for a Venezuelan boat. A few times they took the dinghy exploring through the canals that wove around the marina and through wealthy neighborhoods, eventually ending at the upscale mall.

We all enjoyed the weekly potluck dinners. I relaxed at the pool, caught up on my reading, and tried to come up with ideas for Christmas. I also thoroughly cleaned the inside of the boat. We even learned to enjoy the near-daily, afternoon storms that screamed down the nearby towering mountains.

Getting bolivars was still something we had to do regularly. Jean Claude, who worked at the travel agency, gave the best rate. Since we had long ago run out of US dollars to exchange, we used checks. Jean Claude would take our check and find a "buyer" for it. This usually took twenty-four hours. During that time he would call different people he knew and see who wanted our check.

A check was preferred over cash because it was easier to get out of the country. The Venezuelan currency was unstable, so the locals preferred dollars, but the Venezuelan government limited how much foreign currency, specifically US dollars, they could hold. To get around this, the wealthier class kept bank accounts in the US. About every two weeks or so, a money man left

Venezuela with a stack of US checks and deposited them in a bank in Miami. It was a win-win for everyone.

Shopping was easy in Puerto La Cruz. A series of canals, accessible by dinghy or mid-sized fishing boats, connected all the marinas and the expensive houses of El Morro with Plaza Mayor, a large upscale mall. The mall was a great place to catch a movie, buy DVDs, shop for clothes, or shop for groceries. We visited the mall a few times, mainly to visit the delicious *panaderia* (bakery) to buy *pan de tocino* (fresh-baked bread filled with bacon) or *pan de jamon* (bread filled with ham).

Once a week, a group led by Diane would shop at the fresh market. The first time I visited the market, I was overwhelmed. It started with the taxi. As we stepped outside the gates of the marina, a large car was waiting for us—a very large car. Remember the huge, boxy, American gas guzzlers of the 1970s and early 1980s? Well, they've happily found a home in Venezuela.

Our taxi driver, driving at normal speeds, efficiently ran red lights, drove in the lane reserved for oncoming traffic, and delivered us outside a congested, dirty shopping area that was as far removed from the luxury of Plaza Mayor as you could get. It felt good.

Don't get me wrong. I love a clean, air-conditioned mall as much as anyone else, but since my visit to a fresh market in the Dominican Republic, I was hooked. My heart yearns for the sights, smells, noises, and chaos of an open market, and this one delivered that in spades. Margaret and Ann split from the group, agreeing to meet later at the coffee shop, and Diane showed me the market. She led me on winding paths, through countless stalls of fruits and vegetables, many of which were new to me. Most of the market was covered overhead with plastic tarp that still let in light, while thankfully blocking out most of the blazing sun. I made sure I stuck to Diane's side. If I lost sight of her, I knew I would never find my way back.

I filled my bags with my favorites: oranges, passion fruit, guava, pineapples, tomatoes, potatoes, avocados, and bananas, until they were hard to carry. Diane then led me farther into the market where she introduced me to her cheese man. His cheese shop was next to the rows of small stalls selling meat. A large dead pig hung upside down outside of the first butcher's stall. A young man with a large cleaver was preparing to make the first cuts. Down this aisle was where, if you didn't mind a few flies buzzing around, you bought fresh beef, pork, or chicken. Diane pointed out which butchers had the best products, and I followed her advice.

The beef was grass fed, and most of it came from Argentina. It was tender and flavorful, as was the fresh pork. Our absolute favorite had to be the smoked pork chops. I told the butcher how many *kilos* I wanted and how thick, and he gladly accommodated my request. (The people in the market only spoke Spanish, so my Spanish skills improved dramatically.) We would take the pork chops to the weekly potluck and cook them on the charcoal grill. They were delicious.

Diane led me out of the market and across the busy street to the spice shop. The shop contained hundreds of spices displayed in bulk in glass jars reaching from floor to ceiling. Large barrels of oats, rice, and other grains were spread throughout the store. Smaller barrels contained a variety of nuts, and there were even sections specifically for olive oil or just for chocolate. The colors and smells in the shop filled my senses; a quiet reprieve from the fumes emanating from the car-choked streets outside. I could have stayed there longer, but Diane's shopping style was more of a mission. She had her goods and headed for the door before I even made it to the back of the shop.

Back outside, Diane pointed out the small, Asian-owned stores lining the blocks surrounding the market. These were the same type of stores we had shopped at in nearly every country during our trip. They were the best places to buy paper products, any nonfood items, and American-brand cookies.

Our last stop was the coffee shop and bakery. I bought two loaves of French bread and several mini-baguettes. I ordered a coffee, which turned out to be strong and full of flavor but served in the smallest of cups. Venezuelans are proud of their coffee, which grows high in the Andes and Coastal Cordilleras, and rightfully so. I'm not sure why the cup is so small though. While Margaret and Ann drank their coffee, I walked next door to the beverage shop to get a price on a case of Diet Coke. Finally, I thought, we were done.

We loaded all our bags into a taxi and headed back to the marina, almost. A few blocks down the road, the taxi pulled up to a small store selling alcohol, mostly rum and beer, at discounted prices. I didn't bother buy anything because I really couldn't carry another thing. By the time we returned to the marina, I was hot and tired. Everything I bought was fresh and not in any type of cardboard, so it was quickly and easily stored away. This meant more time for reading and the pool.

We couldn't have been in a better place for Thanksgiving the following week. It turned into quite the international affair. Mini-Market Anne (British I believe) offered her marina apartment to host the dinner. By that time, *Mystic Rhythms'* Richard and Daria had arrived and added to the American constituency of Diane and Harold and us. Ana, who had checked us into Venezuela, came. The French Ann and two other French families were there, including the two girls Tessa played with, along with Anne's Venezuelan granddaughter. Dillon and his mom, Nancy, were there, as was Jacques the boat captain, so French Canada was covered. Margaret and Harold represented the Netherlands.

Instead of turkey, several of us cooked whole chickens, and everyone brought either a side dish or dessert. There was more than enough food. French Ann passed around her rum and passion-fruit drink. It seemed like a tiny bit of passion fruit to a whole lot of rum, as is typical French fashion, but the adults enjoyed it. This was our second Thanksgiving in Venezuela and we loved it. Who would have thought?

The days flew by. We hired Carlos, a hard-working, young Venezuelan, to clean and polish *Alegria*. Sergio, whose wife, Maria, worked for the French travel agency, came highly recommended as a refrigeration expert. We employed him to solve our long-running refrigeration issues.

It was Tristan's birthday, and he wanted a Nintendo game. Nancy drove us to the mall, and Dillon helped Tristan and Tessa get game cards. Afterwards Nancy was running late for an appointment, so she helped me get a taxi to take us back to the marina. I was a little apprehensive—just me and the kids, alone in a taxi in Venezuela, but I was even more so when I saw the taxi we were getting into. It was a small car with tinted windows, driven by a young guy. It didn't seem like a regulation taxi, but then nothing in this country was what it seemed. Nancy gave the driver instructions on where to take us, and we hesitantly hopped in.

As we pulled away from the mall, the thought briefly crossed my mind that we could easily disappear and no one would find us. I could tell by his actions though, that he was as nervous as I was, so I knew we weren't in any danger. Our driver spoke only Spanish, so there was little communication. While we had a fairly easy time conversing in Spanish in Peru and Ecuador, Venezuelan Spanish was much harder. As Nancy explained to me, they tended to clip off the end of their words. I imagined it would be like someone from Venezuela trying to understand the English of someone from Alabama.

The apartment complex where Dylan lived, and where we celebrated Thanksgiving, was in the front of the marina. Taxi drivers always took us to the back, by the marina entrance. This driver took us to the gates by the apartments instead. Two guards stopped our cab. Our driver rolled down the window, and I presume he told them he needed to get in, but the guards took one look at our driver, and the tinted windows, and refused. Our driver pointed to me and said something in Spanish, but the guards had no idea who I was, and only knew that I didn't live in the apartments. They went back and forth in Spanish for a few minutes, and I could tell by their actions we weren't getting in. Our taxi driver was getting nervous. I think he was contemplating being stuck with us forever.

Finally, Tessa saved the day. She rolled down her window and said "Hola" to the guards. One of the guards immediately recognized her and gave her a big smile. He said something to the other guard, who also gave her a big smile. They looked back in the car at me and frowned, apparently disappointed in my choice of drivers. They opened the gate and waved us through. I should have known. Everyone knows Tessa.

On Tristan's birthday, Sergio was still taking up a big portion of our salon, working on the refrigeration, and there was no way I could get into the kitchen and bake a cake. I felt bad and promised Tristan I would make it up to him. Later that evening, Nancy and Dillon arrived with a birthday cake—Nancy's homemade, chocolate-pudding cake. Nancy worked full time as a dive instructor, and in addition to Dillon, she had a young baby to take care of. Some of the ingredients in the cake were hard to find in Venezuela. When did she have time to make this cake? In the US, that would have been a nice gesture; here it was above and beyond. And to think she did this for a family she had known for a very short time, and once we left, more than likely would never meet again. Those were the moments I would keep in my heart forever.

Christmas was fast approaching. Dan and I snuck in a little Christmas shopping at Plaza Mayor. There were a few good toy stores in the mall. We both agreed not to get each other anything, though I dropped several hints for a Swiss Army knife. My love for the knife goes way back. My brother was in the Boy Scouts, and I was fascinated by his Swiss Army knife. Who wouldn't be? I mean, you can cut things, open a bottle, clip something with the scissors, and even eat with the fork. Amazing!

As a sailor, you really need to have a good knife in case of emergencies. Unfortunately Dan wasn't picking up on my hints, so the closest I got was sighing longingly outside the display cases.

Tessa was very worried about Christmas. This would be our first Christmas on *Alegria*, and she had no idea how Santa was going to find us in Venezuela, and if he did, how was he going to get on the boat? Her worry grew when she found out that most Venezuelan children got clothes for Christmas, not toys. Word soon got back to me that Tessa was going boat to boat asking how Santa delivered presents without a chimney. Margaret cornered me one day at the swimming pool.

"Carla. Does Tessa still believe in Santa Claus? Isn't she a little old?" Margaret was from the Netherlands, and maybe they stopped the magic of the season much earlier there. After experiencing Sinterklaas in Aruba, I knew why. The Netherlands version of Santa is vastly different from ours. Their Santa comes from Spain, drags a black servant elf named Black Pete with him, and carries a stick to punish the unruly children. Parents threaten their children that if they aren't good, Black Pete will kidnap them and take them back to Spain. Seriously. Have a magical Christmas kids! Instead of answering Margaret's question, I mumbled something and swam away.

Later, during happy hour by the pool, Harold asked me, "Does Tessa still believe in Santa Claus?"

Okay. Why don't I just get on the loud speaker and announce it to everyone?

"Yes," I replied, sinking low in my seat, expecting to get a lecture.

"Good!" he said. "Don't you tell her any different. The world changes so fast for kids. You need to keep some magic alive for them."

I could have hugged him. He was so right. I still believe in Santa. Do I actually believe there is a guy in a red suit coming down the chimney, delivering gifts? No, but I do believe Christmas is magic. It's the time of year that brings out the best in people. Is that Santa? Who knows? I do know that if I went to bed on Christmas Eve with no presents, I would wake up, and somehow, some way, there would be a gift for me. It may not be a material present, but it would be some kind of gift. Is that Santa, or would it be that magic that moves someone's heart? I don't need to worry about that. I just need to believe, and so does Tessa. Later Tessa told me Harold assured her that Santa came to their boat every year, and he would find ours too. *Bless you Harold.*

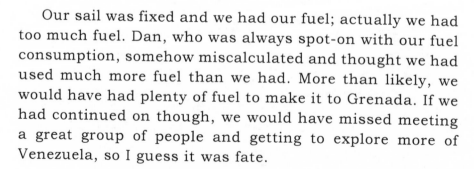

Our sail was fixed and we had our fuel; actually we had too much fuel. Dan, who was always spot-on with our fuel consumption, somehow miscalculated and thought we had used much more fuel than we had. More than likely, we would have had plenty of fuel to make it to Grenada. If we had continued on though, we would have missed meeting a great group of people and getting to explore more of Venezuela, so I guess it was fate.

Later Dan figured out he miscalculated on the fuel because he went by what fuel we normally used for the engine hours. When we were traveling with Jewel, we had to go slow for them, so we put more engine hours on but used much less fuel than normal.

All we needed now was a weather window, and hopefully, a buddy boat. A British couple, Tim and Paula, whom we had met briefly a few days before, said they were heading to Bequia, an island we had visited two years before, for Christmas. Bequia is located within the St. Vincent and the Grenadines archipelago just north of Grenada. We agreed to go together. They had made this trip several times, as had Harold and Diane, and all agreed it wasn't an easy passage. We would be heading into the wind and a strong current. It would be an interesting trip.

We planned to go east to Mochima National Park, anchor there overnight, spend a night at Isla Margarita so our British friends could load up on duty-free goods, and then sail to Bequia. We weren't thrilled about going this way. It would have been an easier and shorter passage sailing back to Blanquilla, then to Grenada, but Tim and Paula really wanted to shop before they headed east, and we decided it would be better to have a buddy boat. The universe had other ideas.

32

Out Thar They Be Pirates

VENEZUELA TO GRENADA

CHECKING OUT OF VENEZUELA WAS just as interesting as checking in. Because the check-out procedure took about a week, we had to have a rough idea of when we wanted to leave. Once we got the paperwork back, we had twenty-four hours, possibly a little more, to actually leave the dock.

We said our goodbyes to everyone the night before. We left with mixed emotions—anxious to get moving again, but sad to leave our community of friends. We followed the British boat out of the marina into calm seas and clear skies. We hoped this buddy-boat experience would work out better than the last one. It didn't.

It wasn't a long trip to our first anchorage, and we planned to be there by early afternoon. Those plans fell apart less than 2 miles out when the Brits tried calling us on the VHF. Two problems were discovered at once—one theirs and one ours. The Brits were taking on water. When they tried to call us, the receiver on our VHF barely picked up the signal even though we were right next to each other. What was going on?

Both of us returned to the marina. So much for our early start. We tested our radio with the other boats in the marina, and we did have a problem. As unhappy as we were about this change of plans, this setback was a blessing in disguise. If we had left on our own, we wouldn't have discovered our radio problem until we needed it for an emergency, which could have been disastrous.

While Tim and Paula sorted out their leak, Carlos the taxi driver took Dan and Tristan into town to buy a new antenna. They came back with a new antenna, and Dan successfully installed it before joining a few other guys trying to help repair the British boat. The leak was discovered around a seacock. The leak was sealed, and we planned on leaving the next day. Since it was Sunday, the marina was officially closed, so the dockhand let us stay overnight, no charge.

We left again early the next morning. We were 2 miles out when Paula and Tim called us with bad news. Their boat was taking on water again. They had to go back and have it pulled out of the water. They wouldn't be heading to Bequia anytime soon. Again, we were forced into the decision to continue on alone.

What were the odds that we would have buddy-boat issues again? Why were we destined to travel through Venezuelan waters alone? Paula and Tim assured us our first anchorage in Mochima National Park would be safe. We hadn't heard of any acts of piracy there, so we waved goodbye and continued onward.

It seemed we didn't have a choice. We couldn't go back to the marina without checking in again. There was really no reason to go back since we would just have to leave on our own again. No one else there was going anywhere anytime soon, which meant no buddy boat. In hindsight, the smartest thing would have been to go back to the marina and leave early the next morning to Blanquilla. From Blanquilla, it would have been an easier easting on up the chain or to Grenada. We weren't thinking that far ahead though, and we continued on with our (their) plans. This was the second time we allowed a buddy boat to influence our decision, and it turned out to be a problem both times. There was definitely a lesson to be learned here about following our own path.

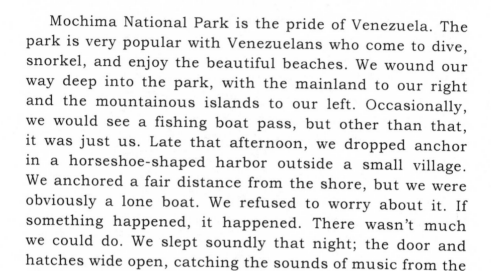

Mochima National Park is the pride of Venezuela. The park is very popular with Venezuelans who come to dive, snorkel, and enjoy the beautiful beaches. We wound our way deep into the park, with the mainland to our right and the mountainous islands to our left. Occasionally, we would see a fishing boat pass, but other than that, it was just us. Late that afternoon, we dropped anchor in a horseshoe-shaped harbor outside a small village. We anchored a fair distance from the shore, but we were obviously a lone boat. We refused to worry about it. If something happened, it happened. There wasn't much we could do. We slept soundly that night; the door and hatches wide open, catching the sounds of music from the shore and the cool mountain breezes.

We left early the next morning. I cooked biscuits and gravy on the way, as we motorsailed to Isla Margarita. Our plan was to spend the night there, then overnight to Grenada. When we arrived in Margarita, we abruptly changed our plans. The last time we were there, two years before, the harbor had been crowded, with at least seventy boats. Even though we knew there had been some crime in the harbor recently, we still expected a good number of boats, but the harbor was nearly empty. A few ragged-looking French boats were anchored and looked like they had been there awhile, but other than that it was a ghost town.

Dan and I immediately got a bad feeling about the place. Something felt off here, and we didn't get a good feeling about staying. After dropping the anchor, we considered our options. We couldn't leave on an overnight passage without knowing the weather. Our satellite phone wasn't giving us a good signal, so we couldn't download the weather. Dan remembered that the last time we were here, we were able to pick up a Wi-Fi signal from one of the hotels on the beach. Maybe he could pick up a signal again. He turned on the computer, and I said a prayer that the signal would reach us. It did.

The good news was the weather looked fine. The bad news was it was deteriorating rapidly for the next afternoon. If we were going, we needed to go now or risk being stuck in Margarita for several days. We agreed to leave. First we needed to drop the dinghy, head into town, and spend the 600 bolivars we still had.

It was the craziest shopping trip. We didn't want to taxi into Porlamar, so we entered the mini-market closest to the dock. Our goal was to get in and get out quickly. I grabbed lunch meat and cheese, Tessa and Tristan pulled bags of chips off the shelves, while Dan found some Polars, the local beer. Most of the prices weren't marked, so we had to wait impatiently while the clerk added up our bill. The first time, it came to three hundred. I urged the kids to get more. The next time it was over four hundred. We indiscriminately grabbed more food. The clerk eyed us nervously. I eyed him nervously. I couldn't escape the overwhelming feeling that we needed to get out of there, now. At this point though, Dan and I were more worried about the weather than pirates. We had 150 miles, somewhere around thirty-plus hours, against the wind and current, with a deteriorating weather window. We would need some luck.

Finally we spent the six hundred, and we raced back to *Alegria*. In record time, the dinghy was stowed, the anchor raised, and we put Isla Margarita quickly and thankfully in our wake. Dan and I kept a sharp eye out the next several hours to make sure no one was following us. Gradually our apprehension faded. Our guardian angel was definitely watching out for us though. We later read that the day before we arrived, a sailboat leaving Margarita had been attacked by a *pirogue* (small, fast fishing boat) carrying five to six men armed with pistols and an AK47. The men in the pirogue fired at the sailboat, forcing the sailboat's crew to return fire with their flare guns. The pirates fled, and the sailboat had to return to the marina in Margarita. The crew was luckily unhurt, but their boat had several bullet holes in its hull.

The early hours into the trip were great. The sky was clear, the wind was low. Tristan stood some watches, giving Dan and me a break. We were making excellent time, hitting 7 knots of speed, in calm seas. Dan casually made the remark that we would be getting to Grenada earlier than we thought. Big mistake. Never, ever, underestimate the ocean.

About halfway to Los Testigos, our speed dropped from 7 knots to 5 knots. The slowing of the boat meant we would be passing Los Testigos at night, which we preferred anyway. Several boats had been boarded and robbed in broad daylight outside of the island. The general consensus was that someone on the island alerted the pirates on the mainland when a lone sailboat left. So far, they were targeting single boats heading east to west, not west to east, but as an added precaution, we sailed at night without our lights. This made it difficult for the pirates to see us, but it also made it difficult for other boat traffic, which may not have been using radar, to see us, so we needed to be extra alert.

As the darkness approached, we all began our night-passage rituals. No matter how many night passages we had completed, they always made me a little nervous at first. I made some soup for dinner, organized our snacks for watches, pulled on my warm sweatpants and sweatshirt, and made sure my iPod was ready to go. (If we were lucky, our Sirius radio would get a signal, and we could listen to it.) Tristan found all our harnesses and laid them out in an orderly fashion. He also found some warm blankets for us to use for sleeping outside that night. Tessa made her usual nest of pillow, warm blanket, DVD player, DVDs, and snacks. Dan made sure his knife was in his pocket, and that flashlights were within easy reach. He visually double checked the engines, checked the oil in our port engine, checked our chartplotter and radar, and reconfirmed our course. Perhaps the strangest thing about this ritual was that it was almost always performed in silence. We were all lost in mental preparation for the long night ahead.

Slowly, the sun dropped below the horizon, and we put on our harnesses. This was the time I dreaded the most; the gathering darkness. Once it was totally dark, I was fine, but for some reason, the growing darkness, on a small boat, in a big ocean, always made me apprehensive.

Not too long after the sun set, we noticed a white light on the horizon, growing brighter and brighter in the darkening sky. At first we thought it was another boat. It appeared to be moving but wasn't showing on our radar. Then we thought it was a light from Los Testigos, but it was too bright for that. Finally, we figured out it was the planet Venus. We had never seen it this bright.

The evening rolled on. Boats appeared on our radar outside of Los Testigos, but like us, they seemed to be traveling without lights. Sometimes, mysteriously, they would appear on our radar, and just as soon, disappear. That was unnerving. We assumed it was a military ship, more than likely the Coast Guard. Sometimes they ran without lights and hid themselves from radar when they tracked smugglers.

I took the first watch that night. Our speed dropped down considerably as the current pushed stronger against us. Shortly into my watch, I smelled something burning. It wasn't a continuous smell, and it wasn't strong, but I could definitely smell it. I chalked it off to someone burning something on the islands, but in the back of my mind, that didn't seem right. When I smelled it again later, it worried me. I thought about telling Dan, but I knew if it meant something was wrong with the engine, he would want to turn back. I didn't want that to happen, so I didn't say anything. By the time I went off watch, two hours later, I didn't smell it anymore.

Dan's watch was uneventful. Our speed continued to drop. When I took over again for my watch, Dan filled me in on our progress. We were barely making any headway at all. Our speed hovered between 2.5 and 3 knots. The current against us increased. I wanted to turn north to get out of the current, but Dan was against it. He thought we should stay the course. I reluctantly agreed for the time being. I looked at the chartplotter, getting my bearings for my watch. Suddenly a glow from the starboard side of the bow caught my attention.

"I thought we were traveling without lights," I said.

"We are."

"Then why is the starboard navigation light on?"

We both looked at the glow coming from the starboard light. It should have been red, but it was brighter than normal and emitting a strange, yellowish-orange glow, flame-colored really. It took us a moment to realize the front of the boat was on fire. Jeez! So much for keeping a low profile. We couldn't have been more conspicuous if we'd tried!

Dan raced to the control panel to turn off the light switch, but the switch wasn't on. It was a short causing the light to burn. We sailed on, like the Statue of Liberty, proudly bearing our torch for all the world and the pirates to see, until Dan removed the control panel and disconnected the power to the light.

Dan had no idea what shorted out the wiring that caused the fire. Fortunately, we spotted it before it damaged all our electronics. I shudder to think what would have happened if we'd shorted out our radar, our GPS, our chartplotter, and our autopilot. I know Columbus sailed across the ocean with only his trusty compass, but we were far from being Columbus. Our flame extinguished, we continued on, in the darkness.

The next morning we were way behind schedule. Dan was adamant about staying the course. He still thought we would be out of the current soon and our speed would pick up. If it didn't, we wouldn't get to Grenada until after dark.

The day passed slowly. Tristan stood a couple of watches again. We never did homeschooling during a passage, so the kids had more free time. We ate lunch, I made cookies, we watched movies, napped, and read books. We kept an eye on our boat speed, took an occasional look at the depth, but in our boredom, never really paid attention to the changing sky. If we had, we would have noticed that at two in the afternoon, the sky grew hazy. At two thirty, we saw a water spout form from a cloud in the distance. Everyone thought that was pretty interesting. There were several murmurs of "wow" and "cool," and I even nonchalantly took a picture of it with my camera. For the record, it is not cool to see a water spout when you are in the middle of the ocean. That should have been obvious to us then. It became very obvious later.

Dan stood watch, Tristan and I read, and Tessa listened to her iPod. I was so engrossed in my book that it took me awhile before I noticed *Alegria* being rocked by the waves. The temperature seemed to be dropping too. Without looking up from my book, I asked Dan, "Can't you go around this?"

"Look up," he said.

I put down my book and was shocked at what I saw. Everywhere I looked, it was gray. It was as if the sky had collapsed around us. The gray was only broken by the angry black of the waves topped by foamy whitecaps.

Where had this come from? Shocked, I asked him, "Have you checked the radar? Is there any way around it?"

"It's a cold front," Dan said. "There's no way around it."

Our streak of outrunning storms had come to an abrupt end. The wind and waves increased. Dan did his best to keep *Alegria* bow-first into the waves. Our situation got serious fast. The waves were averaging around 10 feet, but the 15 feet-plus waves were coming more often. The waves were very short in duration, meaning they hit us one after the other. Most of the time, *Alegria* made it up and down flawlessly, but every so often, one of her hulls would fall off the wave before the other. This caused her to heel at a steep angle, causing some of the cabinet doors inside to fly open. It was unnerving. One time, we fell off the wave so hard, one of the cabinet doors broke its hinges.

There is a tell-tale sound made by the wind in the rigging when the wind blows over 40 knots. It is a high-pitched, scream-like sound. The very sound I was hearing at that moment.

"What's the wind speed?"

"Gusts close to 50 knots," Dan replied, strangely calm.

Not what I wanted to hear at all!

"How far are we from Grenada?"

"About 40 miles."

"How fast are we going?"

A long pause before he answered. "Just under 2 knots."

Under 2 knots? That was just over 1 mile per hour. We might as well have been going backwards! I glanced inside at Tessa. She was engrossed in her snacks and movie. I looked at Tristan sitting next to me. He was devastated.

"What's wrong?" I asked him.

"We are going 2 knots! We are never going to get there!"

I was partially scared and a whole lot fed up. I was tired of this trip. I was tired of it taking so long. I was tired that for what seemed like the last three months there had been one drama after another. And I was really tired of trying to make sense of it all. We had no way of knowing how long this storm would last. Dan was doing a great job of hand steering *Alegria*, keeping her bow into the waves, but it would be dark soon, making it impossible to see the seas.

I changed channels on the VHF to hear if anyone else was out in this weather. We immediately recognized the distinctive voice of the manager of Island Water World in Grenada. We could only hear the manager's side of the conversation, but with the new antenna we'd purchased in Venezuela, and the fact that Island Water World had a VHF repeater that gave them a 70-mile VHF transmission capability, the transmission was fairly clear.

Dan broke into the conversation and asked what the weather was like there. The manager said that a strong front with high winds had passed through not too long ago. Dan told him we were getting that now. The manager said it hadn't lasted too long, maybe a few hours. Dan thanked him, and he wished us luck. That was good news. For now, there was nothing to do but make the best of it. I sent Tristan inside with Tessa. Dan and I put on our harnesses, and I helped him spot waves from the port side.

The waves hit *Alegria* pretty hard. Tristan didn't like it, but Tessa, engrossed in a movie, didn't seem to notice, even when things were falling off the shelves around her. During my watch, the wind gradually retreated to 20 knots and later fell to 12 knots. The waves subsided too, but not before a big one hit us, rocking the boat and causing me to nearly fall out of the captain's seat. Thank goodness my harness was securely attached.

The really good news was that our speed increased. By 2 a.m. we were outside the Carenage (harbor) at St. George's, Grenada. It was such a mental relief to finally be there, but that was short lived. Prickly Bay, located farther south and east, was where we needed to anchor. It wasn't a long distance, but it was a tricky entrance, with reefs on either side. It was fairly well marked, and we had been there before, but we were tired, it was raining, it was dark, and with the ways things had gone over the last several days, we felt it wasn't worth the risk.

What do you do when you are waiting for sun up and you can't anchor? You motor. Slowly. In a big circle. Around and around again.

It was my watch. Dan and Tessa were asleep. Tristan was keeping me company. I had the radar on to keep track of the fishing boats coming and going, most with no lights. One large ship wasn't showing up on my radar. It was running without lights, and Tristan and I noticed it only when it blocked out the lights onshore. It was unnerving, especially when it came so close to us, until we realized it was the Coast Guard. We must have seemed as suspicious to them as they did to us.

With nothing to do but wait it out, Tristan and I watched movies until the sun gradually made an appearance. I surrendered the watch to Dan and fell asleep in the cockpit. What seemed to be hours later, I woke up. I was shocked that we were still moving and hadn't reached the anchorage yet. I hadn't actually been sleeping that long, Dan told me, but we still had a ways to go. When I was circling the night before, I had taken us too far north. Seriously? Would this trip ever end? Frustrated, I went back to sleep.

When I woke up again, we were finally at the anchorage. Prickly Bay was crowded. Some of the boats were already in the Christmas spirit with their rigging decked out in lights. Tristan and I dropped the anchor. Tristan then raised the yellow quarantine flag, while Dan checked the engines. I reluctantly went inside to assess the damage. I was shocked. Books and magazines were strewn across the salon. Bottles and silverware had fallen onto the floor in the kitchen. A cabinet had opened downstairs, spilling clothes. A closet door in our bedroom had been ripped from its hinges. The kids' schoolbooks had crashed at the base of the stairs, making it nearly impossible to reach the head. It was a mess I didn't want to deal with at that moment. We needed to check in with immigration, but first I wanted to take a shower and a nap. The officials had other ideas.

As soon as Tristan put up the quarantine flag, the Coast Guard pulled up next to us, asking where we had come from and wanting to know when we were going to check in. Dan explained that we had just arrived. I added that we'd had a rough passage, the boat was a mess, and we would be in after we cleaned up a bit. They paused for a moment, then said we needed to come in now. Fine. Our prior experiences with Grenadian officials had always been friendly. I didn't know why they were so adamant that we needed to come in at that moment. We unhappily threw on clean clothes, conveniently scattered all over the floor, lowered the dinghy, and presented ourselves to customs and immigration. Apparently we looked harmless enough, and the whole process was quick. Then we came back and took our nap.

The next morning we listened in on the VHF cruiser's net to catch up on the latest news and to hear if there were any boats in Grenada that we knew. The net was full of talk about the approaching holiday and the cruisers' Christmas dinner. If we wanted to join in, we needed to make a reservation soon. Our plan was still to celebrate Christmas in Bequia. As I listened, I noticed the Venezuelan charts sitting on the captain's table.

"I'm going to ask if anyone wants these," I told Dan. At the end of the net, when they called for buy, sell, or trade, I announced the name of our boat and said we had just returned from Venezuela and had a set of charts in great condition. If anyone was interested, they could call me after the net. As soon as the net ended, I heard several boats calling *Alegria*. I took the first one I heard, *Scott Free*.

"*Alegria*. I understand you have charts of Venezuela."

I told him we had several charts for that area, and they were in great shape. He was very interested. "How much do you want for them?"

"Nothing. They're free." I explained to him that a cruiser in Grenada had given them to us before our trip, and now we wanted to pass them along. He was surprised and excited. I told him where we were anchored and described our boat. He was anchored two boats behind us and would be over shortly.

As I gathered the charts together, my mind wandered back to Venezuela, wondering how our friends were doing and how they were getting ready for the holidays. I smiled to myself, remembering how worried Tessa was about Santa finding our boat, and replaying my conversation with Harold about my believing if I had no presents, Santa would make sure I got one. As if she knew I was thinking about her, Tessa appeared at my side. She asked me where we were going to be for Christmas. I knew she was still worried about presents. I assured her that Santa would take care of her and Tristan.

I was a little disappointed about not having a present for Christmas. I was still thinking about that Swiss Army knife back in Venezuela and was really frustrated with myself for not getting it. I knew it would have been expensive though, and I would have felt guilty about it. This year, Christmas would be all about the feelings and not the gifts.

The sound of an approaching dinghy brought me back to the present. Tessa was already grabbing the line and welcoming Scott aboard. We all shook hands and exchanged introductions. He was Canadian, a little older than us, with graying hair and a mustache. He and his wife were in Grenada for a few weeks, waiting for friends. Later next year they were planning on sailing to Venezuela.

Tristan brought out the charts. Dan told Scott that since many of the electronic charts for Venezuela were not totally accurate, paper charts were recommended. I watched Scott watch Tristan gently take off the rubber band holding the maps together and carefully unroll them on the table. Tristan and Dan pointed out different anchorages and discussed the passages. Tessa told Scott about fishing. When Scott was finished looking at the maps, Tristan rolled them back up, taking great care to make sure the paper didn't bend or crease. For some reason, this really impressed Scott. Maybe he didn't expect a young kid to take such good care of things, or maybe he just hadn't met very many cruising kids. Anyway, he complimented us on both Tessa and Tristan and again offered to pay us for the maps.

"These charts are expensive. You sure you don't want anything for them?

I shook my head. "No. They were given to us. Now we're giving them to you."

He smiled. "Well, I never like to go anywhere empty handed." He reached into his pocket, pulled out a rectangular white box and laid it in front of me. Puzzled, I opened the box and pulled out a brown leather case. When I unsnapped the leather case, I gasped. A big smile crossed my face as I pulled out the red, deluxe Swiss Army knife. Santa hadn't forgotten me.

Speaking of Santa, it was time to head to Bequia to celebrate Christmas.

33

What Matters Most

BEQUIA

December 24, 2010 Bequia
(from my journal)

Our 3-foot high, artificial Christmas tree, acquired in the Dominican Republic a few years earlier, was decorated. We had purchased Christmas ornaments in almost every country we had visited, so putting them on the tree was a trip down memory lane. Tristan and Tessa had woven small, multicolor Christmas lights, purchased in Venezuela, through the bimini and around the cockpit. Inside the salon, blue-and-silver-beaded garland was strung throughout, and the glowing Aruba snowman added a festive light. Of course, these lights all ran on electricity, so Dan would only allow them on for a short time, but still, it put us in the spirit.

Bequia was certainly ready for Christmas. The harbor was packed tight. There were easily a hundred boats, several of them megayachts, already anchored when we got there, and more arrived every day. Many of the boats were charter boats, and the anchoring skills of some of them left much to be desired, so we tried to anchor as far away as possible. To make matters worse, large northerly swells rocked the harbor, rolling the boats from side to side. To give ourselves a break, we spent as much time onshore as possible.

On Christmas Eve, we put on our finest clothes, did our best to crawl into our dinghy, which was bouncing crazily behind the boat, and went out for Christmas Eve dinner. We were looking for something different, so we ate a delicious lobster pizza at Mac's Pizzeria. A quick, heavy rain fell while we were eating, but we were protected under the open-air porch. After dinner we lazily walked around the town, enjoying the festive drumming and steel-pan music floating on the warm night air. Close to midnight, we followed a procession out of town and up a steep hill to St. Michael's Catholic Church, an old, small church just off the main roadway.

The night was humid, due to the rain, and the inside of the church was warm. Later, an ocean breeze filtered in through the open windows, cooling the church slightly. We sat in the back, right in front of the musicians with their drums, shakers, and guitar, and next to the chorus. The congregation was mostly locals, but sunburned faces revealed a few tourists. We sat shoulder to shoulder on well-worn wooden pews, and when the singing started, neighboring parishioners shared two aging hymnals with us.

The music, the singing, the ocean breezes, the joy, and the anticipation of Christmas all mixed into an incredible energy, uniting islanders and tourists as one. When the time came for the presentation of the gifts, a church member whispered something to Tristan. The next thing I knew, he was nervously bringing up the gifts to the altar; a moment he will never forget.

When the service was almost over, and I thought it couldn't possibly get better, the lights were extinguished until the small church was illuminated solely by candlelight. The priest was handed an adorable, black baby boy from his proud parents. He walked slowly through the church, holding the baby high as the congregation united in an incredibly moving rendition of "O Holy Night." When we sang the words, "Fall on your knees, and hear the angels voices," a huge swell of emotions welled up inside of me.

I don't know if it was the sight of that incredibly cute, contented baby smiling at the congregation as the priest held him, the old church with its many memories of Christmas, or the fellowship of the people in the church, but for the first time in a long, long, time, I *felt* Christmas. [*End entry*]

Later that night, back on the boat, we watched fireworks and flares being shot over the harbor and heard the numerous boat horns blown in celebration. As I watched the sky light up overhead, I thought about all we had been through as a family over the last four years. There had been many changes in all of us. Tristan had grown into a responsible teenager, confident in his navigation and boat-handling skills. He had an endless fascination with exploring new places, and I could easily see him traveling the world on his own someday.

Tessa had become our world citizen. She was fascinated by people as much as experiences. Her gift was seeing how everyone was alike, not how people were different, and she was unafraid to engage anyone in conversation. Tessa has an uncanny ability to see people as they really are. She would make a great international ambassador.

Dan went from a guy who rarely cut his own lawn to someone we constantly counted on for our safety. He rebuilt the toilet several times, a job I wouldn't wish on anyone, and it seemed there wasn't a mechanical or electrical issue on the boat he couldn't handle. Even when he was out of his depth, he came through for us. We couldn't have done it without him.

And I changed. I learned to let go and stop worrying (most of the time). I learned to stop living my life according to other people's expectations and started living it for myself. We had changed as a family too. Dan and I were no longer parents with two children to look after; we were a team. All four of us were stronger together and always would be.

Gradually, the fireworks faded and our Christmas became tinged with a bit of sadness. We would be leaving in a few days for St. Martin, where we would put *Alegria* up for sale. Within a month after she went on the market, *Alegria* was sold, and we were packing up to return to the US.

34

Full Circle

WE HAD COME FULL CIRCLE. We had sold, given away, or donated most of the boat parts, books, and items we couldn't, or didn't want, to take with us. The cockpit and galley were full of boxes of the things we wanted to keep and would be shipped back to the US. *Alegria* was sold. We were really going back, not *home,* but back, because now we knew that home was wherever we were all together.

The kids at first couldn't understand why we were selling *Alegria.* It was like selling a part of our family. They wanted to leave her at a dock in the Virgin Islands and come back and sail when we could. I told them that wouldn't be fair to her. I reminded them that *Alegria* had sailed from South Africa, through some of the toughest oceans and weather, only to be put in charter in an area of easy, short sailing before we came along and took her on an adventure. She was built for adventure. Now she would have that opportunity with someone else. Sadly, they agreed.

Our last night on *Alegria.* There was a beautiful moon shining on the water. A Van Morrison song came on the radio, and there was just enough room in the cockpit for Dan and me to have one last slow dance to "These Are The Days." It was very romantic. I had my head on Dan's chest, listening to the lyrics, thinking about all we had been through and what lay ahead, trying in vain to ignore the annoying sound of someone rummaging through a suitcase right next to me.

"What is going on?" I demanded.

Tessa, not 6 inches from me, was shamelessly digging through a suitcase, looking for who knows what, in the middle of our romantic moment. Dan and I stopped and stared at her. She glanced up and said, "Don't mind me. Keep on dancing. Pretend I'm not here."

Our last morning on *Alegria*. I walked around making one final check for anything we might have left behind. The boxes were already on their way by cargo plane, but we still had eight large bags and backpacks that would go with us. Tessa and Tristan were with Dan delivering our remaining food, blankets, and various items to Dario, a young homeless man we had befriended on the island. Some of the stuff, we hoped he could sell.

I walked into Tessa's room. Everything was clean. I lifted up her mattress to double check, and I noticed some writing on the platform. I started to wash it off until I realized it was a note Tessa had written to *Alegria*.

Alegria. Thank you so much for taking care of me and my family. Thank you for always being there when I needed you. I love you and will miss you so much.
Love forever
Tessa

I laid my head on the mattress and cried.

I had said my goodbyes to *Alegria* the night before. I had sat on the bow late that night, snug up against the mast; the same spot I used to sit when I Skyped my friends and family back in the US. I ran my hand down *Alegria's* smooth, white fiberglass. She was so much more than a boat to me; she was a friend, a member of our family.

"I'm going to miss you," I said softly. "I'm going to miss our late-night passages together. Some nights it seemed as if you and I were the only ones in the world."

I smiled, remembering the brilliant stars overhead, the whoosh of the waves, and the diamond-like bioluminescence she would leave in her wake.

"Thank you for taking such good care of us and keeping us safe. You changed our lives forever, and we will never forget you. I love you *Alegria.*"

As sad as it was, I knew it was time to go. For the first time in my life I really felt like I had completed something. There was nothing that I regretted doing or not doing or wished we could have done over. It was perfect.

When Dan and the kids came back, we took one last picture of all of us on the trampoline, just as Don had taken the picture of us back in Palm Coast, Florida the day we left. A perfect circle. We boarded the dinghy and headed to shore.

EPILOGUE

THE PLANE TOUCHED DOWN IN Charlotte, North Carolina late in the evening. I faced the debarking of the plane with mixed emotions. A part of me was excited about our new adventure back in the US. Another part of me was scared of what that would mean and how that would change us. We had grown so close as a family. How would that change here?

Dan said to wait until everyone else got off the plane. I stepped aside to let the other passengers rush to their destination. We weren't in any hurry. We weren't even sure where we were staying or what we would be doing. But that was how we had played this all along. We would simply make it up as we went.

The plane was empty now. There were no more excuses to wait. The kids looked at Dan excitedly, and he nodded to go ahead. Tristan took the lead, with Tessa close behind. I followed slowly, deep in thought, trying not to break the spell that had bound us together so magically the last several years. This was really it. As soon as we left the walkway and entered the airport, Tristan and Tessa would be mine no more; they would belong to the world. I watched the back of their heads as they moved quickly down the walkway. It seemed as if, already, there was a distance between us.

I thought back on the many nights playing board games around the table, the singing as we rode the dinghy or walked to the grocery store, the excitement of discovering new places together as a family, the snuggling on long passages, the slow-paced life that allowed us to really know and enjoy one another, and the gift of being together that healed my heart. All that would be memories.

I panicked at the thought and raced to catch up, calling out to Tristan and Tessa just before they entered the terminal. They turned around expectantly, grinning from ear to ear. I wanted to grab them and pull them back to me, holding onto this moment forever—but I knew I couldn't.

"Never mind," I sighed and waved them on. We entered the noisy, bustling airport. The spell was broken.

ACKNOWLEDGMENTS

First I want to thank my wonderful children, Tristan and Tessa. We couldn't have accomplished all we did without you. Thank you for making this crazy adventure so fun, and thank you for putting so much trust in your dad and me. I love you both with all my heart.

A big thanks to my dad, who instilled the travel bug in me when he bought that first truck camper and stuck seven kids in the back for a two-week vacation. I was hooked!

Our trip would not have been possible without the generous help of Karon and Alan Petty. Not only did they bring us everything from a guitar to a cooler, wherever we were in the world, they also kept track of our mail, gave us a place to stay, and kept our Stateside life organized. We are eternally indebted. Thank you to my sister, Linda, and her husband, Jerry, who took in our beloved dog, Rasta. We knew he was in good hands. A big thanks to all my friends, Karen, Dana, and Jennifer, who through late-night Skype calls, shared my world as I shared theirs back in the US. It was so good knowing you were there. Thank you, Karin for providing the best places to write—from a mountaintop house, to a beautiful farm.

Thank you to all the sailing friends we made along the way. I won't list them all, as I am afraid I will leave someone out, but we were in awe of your support and generosity.

And last, but in no way least, a huge thank you to my editor, Renee D. Petrillo. Renee, I can't begin to thank you for your help with this book. You not only invested countless hours on the project, you improved my work and gave me encouragement when I doubted myself. You turned my dream of writing a book into a reality, and there is no way I can ever thank you enough. My wish for you is to realize just how amazing and special you really are.

22285905R00242

Made in the USA
San Bernardino, CA
29 June 2015